BETTER GREAT THAN NEVER

LINDSAY DARE SHOOP

BETTER

GREAT

THAN

NEVER

BELIEVING IT'S POSSIBLE
IS WHERE CHAMPIONS BEGIN

LIONCREST
PUBLISHING

BETTER GREAT THAN NEVER
Believing It's Possible Is Where Champions Begin

ISBN   978-1-5445-1418-5 *Hardcover*
        978-1-5445-1417-8 *Paperback*
        978-1-5445-1419-2 *Ebook*

For Granny Betty, my first editor, who taught me that a preposition is a word with which one should never end a sentence.

And for Kevin "K-Train" Sauer, who never stopped asking…

Because he knows there is possibility within us all.

CONTENTS

INTRODUCTION

THE FIRST OF MANY STEPS.

HAVE YOU EVER PUSHED YOURSELF SO HARD THAT IT MADE you feel like all of your teeth fell out? I know I never did. At least, not until the sport of rowing entered my life.

Imagine: when you cross the finish line, your mind is blank, your ears are ringing, your thoughts are a mess, and your senses are utterly confused. From here, all you can do is wait. Wait until time passes. Wait until you recover. Wait for whatever sensation might come next.

Almost instantly, you taste something oddly metallic on the back of your tongue. A flavor that is warm and creamy, almost sweet. As you try to figure out what it could be, the taste turns bitter, like tarnished silver and warm drool.

Then it hits you. *Could it be blood?* you wonder, *but how?*

At this point, you reason the only possible way you could be tasting blood is that your teeth have fallen out. And as a result, blood has begun to accumulate in your mouth where your teeth once were. So, as you regain use of your hands, you shakily touch your face, then run your fingers along your gums to investigate. *Okay, my teeth are all here. Now what?*

Having confirmed that your teeth are indeed intact, you now shift focus to your next most intense sensation. The one you feel in your feet. An unparalleled ache that throbs rhythmically to the beating of your heart.

Maybe my shoes are too tight, you think to yourself. So you rip open the Velcro closure to free your feet from your shoes, then tear off your socks for good measure. But rather than alleviating the ache, it instead develops into a tingle that feels both excruciating and numb. Preferring numb, you squeeze your feet as hard as you can, hoping that might ease your pain. But it does not. So you release your feet and simply let them dangle from your ankles like two lifeless marionettes. But again, this does not help.

In one final attempt to cure your discomfort, you plunge your feet into the chilly water below, hoping cold immersion will help. *At last...*your pain begins to wane, and you can finally appreciate your newfound level of determination.

Maybe this is what it means to want something so badly you can taste it. That a desire is so strong that it takes on a distinct flavor. I used to think this was just an exaggerated expression. But once I began pursuing my best me through the sport of rowing, I understood it.

Let me assure you, I did not have anywhere near that level of determination when I started down my Olympic path. Quite the opposite. I was awkward and self-conscious. I had insecurities and fears. And even though others saw potential in me, I did not believe I was good enough to amount to much athletically beyond high school. Ultimately, on account of my self-imposed limits, I chose to walk away from sports altogether. Because I did, on the day I finally decided to take up the sport of rowing, I was, by national standards, unfit and overweight.

So no, this is not the story of the Olympic champion who picked up and specialized in her sport with her Olympic dream in mind from a young age. This is instead the story of the Olympic champion whose life first wandered in many directions. Not one of which was toward what allowed me to become my best. Until one day, a stranger reached out and presented an opportunity to try something new. What he presented was only an opportunity though. The decisions, actions, and effort from there were up to me.

My decision to embrace that opportunity by taking on something new, intimidating, and completely uncertain, that was my first step. It was a step I took because, even though I did not know where I could go, I knew I did not want to stay where I was. That step, one that seemed trivial at the time, turned out to be the first of many steps. Many patient, successive steps that grew into tiny confidences. Those small reassurances that showed gradual progress and so encouraged me to discover new things every day. Perhaps most importantly, they were steps taken with friends, family, teammates, and coaches who challenged me throughout the process.

It was with every step I took, challenge I faced, and decision I made to not back down, no matter the circumstances, that my determination grew and eventually gave way to a dream. A dream that gradually transformed from idea into reality on the day my teammates and I raced for gold in the 2008 Beijing Olympics. An event so significant that they remain the most watched Games of all time.

On Sunday, August 17, 2008, my eight teammates and I pushed into the lead within the first minute of the race. From there, we never gave it up. By the time we crossed the finish line, just over six minutes later, we were the first team to bring home Olympic gold for the United States in women's rowing, in any event, over the full 2,000-meter race distance (an accomplishment for which they deemed us worthy for induction into the National Rowing Hall of Fame).

Of the few Americans who have won Olympic gold in women's rowing, I was one of the smallest physically and picked up the sport at the latest point in life. Once I picked it up though and took on gradually greater challenges, I went from being overweight and doubtful to accomplishing something that less than 0.000005 percent of the world's population might ever do.

So when I say that it is never too late to change the way we perceive ourselves, to remove our self-imposed limits, to make the decision to pursue our greatest (or simply better) selves one day at a time, one step at a time, I am certain it is true. So dare to change your mind. Dare to take action. Then stay patient, positive, and determined. For make no mistake, the process of becoming your best, of being proud of the person you can become every day, is a gradual one. One filled with unexpected challenges that can, at times, make every step feel like the first.

ONE

TWO RULES TO LIVE BY.

SUNDAY, AUGUST 17, 2008. SHUNYI DISTRICT, BEIJING, CHINA. *One minute before the start of the women's eight 2,000-meter Olympic final.*

Sitting there at the start line, my nerves momentarily resurged. They were the one final distraction to perforate my consciousness. The one final attempt at disrupting my focus. In our moment of ultimate challenge, worry tried to call my bluff one last time, tried to question how durable my determination had become.

I could not let myself ignore them. My nerves had welled up for a reason—because of how much I cared about what the nine of us were there to do. We were exactly where we had trained to be. At the pinnacle. The line that separated Olympic champions from everyone else.

In through my nose, I took a deep belly breath. My eyes gently blinked closed as my exhale passed my lips. My fingers loosened. My face, feet, and hands relaxed. My major muscles pulsated in attention, ready for their call to action. Meanwhile, my mind reassured me, *You wanted this. We have come all this way. We are in this together. This is what it has all been for.*

The tears. Blisters. Sweat. Frozen, cracked, and bloodied hands.

The frustration. The anxiety. The long days. The weddings and births missed. The rush to work between training sessions to be able to afford groceries. Convincing myself that the cheapest thing on the menu actually is what I want and ordering water by default because it is free.

The snowy Friday nights with one hundred minutes left to pedal on the bike. Literally going nowhere but with nowhere else in the world I would rather be. Teammates by my side.

The sore...*everything.*

The breakthroughs. Those two words of encouragement when needed the most: "Good job."

The laughs. The smiles. The joys. Embracing my being the goofy underdog for the mismatched outfits I chose, either because I awoke in the dark, or it was all I had.

Everything it took just to have the chance to sit in that seat, let alone at that line. The realization that everything that knocked me to the bottom had made me all the stronger. All the more prepared. All the more confident.

My subconscious reassured me a second time, *You already made your choice, Shoop. Only one option remains. Go harder than you ever have in your entire life and hope that your teeth don't fall out.*

One more deep belly breath, and my jaw, neck, and shoulders loosened a little more. Every ounce of my being ready. Finally focused on only one thing: this moment.

I wore the density of my concentration as a cocoon of complete silence. A silence that made it seem as though I had lost my capacity to hear. As everything fell to nothingness, the only sounds I perceived were those that arose from within. Every beat of my heart intensified. Every pulse of my blood clarified. Every chill from every pore amplified. It was as if every one of my cells had awakened and aligned toward my one specific purpose.

Then, as I sat at the threshold of my elevated state of attention, poised with an intent honed over years of training and focusing on what we could become, the start sequence abruptly ruptured the silence. At a most arbitrary moment, the race announcer's monotone voice appeared through my cocoon. And just like that, the thing we had taken all those steps toward was finally at hand.

The race official polled each team one by one over the loudspeakers. With every call, I grinned. The corner of my mouth turning slightly upward. With every country's name, I breathed. The edges of my jaw gritting, then releasing. With every name that echoed, my thoughts were simple: *Breathe. Yes, Shoop. Breathe.* Until finally, they called us.

"United States of America" resounded low and slow over the flat, calm water at the start. I glared through my eyebrows. My heart fluttered up. I exhaled once more to relax my cheeks. I wiggled my fingers once more to relax my grip.

By the time the last of the six names was called, one for each of the six countries strong enough to make it to the Olympic final, I had nothing left to think. All that remained was the start signal.

In those final moments, my nostrils widened as my breaths deepened so the air could enter through my nose and exit through my every pore, signifying my nerves' absolute alignment.

Then, after one seemingly eternal period of time (in reality, only a matter of moments), the announcer's monotone voice droned through the loudspeakers one last time.

"Attention—"

The start command landed on my skin from across the lanes. As I absorbed it, my ears pulled rearward. Every hair on the back of my neck bristled. In less than half a blink, we took off.

"You must see it, then convince your body of what your mind can see." Tom, the head coach of the US Women's National Rowing Team, said to us while we sat huddled at the back of the musty old boat bay. "Then, as you prepare accordingly, let your preparation become your confidence."

Even during a training trip several years before our Olympic final, Tom knew we needed to be confident in order to have even the slightest chance for Olympic gold. In fact, he knew we needed to be more than just confident. We needed to be confident enough to win to come away with a medal at all. So, in order to help us become just that, Tom taught us to trust our preparation because it would gradually build our confidence one day at a time.

Before taking our preparation another step further though, Tom explained one other thing: if we truly aimed for gold, we had to believe that gold was possible. For only once we thought it was possible would we fully embrace the very real and challenging work it would require. This would then strengthen our ability to prepare, which would then strengthen our confidence and fuel our effort through challenge and triumph alike.

That was our cycle. A gradually strengthening cycle of possibility, preparation, and confidence. A cycle that carried on every day, day after day, as we prepared more than ever and believed more than ever. Until the time came to face the ultimate test.

Now that I am on the other side of Olympic gold, I have a far greater understanding of how this cycle ultimately enabled my teammates and me to excel. That is, how our preparation, the ways we addressed our challenges, bridged the gap between possibility and reality. But since the extent of our belief in possibility impacted our preparation, so too did it impact the extent of our reality.

How do I know? I did not emerge from the womb equipped with some superhuman talent or confidence. My parents did not instantly uncover in me some innate ability that made me naturally driven. So no, I did not specialize in one sport—especially not one as rare as rowing—then head down a path toward the Olympics from a young age. Believe it or not, even once I finally made the Olympic team, I was neither the most genetically gifted nor the most experienced, so there must have been something more. Had there not been, I would never have made it as far as I did.

I was the lanky girl who grew up just outside a small college town smack in the middle of Virginia. Rowing was not a thing there when I was young. There were not many suitable bodies of water, which meant there were not any youth rowing teams in the area at the time. Even if rowing had been a thing, I doubt I would have been allowed to pursue it. It would not have been convenient, as it would have been time consuming and too far from where my family lived to make practice attendance plausible.

Considering that we lived ten miles south of town on a small farm (complete with a yard, creek, and a few farm animals), convenience would have been one issue. As for another, my parents worked a lot. My mom was a dental hygienist. My dad was an engineer. Both of their professions required they leave our house early and get home late. Things they were willing to do in order to provide my brother and me with more than what they had growing up.

My mom came from a blue-collar family. Her dad was the local plaster work expert. He died a week before I was born though, so I do not know much about him. I have heard stories that he yelled a lot. I have also heard stories that he was kind and gentle. Both could be true, but I have no way of knowing.

My mom's mom, Granny Betty, as she is known to literally everyone, worked a lifetime as a secretary for my hometown's public school system. She wore three-inch high heels every day despite the bunions they gave her. I bet if you ever caught her scooting around town without her heels, she would be wearing purple Keds in size eight and a half.

Together, my mom's parents raised her and her younger sister (my Aunt Lisa) in the very town where I grew up. To my and my brother's good fortune, most of my mom's family lived nearby. That made the team effort of raising us a tad easier.

Because my dad was one of eight kids, he grew up living simply. He spent a good portion of his childhood in upstate New York, literally walking to school uphill, four miles, both ways. In the winter when the snow was deep, he took to wearing his older brother's shoes. Not because they were all he had but because they kept him from sinking into the freshly fallen soft white powder. That is the kind of practical resourcefulness my dad passed down to my brother and me.

When my parents were in college together, they did not have much extra money to spend, so they saved wherever they could. They went to school all day. My dad worked all night. My mom made their clothes by hand, and she got used to coasting into the driveway on fumes with the car engine cutting out just shy of their front door.

My parents told me they did manage to save a little extra once. To celebrate, my mom spent part of her day cooking a special meal for the two of them. Rather than enjoying the meal though, her effort instead became an emotional nightmare when the table gave out.

The way my mom tells it, she just sat there on the food-covered floor, exhausted, and cried.

As for my big brother, when people say cats and dogs fight, they clearly did not know the two of us when we were kids. Our parents even expressed a fear that we would never get along—a fear they maintained until we were both well over eighteen and my brother had gone off to college. What else were they to think given that we once got into a car accident while fighting over which radio station to listen to on the way to school one morning?

It was April Fools' Day. It was drizzling. My big brother was driving our grandmother's Volvo 240 DL, the one without a passenger-side mirror (apparently that was an upgrade back then). The car was a 1983, which to my brother and me, even in 1997, was new. As our grandmother's Volvo danced its 180 around the center line of the old country road that linked our house to town, I stared into my brother's eyes, clutching my armrest for dear life. When the car finally came to a halt on a half-dying tree of a fencepost, the glass from the rear window shattered and exploded toward us into the front seats. Once all was silent, I turned once more to my brother, making eye contact with nothing better to say than, "What did you just do?"

The long, winding country road out to where I grew up was remote enough to be labeled a rural route for most of my childhood. It was the kind of road that meanders away from civilization, gradually exchanging houses for trees along the way. The kind of road that trades cats asleep on porches for cows grazing in fields. The kind of road that leads to long, slow drives stuck behind tractors with nowhere to pass. And the kind of road that rolls through a rural landscape with hills that are nearly impossible to climb when the snow falls in winter.

Living away from town made visits by school friends few and far between. So, when we were young, my brother had no choice but to spend time with me—probably more than he would have liked. It was for that reason, and because no one who lived nearby had daughters my age, that I grew up with mostly boys. Boys who chased me around the yard with sticks and rocks, but who also let me join in their adventures from time to time.

Trying to keep up with those boys meant that I spent a lot of time either ostracized or learning how to throw hard and run fast. My only options since I knew that if I were caught, doom at their hands most certainly loomed. They often broke into teams and built forts, from which they dropped or launched things, typically anything hard enough to leave a mark, like unripe pears, rocks, or broken bricks. On the day they introduced dropping things, my big brother took a brick to the top of his head from a second-story hideout. That day's game ended abruptly with my brother rubbing mud into his scalp wound for his entire trudge back up to the house from the woods.

A few years in, we had no choice but to wear bike helmets when we played together.

My big brother and me.

You could say that growing up in the country with a rough-and-tumble attitude toward fun and games prepared me for nearly anything physical that came my way. Especially since, when you are young and the only girl, it is a badge of honor to keep up with the boys. Much to my parents' relief, I, in time, migrated away from backyard teams toward organized sports. A transition that initially occurred due to one practical purpose: necessity. Yes, I became an athlete not as much for talent, as you might think, but rather, necessity.

Sports passed time. In a pinch, they proved to be decent substitutes for babysitters by extending the school day until after five o'clock, when my parents got off work. And since my parents worked those long days to provide more for my big brother and me, the idea of free babysitting was a welcomed relief. Our mom and dad took turns picking us up from practices so that one or the other of them could work late or run errands. Given everything they did and how remotely we lived, I was often asleep well before whichever one of them it was who ran the errands made it home for the night.

Sports also provided an outlet. Because they were an energy vent that ensured I was not overwhelmingly energized when I got home, sports dampened my ability to inundate my parents with story upon story of what happened to me at school on a given day. This bought them time to decompress before my wave of words began. If you asked my parents, no amount of playing during and after school could dampen my stories.

The third reason I say I became an athlete out of necessity is that I recently learned that I nearly drowned in a lake when I was two. When my mom looked up from where she was sitting and saw me bobbing there in the water, her heart all but stopped. She jumped up and ran to my rescue while a friend ran for my brother, who was playing happily nearby. Almost immediately thereafter, my parents enrolled my big brother and me in swimming lessons.

So you see, I did not find my way to becoming an athlete because of some innate talent. It was instead because my parents wanted me to survive my childhood. Swimming lessons were the start. Then from there, once my family realized how many practical purposes sports serve, I dabbled in nearly a dozen different ones until I turned seventeen.

I swam, took diving classes, rode horses, and did gymnastics. I played basketball, soccer, field hockey, tennis, volleyball, beach volleyball, and was the only girl on an otherwise all boys baseball team. If you consider ballet a sport, I even took ballet.

Dance was probably the one endeavor my mom secretly hoped I would have been the best at. Either that or piano. Much to her dismay, I have two left feet and not a musical bone in my body. So instead of learning music or dance, by growing up with mostly boys, I learned that throw hard and run fast were two rules to live by.

January 2014,

When we were kids, we made up our own games. We thought we were so clever back then when we dared each other to jump from the second story of the barn or across the widest parts of the creek. We even played with arrows, rocks, sticks, and bricks...Honestly, I cannot believe we don't have more scars.

TWO

LENGTH OF LIMB.

HAVE YOU EVER SEEN A DOG THAT IS A LITTLE ON THE larger side but also has a smooth coat that looks a bit baggy? Based on appearance, you get the impression that the dog could just as easily be a puppy as it could be full grown. Being the detective that you are, you glance down at its paws. They are large and floppy compared to its lanky legs. There you have your answer. That dog is a puppy with a lot of growing left to do.

That was me. I have been on the lankier side since birth. Fingers, limbs, feet. I wore a woman's size five shoe when I was all of six years old. I have been taller than the average American woman since sixth grade, when I stood five feet five inches. Now that I am fully grown at six feet one-half inches, I am taller than the average American man.

Growing up the tall girl whose pant legs and shirt sleeves never seemed quite long enough, my height has guided me toward or away from certain things pretty much forever. For my height, I got to start riding horses earlier than most kids. For my height, I got to start kindergarten earlier than most kids. And for my height, people have made assumptions about me for as long as I can remember.

With early length like mine, people often thought I was older than I was. Which came in handy at times. Like when four-year-old me fell in love with horses and was dying to take riding lessons. The trouble was that the local farm did not usually allow kids to begin riding until they turned five. The reason being that it was a safety hazard. Had I lacked leg length, I would not have been able to grip the saddle. Had that been the case, I would have spent every lesson falling off.

Despite my being younger than her usual students, my British-by-way-of-South-Africa instructor took one look at me and made an exception. "Length of limb," she said. "She has length of limb."

September 2000,

I spent many years a little girl, a dreamer, but mature beyond my years they'd tell me. Sometimes I thought it was true too. Then I examined an old photo album. Turns out I was just a big kid until I was at least sixteen.

My "length of limb" enabled me to enter kindergarten when I was just four too. My birthday fell late in the year, which meant I would not turn the standard five by the beginning of the school year. At the time, parents could choose to enroll their kids early or keep them back until they turned five. My being a tad taller made my parents' decision easy. A decision with which my elementary school teachers wholeheartedly agreed.

The summer after kindergarten, our parents signed my big brother and me up for one of the local swim teams. It lightened their busy workdays, given that they could take us both to the same place at the same time.

Even though I was just five when we started, my leg length earned me a time that, when categorized by national speed standards, was better than average when compared to a lot of the other kids my age. Such speeds meant that I tended to race against girls who were older than me. My "racing up," as we called it, helped my teammates because I filled a gap in our roster. Ultimately, that helped our whole team earn more points than it would have otherwise. Even so, we did not win that many meets.

Elementary school, me swimming breaststroke.

By the time I hit second grade, being lanky and having grown up with those boys who taught me to throw hard and run fast earned me schoolyard respect because I could kick a football better than anyone else on my first try (the boys and girls alike).

We were all out on the school playground one afternoon taking turns tossing a football to one another. We were not holding it on the ground as you normally might with a football. No. Place-kicks were not challenging enough for us. Instead, one of us would haphazardly chuck the ball into the air, while another of us aimed to kick it before it hit the ground. Much like playing in the backyard with the boys, when I was at school, we also made things up and creatively upped the challenge as we went along. Midair football kicks were no exception.

Before my turn, not a single second grader managed to connect and actually kick the ball. With every miss, we all laughed hysterically at how ridiculous it looked to awkwardly swoop one leg high into the air, attempting to kick the ball as it flipped by, hit the ground, then bounced erratically away. Toss after toss, swooping kick after swooping kick, everyone missed. Until finally, it was my turn. As the ball flipped haphazardly toward me, I kept my eyes focused on the center of it, prepared my kick position, then swooped my right leg into the air.

Thwump!

I kicked it. On the first try. Not only was I the only girl to kick it; I was the only second grader to kick it. We abruptly ended the game there, which left me to reign over the schoolyard for the rest of that afternoon.

Things like kicking that ball came easier to me because of my size five shoes. Simply having a larger foot increased my odds of connecting with the ball. I did not have the heart to tell the other kids that I was just as shocked as they were by what I had done. Impressing them felt great, so I savored the moment for as long as I could. Schoolyard respect was indeed a key to feeling good about myself when I was six.

Even there, on our elementary school playground, those small steps with small successes were the little reassurances that made me feel I was good at something. That encouraged me along the way. As I left the playground that afternoon, I walked a little taller, one step at a time, chest upward, face to the sun, my heart emboldened by my newfound elementary school confidence.

I discovered a sense of joy, a happiness from kicking that ball. A sense of wonder in how those little reassurances made me feel. So from there on, I moved in the direction of things that could help me feel that way as often as possible. In the direction of what might suit someone like me. Someone taller than average. With arms and legs longer than average. Feet bigger than average. One of the few girls who could keep up with the boys. Which guided me toward even more sports.

I was eight when I started playing basketball. Third grade. We called ourselves the Purple Team after the purple T-shirts we wore. That was the distinction the YMCA used then—one based solely on the color of the T-shirt your randomly assigned team was given. We practiced at random too, playing on courts that were shorter, shooting on rims that were lower (eight feet rather than the standard ten feet high). Games consisted of running in circles without much clue as to how the sport worked other than attempting to shoot the basketball through the hoop and to make steals as often as possible. Steals are easier when you are eight and no one is good at passing the ball yet.

Our coach was tall and had curly brown hair like mine. She smiled, laughed, had tons of positive energy, and in my eight-year-old eyes, was amazing at basketball. After we finished our Purple Team's season, having won all of our games against the other third graders, I once more walked a little taller, one step at a time, and looked forward to playing basketball again. I also hoped we would get to have our same coach again. Over the course of our very short season together, she made me think that maybe I could grow up to be like her. That maybe I could be that athletic and cool one day.

By fifth grade, field hockey and soccer joined my sport skillset. At nine years old, I finally got to play on teams tied to my school. With fifth grade being the youngest grade for which my school had organized teams, those two field sports, along with basketball, occupied every season of the year throughout middle school. A reasonable basis for the mutterings that I might be maturing into an "all-around athlete."

Late in the summer of the following year, I walked downstairs into my family's living room and pushed the silver click-on switch of our old Sony television. For my entire childhood, when it came to television, we relied on the massive metal antenna—one that looked more like a clothesline from the 1970s—that lived on the highest part of our pointed two-story tin roof. That August before I started sixth grade was no different.

We had neither cable nor satellite, which left me with all of four channels to choose from (sometimes five, depending on how clear the sky was that day). Because I knew NBC was the most reliable, I started with NBC.

When I pressed my ten-year-old belly up against the glass television screen to reach for the small bunny ear–shaped antenna that sat on top of the TV itself, I could feel the static electricity playing with the lint on my T-shirt. As my belly tingled from the static, I began adjusting the TV antenna toward a position that would allow me to most clearly watch NBC. With one hand still on the bunny ears, I craned my neck, chin to my chest, to assess the image on the screen to be sure my adjustments were helping. Eventually, the snow-like fuzz on the TV screen softened into a tolerably clear picture.

When the image clarified and no longer strained my eyes, something foreign to me appeared on the screen. The only thing I could come up with at the time was that it reminded me of small water bugs. The little black kind with a skinny body and two even skinnier legs sticking out to its sides. The kind that skim the surface of a pool or creek during the summer. Usually their skinny little legs move in unison, back and forth to propel them, gliding rapidly yet delicately across the water.

As my eyes fixated, and I attempted to understand what I was seeing, the NBC commentators' voices chimed in. With their help, I finally realized that what I had stumbled upon were not water bugs (of course they were not). They were something similar when viewed from above though—tiny one-person boats separated by lane lines as if they were in some gigantic version of a swimming pool during a swim meet.

Before my mind had a chance to wrap itself around what it was seeing, the television cameras switched from that above view to a side view to a front view, then back again. At every switch of the camera's angle, each image became increasingly more confusing than the previous. Meanwhile, the two commentators carried on in the background. Needless to say, no matter which view I saw, I understood neither how nor why the people in the boats could face in one direction but race in the opposite.

Because the Summer Olympic Games only happen every four years, they dominated NBC's airtime on August 2, 1992. So the Olympics was apparently what I had come across on our old Sony TV that day. It was Barcelona. The women's single race. One of the fourteen rowing events held at the Olympics. As I watched, I could see that it was a women's event. One woman per boat. Two oars per woman. Which, apparently, made them look like tiny water bugs when viewed from above.

During the (seemingly endless to my ten-year-old mind) race, I distinctly recall the commentators diverting from the race itself to tell a background story about one of the women who was leading the pack. She was the favorite for that particular event heading into the Barcelona Olympics. She had won the previous year's World Championships—the international race that happens during each year that the Olympic Games do not. However, during the final months before the Games, right when she should have been completely focused on nothing but her training routine, the woman the commentators spoke of had gotten into an accident with another boat during training. An accident that left one of her legs severely injured.

Now that adult me understands what I do about rowing—for one thing, that it is not an arm sport but, rather, a leg-dominated sport, a sport where speed comes mostly from strong legs that push to drive the boat forward—I realize just how debilitating a leg injury can be.

Due the extent of her injury, the woman's doctors told her she might never row again. That she should give up her Olympic dream. But instead of giving up, following several surgeries and many weeks of physical therapy, that woman carried on with her Olympic preparation despite her dire predicament.

She could have easily called it quits at that point, and people probably would have understood. But no. She made her way to the Olympic final in the women's singles race—the very race ten-year-old me stood watching—despite her odds. That is what kept me glued to the screen on August 2, 1992, even though I had never heard of a sport called "rowing" before.

By the time the women in the race crossed the finish line on that August day in 1992, the one who had overcome that debilitating leg injury came away with the bronze medal. Third place at the Olympic Games just a few months after she was told she would never row again.

Those eight and a half minutes I spent confused by the tiny water-bug-like boats on the fuzzy screen when I was ten were all I would learn about rowing for the decade that followed. As I said, rowing was not a thing where I grew up. Even if I had come away wanting to take up rowing right then and there, it would not have mattered. I knew of no nearby teams, nor was there internet searching by which I could find one. There was no googling, no streaming video, so no on-demand replays. Instead, I buried rowing deep within my ten-year-old mind.

One thing I did not bury, though, was the story the commentators shared about the woman who overcame injury to take bronze. I was in awe. Her story was inspiring. She made me wonder about the kind of physical and mental strength it took to be an athlete at her level—a real athlete, an Olympian. With the number of different sports I was interested in then, I could not help but think of how incredible it would feel to one day be like the women who raced in the Barcelona Olympics. But I was ten. I knew I had a long way to go before I could become a real athlete like them.

While sixth grade came and went, field hockey, basketball, and soccer continued to anchor my afternoons. But because I was another year older, both school and sport demands increased. More homework. More games. One or both on every day of the week. Long drives home after practice or a game. Up late to finish whatever school assignment was due the next day. Spending the school year like that would make any sixth grader eagerly anticipate the freedom of summer vacation. Which I did because summer was a time to play without having to think about school.

As they did from time to time, my aunt, uncle, and two younger cousins made the long, winding drive to visit us out at our house one summer Saturday. We usually grilled hotdogs and hamburgers, had a picnic, then played games in the backyard. As for this particular visit, our chosen backyard game was baseball.

After lunch, we gathered what equipment we had, then headed to the yard, where we used pine cones to mark the bases for our makeshift playing field. After that, we assigned a batting order, and my brother, cousins, and I took turns swinging at the pitches my uncle threw our way.

When my turn at bat came, I stood ready, bat in hand, and facing toward the small field where our horses and goats roamed. My uncle then pitched my brother's blue baseball toward me. I never had formal coaching in baseball before then, but I had learned through trial and error to keep my eyes on the center of the ball—the very approach that helped me kick that football back in second grade. As the dark-blue dot of a baseball neared me, I swung.

Thwack!

When I made contact with the ball, the vibrations from the

bat stung my hands a little. I did not mind. It was a small price to pay for the satisfaction of watching that blue dot sail over my uncle's left shoulder toward our makeshift right field. As the ball soared away, my uncle barely moved. He only turned slightly as he watched the ball make its arc, come to a landing in the yard, roll down the grassy hill, then disappear.

"Hey," he said, turning back toward me with a semipuzzled smile on his face. "Do you want to play on my farm league baseball team?"

He was coaching a team of kids who were too young for little league. The season had already begun, but my uncle said he would call the other coaches to ask special permission for a late roster addition. If the other coaches approved, I could join the team the following week. Of course, I was interested. I liked batting, and I had never been on a baseball team before.

One week later, I went to my first baseball team practice. A week or so after that, my first game. At eleven years old, I was the only girl on our team. I could hit and throw as well or better than any of the boys. I was also the tallest. When my turn came to step up for my first at bat during my first game, I pulled on my protective helmet, grabbed my favorite bat, walked toward home plate, and showed everyone there that I was the tallest out of all the players on either team.

After our game that day, my uncle pulled me aside and told me that as soon as the coach from the other team saw me walk out onto the field, he immediately wanted to know who I was. My uncle told him the truth. That I was his niece. You see, when my uncle called the league to ask if "his niece" could join late, the answer quickly came back as "Yes." The other coaches sold me short because I was a niece and not a nephew.

My uncle, though, he knew better than to sell me short because I was a girl. He was tall, athletic, and radiated positive energy through his smile. To me, he knew everything there was to know about sports. So after I hit a few into the outfield during my first baseball game that day, then learned just how much someone like my uncle believed in me, I walked a little taller, reassured, one step at a time, toward the car.

As I climbed into the back-left seat of my parents' car, I looked down at my navy-blue team T-shirt, then kicked a little reddish-brown dirt from my cleats. It was dirt I had collected rounding the bases during my very first official baseball game. I could not help but grin as I buckled my seat belt.

During the forty-five-minute drive home with my parents and brother, I started to think that maybe those mutterings of my becoming an all-around athlete might not be so far off. I also could not help but wonder if I could be as athletic and positive as my uncle one day.

My uncle David and me after one of my first baseball games.

THREE CONDITIONS.

I ALREADY TOLD YOU THAT I GREW UP JUST OUTSIDE A SMALL college town. And when I say, "just outside," I mean sixteen miles. About twenty minutes by car. Forty-five if you get stuck behind a bus. What I did not tell you, though, is that the town itself is home to the University of Virginia. So like most kids from my hometown, I followed all kinds of Virginia sports when I was young. I followed them in the paper, watched them on TV, and when I got into middle and high school, I even got to watch them in person. To me, the Virginia Cavaliers were celebrities. Heroes in my young eyes.

The day I sat near the baseline in the old University Hall and watched the Virginia women's basketball team play, I witnessed firsthand what it was like to be fast when the Cavaliers' new forward sprinted from the opposite end of the court toward where I was seated in the stands. She then received a pass near the baseline. When she did, I could tell by the look on her face that she knew she was going to score.

In one smooth motion, the Cavalier forward received the ball, squared her body toward the hoop, then shot with finesse. Her three-pointer seemed effortless. After the sound of the basketball's textured rubber made its trademark *swish* through the net, she took off toward the other end, her long blonde ponytail whipping in satisfaction as she spun. My jaw dropped as I watched her sprint away.

She was a few inches taller than me. She was faster than me. She handled the ball better than me. And she definitely shot better than me. To me, much like the women I had watched in that Olympic rowing race on NBC a few years before, this Virginia Cavalier was a real athlete.

I was in middle school then. I was sure she had been in middle school at some point too. Which made me wonder how she had gone from middle school skill to college caliber. As I watched in awe, I wondered what it might feel like to be as fast and skilled as her one day. *Imagine. Me. Good enough to play in college.*

By the time I was twelve, basketball was my constant. It was common in my hometown and one of the few sports offered by my school. My school was small. The kind where everyone knows everyone, where most of your classmates and teachers remain the same from year to year, and where, because it is somehow meant to make things easier, you have a dress code. Even though many of my school's qualities made things easier for my family, having a dress code did not. If anything, it made things harder. Particularly on game days.

On top of its standard obligations, my school required those who played sports to dress up on game days. For girls, that meant dresses, skirts, or dress pants. All of which I dreaded wearing because tall-sized clothing designed for girls my age did not exist when I was in eighth grade. As for shoes, forget it. When my feet grew four sizes in one year, my mom and I both knew that I was destined for large feet. On the day my feet grew to size ten, I looked down at my lanky toes and wished they would stay put at that ten. Although I knew I did not have direct control over them like that, I figured one quick wish could not hurt. When my feet finally reached size twelve (twelve and a half on the right), boys' shoes became my only option.

My last hope for girls' shoes came and went when a friend of my mom's called her about a store that supposedly carried size twelves and was a mere ninety-minute drive from where we lived. The moment my mom hung up the phone, I heard hope in her voice, which gave me hope too. We made the trip as soon as possible after that.

Maybe they'll sell girls' shoes in my size, hopeful twelve-year-old me thought as I sat on the cushioned bench in the front corner of the store anticipating the wonderful choices I was about to have. When the store clerk walked toward me carrying four large shoe boxes, I daydreamed he had so many options that he simply could not carry them all at once. Unfortunately, I soon discovered that was not the case. Four pairs were it. Every pair unisex. Every pair too wide for my narrow feet. Knowing how far out of her way my mom had gone for me that day, I contemplated my four options, then picked the most feminine pair among them—a pair of dark brown leather sandals.

As my mom and I left the store, I was disappointed by having to settle for boys' shoes. I could tell that my mom was disappointed too. Mostly because she knew by the look on my face that I had gotten my hopes up.

During our ninety-minute drive home, my mom and I talked about my new shoes. She asked me questions about them, then started to describe them. Eventually, the way she spoke about them made me think maybe, just maybe, my new shoes were more feminine than I thought. The only thing missing was a little heel she said. I was tall, I did not need the heel to be graceful she said. Plus, flats would be more comfortable during my long days at school.

Dressing up made me nervous, so anything to make me feel less self-conscious was a good thing. By the time we got home, my new shoes had grown on me. Albeit slightly, I looked forward to wearing them on the day of my next basketball game. A day that came shortly after our trip to the shoe store.

On the morning of my next game, I dressed for school in my long light-green dress, the one with the leaf print and the brown buttons down the front. I wore my favorite white capped-sleeve T-shirt underneath, and of course, my new shoes. I even wore my hair down—something I rarely did unless my mom made me. On my way out the door, I walked with my chest up and stood a little taller than usual. As I climbed into the back-left seat of my dad's car, I wondered, *Is it possible that I feel good about my outfit?*

During our long, slow drive toward school on that late fall morning of my eighth-grade year, the scent of my shoes' fresh leather permeated the car. When it did, my stomach turned a little. Maybe the smell and the curvy road made me carsick. Maybe I was nervous about my upcoming game. Either way, when we pulled into my school's parking lot, I took a deep breath, closed my eyes as I exhaled it, and planned to behave as if nothing about my outfit was out of the ordinary. I figured, that way, no one would notice that I was wearing boys' shoes.

Once I had taken my deep breath and felt a little calmer, I said goodbye to my dad, walked into school, and pretended I had no idea I was dressed unusually. Then, as I navigated the hallway, I did the same. When I stopped by my locker, the same. And when I chatted with friends, then headed to Latin class with one of my favorite teachers, the same.

I arrived a little early for Latin, took my seat, fiddled with my notebook, then organized my papers. While I situated myself, I thought about how my day had passed pretty typically thus far. No one had pointed out my dress or my hair or my shoes, so I began to relax about my appearance and thought that my mom might have been right. *Maybe I do look nice.*

Just before the bell rang, my remaining classmates filed in.

One by one, they walked by laughing or chatting, then took their respective seats. With every person who passed, I settled more comfortably into my seat, and I became less anxious about my appearance.

Right as my stomach began to ease for the first time since I left home, a whisper of a male voice crept over my shoulder and crawled into my right ear. "Hey. Nice Jesus shoes," he said. "Where'd you get 'em? Kmart?"

I pretended not to hear what my classmate said, so I did not respond with something clever. Instead, I discreetly inched my heels up the legs of my desk to hide my shoes under my dress and out of sight.

Rather than continuing to sit tall, chest up, pleased with my touch of newfound confidence in my appearance, my chest deflated, I slid down slightly in my chair, and my shoulders hunched as if to hug my heart. As if to shield it from the hurt of the boy's words. It was a hurt I was not used to. One that swept away every increasingly comfortable and confident step I had taken that morning.

My new brown leather sandals, the ones my mom and I drove all that way to find, only made it through a few hours of my school day before being identified as for a boy and labeled "Jesus shoes." Because of how many games I played during the year for my school's teams, I had to dress up often. That meant I felt awkward often, and I had to pretend it did not bother me. Often.

After the boy's comment, I could not wait for the day to be over so I could change out of those shoes and back into the comfort of my team uniform, gym shoes, and practice. Back to where I felt special for being tall rather than awkward. Back to where I could kick or hit the ball far, throw hard, and score points. Back to where these little reassurances gradually built my confidence.

Sports were my place to shine. I was cool there. While wearing my team uniform, no one could make fun of my clothes or my feet or my shoes because, let's face it, basketball shoes tend to look like boys' shoes anyway.

Because I was the tallest girl in my grade, by the time I was twelve, and I had played basketball since third grade, my school team's coaches dubbed me full of "potential." So they suggested I focus on basketball by skipping junior varsity and trying out for varsity right away. I was not even in high school yet, but since my school allowed it, and I trusted the coaches, I figured I would do what they suggested. Just in case they were right about me and my potential. Plus, if I wanted to be anything like the athletes and coaches I admired growing up, taking on tougher competition was a step I needed to take.

On the afternoon of the varsity tryout, I got dropped off at the community facility where my school's basketball team practiced. I stood there on the concrete curb outside the building for a moment to collect myself before walking in. As I sized up the brick facade, I took a deep breath, exhaled it, then walked toward the building's small glass-door entrance. When I approached the doors, I briefly caught my reflection in the glass. I was dressed in my gym shorts, T-shirt, and basketball shoes. I wore sweatpants over my shorts and my winter jacket to ward off the chill of the season. A chill made a tad nippier by my growing nervousness. After sizing myself up, I walked in alone.

When the door closed behind me, my eyes and ears first fixated on the whiteness and flickering buzz of the lobby lights. Then the low electric hum of the vending machines. Until finally, the faint echoes of rubber pinging against wood. When I heard those echoes, I knew where I needed to go.

With that faint rubbery pinging as my guide, I continued through the lobby toward the gym, where the familiar sound of basketballs against freshly varnished wood intensified. With every step I took, my goose bumps grew firmer on account of my nerves, and I breathed deeper. While my body subconsciously prepared itself to fight or flee, I realized that this was no ordinary tryout, as the coaches had suggested. This was different.

I had tried new things and had joined new teams before. I had experienced new coaches and had met new teammates before. However, the step I was about to take by going from middle school to varsity sports was a new kind of step. It was the single largest step of my eighth-grade life.

As I stood there on the cusp of making the step up to my school's varsity team, I finally processed what it meant: I would no longer be compared to just the girls my age but to the high school girls too. When that hit me, I realized I was not about to take another gradual, manageable step. I was about to take a leap. One that made even my size twelve basketball shoes feel small.

By the time I reached the gym, about to take my first step onto the court for my very first varsity basketball tryout, the sport that had nudged me gradually forward through each of the five years I had played it suddenly intimidated me. As the demands and expectations of playing for my school's varsity team struck me one rubbery pinging echo at a time, my nerves swelled further, my goose bumps prickled, and my arm hair bristled.

Up until the moment I walked into the gym that day, I had the impression that the varsity coach would teach me everything I needed to know. Gradually. So I could gradually become more confident in my basketball skills. However, when I peeked into the gym and saw the first of many basketballs *swish* through the ten-foot rim, I panicked and assumed every other girl at the tryout was better than me. So I quickly changed my mind. I did not check in with the varsity coach as planned. I did not warm up with the rest of the girls as planned. Instead, I chickened out and backpedaled toward the bleachers to watch.

When the coach found me hiding from sight (and further embarrassment), I pretended I had not come to try out for the team and was only there to observe. To learn for next season when

I felt ready for varsity. In reality, the junior varsity team, was less intimidating and what I felt prepared for.

Because the varsity coach knew he could not force me to try out, he agreed to let me play JV under a few conditions. First, that I would try out for the varsity team the following year. Second, that I would play for the JV team provided that whenever JV did not have a game, I would dress in uniform and play with varsity. That way, I could grow my confidence against JV competition but also periodically test it at the varsity level. The third condition? That I would call a local club team coach to see if I could join his team too. His team was comprised of only the best players in the area, all collected from different schools. So if I truly did want to improve to college caliber one day, joining his team was a must.

All three conditions the varsity coach presented were supposedly the next steps toward becoming my best at basketball. Steps that would prepare me to play at the next level: college. So I agreed to everything the varsity coach told me.

At twelve years old, I played for three basketball teams at the same time. I practiced or played the sport every day of the week, including Sunday nights. By playing that much basketball, my free throw percentage improved because we finished every club team practice with no less than twenty shots from the foul line. We ran sprints for missed shots, both individually and as a team. Push-up holds were the norm for poorly executed plays. And at the end of most practices, we scrimmaged our dads. The idea was that being knocked around by people much larger and stronger would surely prepare us for anything our twelve- and thirteen-year-old opponents could do.

During club team games, we knew when it was time for a substitution when our coach would whirl wildly toward the bench, arms assertively outstretched, armpits stained in sweat, a tiny pearl of spit flying from the corner of his mouth, his shirt partially untucking itself as he spun. He would scan the row of us sitting on the bench, then look back at the court, then back to the bench again. While we knew it was time for a substitution, we never knew who would be the one selected. Only when I would feel him lock his grip around the edge of my jersey to slingshot me toward the scorer's table did I know when it was my turn. I knew to sprint, too, because he could just as quickly change his mind and yank me back to my seat.

The first time he yanked me back, he snapped at me and insisted that my lack of speed demonstrated that I did not want to play as badly as my teammates. He told me to let him know when I finally decided to sprint. Only then would he again consider putting me in a game. In reality, I was not as fast as my teammates. I was still that awkwardly lanky puppy who had a lot more growing to do.

Little did he know that I sprinted faster for him that day than I ever had in my whole life. I had spent so much time riding the bench that I really did want to play. But with every passing minute I sat, the idea of playing made me increasingly nervous. I imagined myself ruining a play or missing a shot, losing the game for my team. Considering I had a front-row seat to every word our coach shouted toward my teammates on the court, my hesitation intensified. Sometimes I would think about how my club coach reminded me of the coaches I admired growing up. Most of the time, though, he made me nervous.

Every now and again, my old national rowing team teammates will bring up stories about what our rowing coach, Tom, used to say to me. They will laugh at the odd things he used to come up with and wonder how I always took them in stride. Compared to my club team basketball coach, I never considered anything Tom said as harsh. Just creative, honest, and clear.

As I moved up from middle school to varsity and club basketball teams, not only did the coaches intensify but so did the demands of sports altogether. The players got bigger, more experienced, and more skilled. Practices got longer, with more drills and more plays to learn, while games became more challenging in every way. As a result, taking things gradually did not seem fast enough, so I began to question every step I took.

Before eighth grade, school and sports increased in challenge one step at a time. But with eighth grade flying by and high school approaching, I began to feel myself taking oddly hesitant steps. Rather than steadily stepping forward, my progress slowed, so I hesitated even more. The more I hesitated, the more I doubted. The more I doubted, the more I felt as though my progress had all but stopped and, with it, the very idea of ever becoming good enough to play in college.

On the day our club coach offered us one-on-one meetings to discuss what we each needed to do to play basketball in college, my teammates were excited for their meetings. Despite my doubts, I went along with the plan and took him up on the offer too. Imagine if I had been the only one who chose not to take a meeting? I would never have seen another second of playing time.

On the afternoon of my meeting, my coach and I sat down under the screened-in porch of his house to review what I needed to do to play college ball. He assumed my motivation to play for three basketball teams at the same time was that I was certain I wanted to play in college.

According to him, the key to my being recruited was one thing: preparation. He told me I needed to keep improving my skills, my dribbling, passing, shooting, and rebounding. Plus, I needed to improve my strength, speed, and aggression. He spoke of patience, consistency, and dedication. He told me I had the potential for it all. He also told me his plan.

Over the years, he had compiled a step-by-step workbook specifically designed for athletes who wanted to play college basketball. He refined it every year to the point that it was foolproof. He told me his advice and drills would help me stay in touch with basketball year-round which would ensure my steady improvement.

By the end of our meeting, we had reviewed his entire plan for me, and I learned one key takeaway: playing basketball for three teams, practicing or playing every day, was only the beginning. In order to step up to the next level, to become college caliber, I needed to practice multiple times a day, with multiple coaches, and on my own. Plus, become stronger, faster, and more aggressive.

Everything about our meeting boggled my mind that summer before ninth grade. Nevertheless, I accepted his advice and workbook with open palms and got to work right away.

My dad took my brother and me to the middle school near our house that very evening. As the sun started to set and the gnats grew thick in the warm, damp air, I did layup drill after layup drill, elbow jumper after elbow jumper out on the old, weathered asphalt court behind the school. I had day one officially on the books. I remember it well, for day one was both the first and the last day I followed any of the notes in that workbook.

The amount of time it took me to complete that first day of drills—supposedly one of the short, easy days—seemed like forever. And if a short day seemed like forever, the idea of what it would take for me to become college caliber was more than overwhelming. It seemed downright impossible.

My fledgling confidence was not yet firm. It was still forming, so even though I was proud I had completed day one, I faltered from there forward. I further questioned myself. I began doubting things I had never doubted before. I even wondered whether what I admired in my coaches, teammates, and childhood heroes was possible for me at all. I could not see it at the time, but with every hesitation and small comparison I made, I was unwittingly empowering doubt to limit my forward steps.

I was on the cusp of high school and varsity sports, and the very things that had long helped me learn and grow were transforming into intimidating and uncomfortable experiences. So while I weighed what it would take to play college sports, part of me began to question if I was good enough to play even high school varsity.

Despite my internal debate, I did not break my promises to my school's varsity coach. Later that year, in the fall of ninth grade, I followed through on his last remaining condition. Instead of backpedaling and hiding behind the bleachers, I took a breath, exhaled it, and made the varsity basketball team. I may not have felt I had next-level potential, but I did enjoy playing sports and spending time with my teammates.

January 2014,

I swore I would be committed to the notebook of drills. They told me I needed to be stronger, keep the ball higher, play to my strengths. But I preferred finesse.

FOUR

BUT IF YOU'RE AN ARTIST.

A FEW MONTHS BEFORE I MADE THE VARSITY BASKETBALL team, I tried out for varsity volleyball at the recommendation of some friends. They felt volleyball would complement our main sport basketball through its jump requirements and similar on-the-court conditioning. I was thirteen and a high school freshman. I looked up to my friends because they were older. To me, they were cool, so of course, their idea made sense.

Up through ninth grade, I had played basketball most consistently, which (understandably) made people presume it was my favorite. But once I began playing volleyball, that changed. To me, volleyball was new and different. And while I initially picked it up freshman year because of my friends, by sophomore year, it became my favorite sport thanks to our new coach who opened my eyes to something I did not know was missing.

On the first day of the fall season during my sophomore year, our new volleyball coach, Coach Morse, walked onto the court with a smile on her face. At first glance, I got the impression she was part nervous, all excited, and most certainly tall, athletic, and positive. The fact that she had been an Academic All-American during her college years put me in even more awe, so I eagerly anticipated her knowledge.

From day one, Coach Morse had a plan. One that started with basic skills. Every day. Simple repetitive drills. Sometimes small games at the end of practice if time permitted. She taught us the proper techniques for passing, digging, serving, and hitting. She taught us the different sport positions which eventually became plays. She even taught us about team cheers because they could help us to regroup after nearly every play. Everything Coach Morse imparted came with insightful tips that made the sport itself more enjoyable and all the easier to understand.

During games, she would sit quietly and take notes. She always focused on what we did, but never shouted. Instead, she gave us pointers from the sidelines with careful direction.

Though volleyball is a team sport, after every game, we each received a tally of our individual "points" we had earned in that game, which were based on our coach's rating system. We accumulated these points for every pass or serve we made. Passes were rated zero to three based on how much effort it took our setter—the girl who set the ball up to be spiked (who was usually the second person to touch the ball in a given play)—to do her job. Serves were rated on whether we made it over the net and also if we aced it (which would immediately score a point for our team).

Toward the end of one of our games late in the season, the coach I so looked up to smiled at me, then very casually made a comment as I passed her. "Nice work, Miss Consistent."

Because of the rating system she kept, Coach Morse could see that the majority of my passes were regularly better than average. I rarely, if ever, scored zero, while the rest of my skills reliably helped our team score points. Because I focused one pass or hit at a time, I did not notice anything special about what I was doing. Rather, I happily worked hard with my teammates. This all added up to my enjoyment of absolutely everything we were building together one drill and one day at a time.

Because I had never received a compliment like "Miss Consistent" before, I could not help but grin.

The way we trained seemed so simple that I at first wondered why we spent so much time on skills and so little on playing during our practices. But when our tiny daily improvements began to show through the games we started to win, I no longer wondered. We were taking steps and gaining traces of confidence as a team. When we found ourselves fighting our way through a three-and-a-half-hour match in the state tournament during our first year with Coach Morse, I fully appreciated the importance of the little things she taught us.

Because of her methods, it took just two short seasons for volleyball to overshadow basketball in my mind. All thanks to the coach who taught me the true value and meaning of consistency by mastering the basics. She trained us to do the simple things incredibly well and taught us that working together would carry us the farthest. To me, that made it all the more enjoyable. In fact, I enjoyed volleyball more than any sport I had ever played before then.

Of all the things people ever suggested to me during high school, enjoying what I chose to do was never something anyone stated outright. But given that I found myself drawn to the sports and school subjects that I enjoyed, I came to trust that enjoying what I did was important to me. I just did not know what specific pursuit after high school would allow me to accomplish that.

By the time I was told I should be thinking about college, here is what I knew: I had gone to school and played team sports for basically my entire life. In school and athletics alike, I picked things up to a decent level of proficiency by making gradual progress one step at a time. I learned that when demands ramped up too quickly, as they did with basketball, I questioned myself, which caused my progress to hesitate.

When it came to my studies, I did my homework and paid attention to my teachers. I never skipped class and was never late unless excused. Such simple tactics helped me earn good grades—all A's with the exception of history. I was terrible at history. As it turns out, history is pretty difficult if you do not like to read (which I did not then).

If I had to pick a favorite subject, it would have been art, followed by Spanish, then math or science of any kind. All on account of my teachers, who (like my favorite coaches) helped me gradually learn.

When fall of senior year arrived, I could no longer simply think about college. I needed to make decisions about it. I had not given college much thought before senior year apart from periodic conversations with my mom about what I might do for a living one day. She emphasized the importance of self-reliance and independence but never once pressed me toward any one thing. She simply told me that I could "do just about anything to support myself." Especially if it was "just me."

The day she said I could even work at McDonald's to support myself, I figured she was joking. But she was serious. Though I am pretty sure she did not want me to work in fast food.

Other than my mom's open-minded guidance about "doing anything to support myself," my only college consideration was that California seemed like an interesting state. I saw UCLA on TV once, and I liked their school colors. Despite my intrigue, I never even looked into applying to UCLA.

Instead, I applied early to only one school. The one I thought was the most affordable. The one that was sixteen whole miles from where I grew up—the University of Virginia (UVA). With my application in by November of senior year, I could know where I was headed before most of my friends even started looking. And since I did not consider myself college athlete material, I was fine with the early commitment.

By spring of senior year, despite my hesitations and doubts, I had invested enough in volleyball and basketball to become decent at both. In basketball, there were times when I scored more than twenty points in a single game. In volleyball, I could set up plays, make blocks, ace serves, and pass accurately. In both sports, my progress earned me awards like Most Improved, Most Consistent, and eventually Most Valuable Player. Initially, these honors came at individual tournaments. Then for my school's conference. Then its league. Until finally, I earned it for the entire state of Virginia.

But here is the thing. For every indication of my improvement, my self-doubt made me question it. I had watched Olympians, college athletes, my coaches, and even my own teammates win medals, score points, jump high, hit hard, shoot well, and run fast. Their very existence demonstrated the kind of strength, speed, talent, knowledge, and commitment it would take to compete at the next level. By comparison, I felt I could never be like them. I was just a tall girl at a small school, where I presumed my skills only stood out because there were not many other female athletes. I assumed that once I was outside my own school, people would realize I was quite average.

It was with these assumptions in mind and high school graduation upon me that I felt I had no choice but to abandon athletics and focus solely on academics. This meant that when high school basketball ended for me, it would be the first time in fifteen years that I would not have a team to call my own.

On graduation day, I stacked into formation on the back stairs of the venue where our ceremony was held. In pictures from the event, I am standing with my eyes closed, preparing to throw my cap. They told us we could pretend but that we should not actually throw them. If we did, they said we would get into trouble. We were told not to do a lot of things, so I did not throw my cap that June morning.

Two and a half months of summer freedom later, it was time.

On move-in day, I procrastinated all morning. The place I had known for seventeen years as my house had somehow turned into my parents' house overnight. An entire childhood under one roof, and *poof*, I woke up in a bedroom that was no longer mine. It was instead an unfamiliar space filled with cardboard boxes.

All of a sudden, the guidance I was used to having, the suggestions about what I should do were gone. My path was my own, and for the first time in my life, it did not include sports and teams. I was seventeen and self-conscious of the fact that I was six feet tall and wore a size twelve shoe. I slouched in accordance with my friend's heights. I wore baggy clothes because the sleeves and pant legs were never long enough in regular-fit sizes. And having succumbed to a consistent stream of self-doubt, I did not dare take on college athletics. Instead, I played it safe.

I was bound for the University of Virginia to pursue academics, not sports. My plan was to focus on school, study whatever was required and whatever I enjoyed. Those were my next steps. The ones that made the most sense. I stopped playing sports and prepared to major in Spanish, minor in art history, and take as many art classes as I could.

Over the years, I had gravitated toward art and Spanish for many of the same reasons why I was drawn to my favorite sports. Not only had Spanish and art become enjoyable, but they had also come most easily to me, which increased my enjoyment of them. And since my mom consistently reiterated that I could "do anything to support myself," I figured those subjects would somehow work. They were my best plan for enjoying what I chose to do. The only thing I was sure about anymore.

When I told people my major and minor, most assumed I wanted to teach. I was told to be a teacher so often that it made me think it was the only thing people interested in Spanish and art could become. So I took to grinning and staying quiet since I had yet to form "a real plan" past college. Spanish and art made me happy. That was as far as I had gotten.

A few months after my freshman fall at UVA began, I drove out to my parents' house for an impromptu visit. I had officially shifted focus away from sports and toward art and Spanish, so was excited to share an art project I had been working on. The focus I discovered in art was the kind that kept me up all night, hours passing in a blink. Only when the pitch black of night made its shift to the bluish grey of morning would I realize how long my creativity had flowed. I was proud of my commitment, so I could not wait to show it off.

At a school like UVA, I had options. Moving from my small high school with a short list of classes to a large university with seemingly endless possibilities allowed me to pursue all kinds of interests on top of Spanish and art. Based on my logic at the time, I anchored my schedule with those two subjects, then built one of everything else around them. I included in my schedule such courses as environmental policy, oceanography, astronomy, art history, cinema, and anthropology.

On the afternoon of my impromptu visit with my parents though, as I excitedly shared my diverse class schedule and showed off my artwork, something unexpected happened. Rather than being utterly pleased, my mom's advice about what I could do to support myself took on an addendum.

"Yes, you can do anything." I could hear the hesitation in her voice as she continued. "But, Honey, if you're an artist, you might starve."

From that visit forward, my parents became a bit more cautious whenever we discussed what I might do for a living.

Considering my mom's new words of caution, I could not help but question my choices. Art and Spanish were what I enjoyed. Having given up sports, they were all I had left. Apparently though, what I had long enjoyed, what had long guided me, were no longer viable options. Which meant I had new decisions to make. Unfamiliar decisions. Intimidating decisions. Decisions that led me into uncharted territory, where I stumbled upon some startling realities.

September 2000,

I guess I don't know what will happen in the future...I wonder where I will be in a decade, a year, a month, a week, a day. I once thought I could be one of those people who is successful. But now I know that might not be what makes me even remotely happy.

FIVE

I USED TO BE.

WHEN I PLAYED FIELD HOCKEY AND SOCCER BACK IN MIDDLE school, I was the goalie for both teams. I preferred being the goalie because I got to run less than my teammates. I hated running back then. It embarrassed me because I was the slowest. So slow that I once got the field hockey team's Turtle Award for being the slowest.

My distaste for running notwithstanding, late in the fall of my first year at UVA, when my lifelong friend, Victoria, invited me to run a 5K with her, I threw caution to the wind. The event was a fundraiser for UVA, the entry fee was cheap, and the start location was across the street from my dorm. For as much as I trusted Victoria and as easy a setup as the race was, I could not say no.

On the morning of the race, I dressed in my best 5K-in-November running attire, laced up my old sneakers, put on a long-sleeved T-shirt, and cinched the waistband of my favorite mesh shorts. After double-knotting my shoelaces, I headed out the door, then made my way down the short slope that led from my dorm toward the parking lot where the race organizers were busy setting up.

Everything about the morning epitomized fall in central Virginia. The brownish-green remnants of dry grass that crunched faintly under my feet. The parched, curled leaves lying carefully on the bald dirt patches that dotted the grass. The sun that tried to shine some semblance of warmth down on me through a cloudless sky. The crisp, cool morning air that filled the space between me and the sun.

I have played a lot of sports in my life, I thought to myself as I strolled toward the start, where I would await Victoria's arrival. *This is 3.1 miles. I know I don't run, but I should be able to do this.*

After Victoria arrived and the time came for the race to start, the organizers arranged us across the parking lot in a straight line. They did not stage us with tape or rope. We did not have GPS trackers or chip times. It was not that kind of race. I was not that kind of runner. Truthfully, their low-key style made me feel better about my casual approach to the event.

In the final moments before we got underway, I paid little attention to what was going on around me and simply continued chatting with Victoria. Then, right as I was midsentence, the race organizers made a quick announcement, and we abruptly took off.

We began at a jogging pace. A pace that allowed us to chat. A pace I imagined us keeping the whole race through. But as the energy from the crowd invigorated her, Victoria picked up her pace. When I attempted to increase my speed with hers, my words shortened. Until they eventually trailed off in exchange for a labored breathing. It was a shortness of breath I had not felt in at least six months. Not since high school.

As we navigated the small crowd at our accelerating pace, we made quick work of the pack, passing our competitors left and right. Wherever Victoria ran, I followed. Every time she passed someone new, I did too, so I gained a little confidence despite my labored breathing. *I am faster than some of these people*, I thought.

Within a few minutes at our quickened pace, I began to

wonder, *Okay, we've passed enough people. What's the plan now? When do we hit our real pace?*

By the time I mentally repeated that pattern a few times, I realized I had misjudged Victoria's intentions. She was not there to go for a morning jog, enjoy fall, and chat with me. She was there to run. And fast. Maybe even win.

Without the same fitness as her, my pace faded. And while my body begged me to slow down, Victoria urged me to speed up.

"I'm going to run ahead if that's okay?" she effortlessly asked.

"Go," I gasped.

To avoid the embarrassment of her realizing how unfit I was, I let her get some distance ahead before I slowed further. As sweat continued to build on my brow, I barely made out her image as she flew ahead, crested the upcoming hill, and curved out of sight. That was the last I saw of her until the race was nearly over.

A few rounds of circular thought later, it was my turn to face the hill. As I did, my effort increased with every step up the incline. With it, my capacity to hear faded and gave way to something new. A dull ringing. My body was begging me to walk.

I can't walk, I debated internally. *I've played sports my whole life. This shouldn't be so hard.*

As if the entire experience had not already been demoralizing enough, fate decided to rub salt into my growing wound. About the time I made it halfway up the hill, I glanced over my shoulder when I heard an odd sound overtaking me from behind.

At first, it was in my periphery, so I could not tell what it was. But as it gained on me, then came into full view, I realized that the source of the strange sound was a person. Let's just say it was an older gentleman. One of the runners Victoria and I passed at the beginning of the race. One of several I assumed I was faster than solely based on appearance. He must have been at least seventy-five and appeared haggard. His knees were knobby. His elbows and ankles pointy. Even his socks appeared haggard as they loosely slouched down his thin calves toward the tops of his well-worn shoes.

Nothing about his appearance mattered though. Socks and all, as we both ascended the hill, he came level with me. As he overtook me, it was clear he was going to reach the top first, and there was nothing I could do about it. To make matters worse, he was not even running. He was, to my mortification, speed-walking.

Not even the depths of my imagination could have mustered a good enough excuse for why I had just been eclipsed by someone who was walking. How my running pace had become slower than that of an old man's walk, I did not know. What I did know: I definitely could not stop.

I lumbered along in my defeat until I finally made it to the last mile. At which time, Victoria, who had vanished early in the run, reappeared. She had finished the race so far ahead of me that she had time to recover, wait, then jog back to find me. In total, by completing her race, then my race too, she covered more than four miles in the same amount of time it took me to run 3.1.

You might think that a demoralizing finish like that (not only behind my friend but also an elderly speed-walker) would have made me analyze how my fitness was deteriorating. But for whatever reason, it did not. Instead, I excused my loss because I had never been a runner by any stretch. I had never enjoyed running, so I was okay with telling myself I would never be good at it.

My poor running performance was not my only forewarning. Other aspects of my life were deteriorating in unexpected ways too.

I spent the majority of my second year in college working at a local bagel shop. I snacked several times a shift on fresh-from-the-oven bagels and frozen yogurt. The best bagel you will ever taste is one hot from the baking rack. If your skin can handle the scorch, try hollowing it out, then letting it sit for a minute. As it cools, the outer layer creates a delicate, crisp texture that is unparalleled.

A few years after I stopped working at that shop, someone told me that one bagel was the same as eating five slices of toast. I rarely hollowed the dough back then, so I probably consumed the equivalent of a whole loaf of toast every day I worked.

I ended each shift belly full and feet sore. The thighs of my shorts slathered in butter-flavored pan and grill grease from wiping my hands on my aprons. Because I drove home each day reeking of garlic and stored my work shoes in the trunk, the smell eventually permeated my car. At least my bedroom did not stink.

On my days off, I hung out with a group of guys who lived near campus. Only one of them was also a full-time student. The rest worked or went to school part time. We tended to stay up way too late watching basketball and theorizing about politics and religion. Because they are two topics which let people be both simultaneously opposed and yet correct, our conversations could last hours.

The more bagels I sliced and late nights I spent watching basketball, my grades, unlike my weight, gradually dropped. I found it impossible to arrive to class by 9:30 a.m., as meeting friends at Burger King for Croissan'wiches seemed more appealing. I eventually turned into that flaky coworker people had to cover for because I called in late to skip shifts at random. I started avoiding old friends and was only moderately dedicated to any aspect of my life, which made none of the things I was doing remotely fulfilling.

Before college, my parents, teachers, coaches, teammates, and sports kept me on track. I arrived on time unless excused or if my brother and I got stuck behind a bus on our morning commute to school. I paid attention and took notes, never skipped class, and always did my homework. I asked and answered questions and noted which details my teachers repeated. That was how I knew which topics were essential to make the grades.

After I got used to arriving late for class though (sometimes not arriving at all), I could no longer pay attention nor take notes nor highlight the important points. Which meant I could no longer make the grades.

On one Burger King–filled belly of a morning, I arrived miraculously on time to Psychology 101. I settled into a seat toward the farthest back left of the massive lecture hall and plopped open my spiral notebook. A few words into the lecture, instead of teaching us more about the human mind, our professor divulged that he would instead review our most recent test.

A test? What test? I did my best to hide my shock as I looked around the 350-person capacity room. *I can't be the only one confused here*, I internally rationalized.

Evidently, I had foregone enough classes in a row that fall to not only miss a test but also the reminders about it, the review sessions leading up to it, the subsequent debates among my peers about how the test went for each of them, plus our professor's discussion of when he would have our grades finalized. Seeing as how I had only attended four classes by that point in the semester, I knew I was bound to miss a few things, but never did I expect to miss a test.

The lecture hall's immense size had allowed my absences to go unnoticed previously. So on the day I discovered my critical mistake, I stood up right away and walked out. Once again unnoticed.

I wallowed in my personal bout of shame for a few hours, then I eventually reached out to my professor to schedule a meeting. That very afternoon, I sat down in the contoured hard plastic chair by the door in my professor's office, and I tried to hold it together. With my back literally against the wall, I could no longer restrain myself. Before either of us got out a single word, my chin puckered as I broke down into an uncontrollable gush of tears. Never before had I been so irresponsible.

One good thing happened that day: my professor took pity on me. He did not have to, but he did. He allowed me to take a short answer rather than multiple choice version of the test I missed.

I attended Psychology 101 four times that fall semester of my second year at UVA. But because of my professor's compassion, I squeaked out a C-minus. I was lucky. It could have been worse.

Another year passed. It was finally the late fall of my third year at UVA. And while my grades continued to drop and my weight continued to rise, an odd sense finally started growing in the pit of my stomach. Something did not feel right. Something was missing.

One of my best friends from middle school had spent most of her life swimming twice a day, year-round—a dedication that earned her a place on the UVA swim team. I admired her work ethic. I considered her a real athlete, one with a plan.

Because we had been friends for so long, we thought it best not to live together even though we went to the same university. Instead, we made a point to visit whenever her busy schedule permitted.

On one such occasion, I stopped by the house she shared with several of her swimmer teammates. Their plan for the evening was to watch TV and paint their nails. They seemed like a fun group. The kind of people I would have enjoyed being friends with.

Shortly after I walked into the living room, one of the girls looked up at me with a curious look on her face. "Don't I know you?" It came out more like a statement than a question. "I've seen you around campus. You're an athlete, right?"

My face flushed and my mind blanked in response to her suggestion. I was at a loss for words, so I laughed nervously. That was my natural instinct whenever I did not know what to say. It happened with questions about college sports, being a Spanish major, and now about being an athlete at all. It reflected exactly how I felt about myself.

"I used to be. But not anymore," I stammered as I shyly looked away.

"Oh, I just assumed," she said.

The baggy, navy-blue Virginia sweatpants I was wearing had given her the impression. I had nabbed them from my dad's closet before I left for college. They had been a permanent fixture in my wardrobe ever since. So to her, I looked the part.

Not until then did I realize how important teams were to me. They were part of who I was. A longstanding component of my identity even though I had not been part of one for nearly three years by then. So that feeling in my stomach, the one that told me something was missing, it arrived once I knew how much I missed being a teammate.

The trouble was, just as my grades had become subpar, so too had my health habits. I was nearly thirty pounds heavier than I had ever been in my life because I exercised very little and enjoyed fast food for breakfast a lot. Pizza Hut breadsticks were not uncommon, and Franken Berry cereal was my go-to snack. I did not drink sodas very often to avoid cavities, but I did love gummy candy, particularly the kind with sugar crystals that made them sparkle.

Needless to say, as I progressed through my third year in college, I should not have been surprised that I could not run a 5K, that my running pace was slower than a speed-walker's, and that being a young woman well over two hundred pounds was about to be my reality.

I was definitely in unfamiliar territory, confronting startling realities.

September 2000,

I should have gone away to school and played volleyball and basketball. If I had, I wonder where I'd be now. Who knows? I shall try hard. Although I constantly seem to trip and stumble. Please help me to not fall on my face.

SIX

I WISH I HAD DONE CREW.

ON THE NIGHT OF FRIDAY, NOVEMBER 30, 2001, A MATTER
of weeks after I spoke the words, "I used to be an athlete, but not
anymore," I awoke in the middle of the night, tossing and turning.
Had it been a typical Friday, I would have been out to dinner
or at a party with friends. As for this particular Friday though,
nothing felt typical. For whatever reason, I was tired and did not
feel like being social. So instead of going out, I was at home in
bed having trouble falling asleep.

It was one of those nights where no matter what I did, I
simply could not relax. And even though my mind begged for a
much-needed time-out, I just could not get those words out of
my head. *You're an athlete, right? I used to be. But not anymore...*

So began my futile fight with sleeplessness that Friday night.

At first, I sprawled onto my stomach like a starfish (as usual).
No sleep. Next, I turned to my left. No sleep. I then gave the right
a shot. No sleep. As a last resort, I flopped onto my back, stuffed
one pillow under my knees, then fluffed another behind my neck.

Still no sleep.

Around and around, I tossed and turned, flipped and flopped.
I rolled and rotated through various positions until my legs were

well entangled within my sheets. I made circles with my eyes beneath closed lids in an attempt to distract my thoughts. I randomly counted numbers and started over every time I lost my place. Usually by the count of seven.

I even went so far as to picture sheep. Yes, I actually counted sheep.

Do not open your eyes, my mind insisted. *No matter what, do not open your eyes. Eyes closed. Eyes closed. Eyes closed*, I repeated internally. *Please. Just. Stay. Closed.*

With each successive thought, I clenched my eyelids all the more tightly. I had to restrain my vision to ensure I stayed that one step closer to sleep. I knew that if my eyes opened for even a millisecond, I would have to start the whole process over.

Despite my best tactics, my eyelids gave into their temptation like two defiant little children. I blinked, and that was all it took. A brief flash was enough for me to catch sight of my alarm clock.

Although my eyelids immediately slammed shut, it was too late. Those piercing red digits had already seared their image. In that one small moment, I became excruciatingly aware of the fact that it was 12:01 a.m. and I had been tossing and turning for more than two hours.

Defeated, I rolled onto my back again and gazed helplessly at the dark ceiling above me, hoping my mind would stop racing.

Still no sleep.

I knew what I had to do. My only remaining option was to get my thoughts out of my head and onto paper. I had to expose every last one of my thoughts to the world should I ever want to sleep again.

I clicked on the dim little light that hung above my nightstand. I then sat up and paused there staring vacantly at the wall to let my eyes adjust to the light. Once my eyes had adjusted to a blur, I walked across my room, grabbed the first notebook I saw, then headed back to my bed.

Sitting there on the edge of my bed, one foot resting on the floor, the other tucked warmly under my thigh and blanket, I flipped through the pages of my little notebook with the lighthouse on the front and back covers. At the first empty page I found, I began deliberately and legibly writing. But as my thoughts clarified, my handwriting hastened.

With each passing line, my clarity devolved to desperation. With my desperation, my writing digressed to a blur. From my usual calligraphy-like cursive, my style became more like the scribbles you make when you check to see if a pen is running out of ink. Legibility was the least of my worries on that restless November night though. Continued restraint was the last thing I needed.

My thoughts flowed until my vision blurred and my hand cramped up on account of my writing speed. So I came to a stop and looked back at what I wrote. It was not pretty. It definitely was not eloquent. But it was the truth.

It was a truth whose seed was subconsciously planted the day I played my last minute of high school sports. A truth my body felt as I gained weight and lost sleep. A truth my mind knew as I skipped class and my grades dropped along with my focus and my happiness. It was a truth I had harbored long before my pen and notebook displayed it that night. A truth that my mind had apparently concealed until reality prevented me from sleeping another wink.

November 30, 2001,

12:01 a.m. You gotta reflect! Exercise and reflect! That is all I can say. Being so exhausted that you can barely move. That is the best feeling in the world. That and sleep and loving people.

I don't have much to write, at least not that I wish to start with right now. I am too "sheepy" for all that right now. I don't know. I just don't know.

Who will I be? School is almost over for the semester. And now that I am where I am, I wish a thing or two were different. I wish I had done crew. I wish I were not a lazy bum, then I may have actually been something. The world will never know, and that includes me.

I wish I had done crew, I whispered as I reread my words carefully. I am not sure why my mind jumped that November night to a conversation I had with Kevin, one of my mom's friends, nearly three years earlier. He had noticed my height back when I was in high school, and being a rowing coach, had suggested I try rowing. I did not take him seriously at the time though, and apparently, that was something I had come to regret and reflected on that sleepless night.

I reread my words, twice, closed my notebook, capped my pen, and clicked off my tiny bedside lamp. I gingerly unfurled my right foot from beneath the back of my left thigh and shook it lightly while it tingled itself awake. I then slipped back under the covers, rested my head upon my pillow, and patiently anticipated dawn. As sleep finally approached, ink-stained fingertips and all, I meditated on what I finally had the courage to admit, then gradually drifted away.

I wish I had done crew...

SEVEN

IT'S NEVER TOO LATE.

AFTER MY LATE NIGHT OF TOSSING, TURNING, AND THINK-ing, I slept in later than usual the next day. Luckily, it was a Saturday, so I did not have class. I can only imagine how my lack of rest would have impacted my brain power had it been a week-day. By the time I crawled out of bed, not only was I delighted to find that my thoughts had calmed, I was pleased to discover that it was also unseasonably warm.

The entire fall of my third year was just that. Unseasonably warm. I do not mean a little warmer. I mean the type of weather that makes you wonder how such dramatic swings happen at all. It was the kind of warm that leads to unusually high amounts of rain. The kind that makes front-page news throughout North America. The kind that allows you to spend more time outside than you would otherwise. The kind that makes you think that maybe things do happen for a reason…but only in their due time.

Saturday, December 1, 2001, arrived with not a single cloud. It was sunny and seventy degrees, with the kind of blue sky that typically only comes during the low humidity of spring. An ideal day to be outside for the last home football game of the season.

Before making my way to the stadium for the game though, I

walked to the campus pool to meet up with an old roommate. She and I had planned to start our morning by supporting the swim team at its annual invitational swim meet. We would cheer on some of our friends at their meet first, then head to the football game after that.

The swim meet was a weekend-long event. The building where the meet was held, the Aquatics and Fitness Center (the AFC), usually gave priority to swimming on such occasions. However, because standard procedure during football games was to close the AFC, the two sports had to compromise. This was a first, as the football game had been rescheduled from earlier in the year due to the tragic events of September 11, 2001. So not only was the weather an anomaly, the swim team's overlap with football was too.

Luckily, the negotiation for that special Saturday was relatively simple. The majority of the AFC remained closed while the pool was kept open. The main doors to the building were otherwise locked. The lights, televisions, radio, and machines in the gym were off. The two-story entryway was dark. Only one row of lights near the pool end of the building remained on. The massive space was empty and silent except for the occasional cheer that escaped whenever people opened the pool deck doors.

As if the lack of lighting and personnel were not enough to signify that the gym was closed for the day, temporary white fences were also put in place. The physical barrier would funnel people toward the pool and away from the rest of the gym. As far as I could tell, no one ventured past those fences…until I came along.

After most of our friends were done with their swimming events, I decided I had seen enough and was ready for football. In anticipation of how crowded the stadium would be, I figured I should use the restroom before leaving the AFC. Trouble was, the only one was on the other side of those temporary white fences. That meant I would have to hop over and risk being caught if I wanted to use the restroom.

As I scanned the large corridor, I weighed my options. When I did not see anyone around, I went for it. I hiked up my pants, then flung my right leg over a sturdy section of fence. I then shifted my weight up and over, then hopped a little to clear it. With my right leg safely on the ground, I windmilled my left high in the air like a slow-motion roundhouse kick. Once I successfully made it over without falling and with the coast still clear, I snuck off to the bathroom.

Mission accomplished, I walked back in the direction from which I came, then headed toward the freedom of my afternoon of football...or so I thought.

On my way out, I realized I was no longer alone. I noticed the figure of a tall, athletic man walking in my direction, then past me. He and I must have had the same plan, and by the look of it, he knew he was not supposed to be there either. At first, I avoided eye contact, thinking that if I did not look directly at him, he would not see me. But that is not how it works. We were in a wide-open space. He could definitely see me.

When we attempted to nonchalantly pass one another, I swore I heard my name, so I paused for a second, then turned. It was one of those moments when you see someone you think you know, but because your reaction is delayed, it is not until fifteen feet later that you swear you know them. So you glance to be sure.

As it turned out on this particular Saturday, not only did we both do a double take; we realized we knew each other (sort of).

Nearly three years before, during my senior year of high school, Kevin, the head coach of the UVA rowing team, came up to me after my school's Winter Sports Award Ceremony, because I was tall, and he had heard I was athletic. My mom had apparently been embellishing stories about me for some time. She was his dental hygienist. That is what they do.

Originally, everything about Kevin's persona intimidated me. He was the tallest, most broad-chested, deep-voiced man I had ever met. As he towered over me on the night of my school's award ceremony, he smiled kindly and spoke calmly, though deeply. He introduced himself first, then went on to suggest that if I chose to go to UVA, I should think about joining the rowing team. He implied I could be good at it.

Because I had never rowed before and I had a distinct impression of what it took to be a real athlete, Kevin's suggestion seemed impossible. I assumed it was too late for me to try something new, let alone be any good at it, so I did not take him seriously at the time. However, on this December Saturday when we crossed paths at the AFC, I reconsidered.

Despite the darkness of the AFC atrium and the three years that had passed since we first met, Kevin recognized me. Not only that, he called me by name.

Compelled by one of his many great qualities, Kevin spoke to me despite my being a relative stranger. He is the kind of person who always seeks opportunities and pursues them. He puts care and compassion for others into the world at every possible moment. I do not know if he will ever realize that by always reaching out, by ceaselessly searching, he has managed to impact countless lives.

I consider myself one of the luckiest ones. For with one small, direct statement, he presented me with an opportunity to alter the course of my life. By just how much, neither he nor I could have anticipated. At the time, it was only a simple hello.

"Hey, Lindsay," Kevin said very plainly.

"Hi, Kevin," I replied, also very plainly.

Wearing one of his trademark smirks, his next words were without hesitation. He cut straight to the point. "You know, it's never too late to row."

Most people might have led with something more like, "How are things?" Or "Your mom cleaned my teeth the other day." Or even, "What have you been up to these past three years?" But that is not Kevin. He is not most people.

Upon his fateful suggestion, I replied, "You know, I'd like that."

During our brief exchange, he reached into his pocket and pulled out a Virginia Rowing business card. The card looked like he had sat on it quite a few times, but it had everything I needed. He told me to give him a call so he could connect me with the novice coach. I assumed I would find out what "novice" meant soon enough.

That was it. We shook hands, smiled, then parted ways.

I have no idea where Kevin headed after that. As for me, I walked over to the football stadium and sat on the hill behind the end zone near the student section. I found a dry place on the grass, rested my elbows on my knees, then closed my eyes as I tilted my head upward to let the sun warm my face. That December first was indeed a beautiful day.

Not long after our chance meeting, I pulled out Kevin's card and gave him a call. I was finally ready. I was tired of being mistaken for an athlete. I would much rather be an athlete.

The Virginia Rowing Team has long been one of the best programs in the country. That made my likelihood of standing out among such competition small, my future definitely uncertain. But it was a risk I had to take. For although I was not sure of what would come next, I knew without a doubt that I did not want to stay where I was. I figured anything would be better than my doubt-filled, aimless path.

Just one night before that chance meeting with Kevin, when I had written, *I wish I had done crew*, my dreams had been nothing more than wishes. They were barely ideas that could not be made real because I kept them to myself. I did not grasp the importance of outwardly sharing my dreams then. So I could not understand that expressing them in the face of uncertainty was a necessary step toward real pursuit. My subconscious, though, it knew better. So it forced sleeplessness on me to guarantee that my dreams could come to life. Literally awakened, my subconscious made me admit how I felt even though I did not know how or where to start.

When I was seventeen, I would not have mustered the courage to make the call. I would have hidden or pretended that I did not recognize Kevin at all. But at age twenty, I had just enough nerve to call a relative stranger to find out what I needed to do to try out for a sport that I knew nothing about.

If you had been a fly on my bedroom wall the night before I bumped into Kevin at the AFC, you would have watched me cry. You would have looked on as I frantically scribbled in my notebook with a red pen. You would have heard me mutter to myself about what I wish I was and about my longing that it was not too late for me.

But just as Kevin said, I would find out soon enough, it is never too late.

January 2002,

Think of the one thing that scares you the most. Sometimes you have to think hard about it. But sometimes, you know it off the top of your head. I saw mine one night in a dream...

EIGHT

IF YOU HAVE ANY QUESTIONS.

IT WAS NOT UNTIL I WAS HOME FOR THE WINTER HOLIDAY that I told my family of my decision to join the rowing team. There was not much to tell at that point. All I knew was where and when I had to show up for my first day, and that I should wear some tight pants (whatever that meant) and my sneakers. Because my mom entered the gym world with aerobics in the 1980s, she was the queen of formfitting exercise outfits. That meant she could help me with the tight pants. The rest was up to me.

On a snowy Wednesday in January at the start of the spring semester of my junior year at UVA, I drove my eighteen-year-old Volvo across campus for my first day of rowing practice. I pulled up to the giant metal-and-brick block of a building known as "the Cage" and found a parking spot close to the building's tiny glass entrance. When I got there, I was surprised to find that cars were in the lot, but no people were milling around. Not a soul in sight. Despite the strange sense that being alone gave me, I headed inside to go find the team.

Back before the fall semester ended, Kevin had gone out of

his way to show me around the team's indoor facilities. So on my first official day of practice, I was mildly familiar with the Cage. All I needed to do was to remember which way Kevin and I had walked on the day he had shown me around.

When I walked into the Cage, being inside jogged my memory. I recalled passing through two sets of wooden doors, and if my memory served, I had hung a right after passing through both. I also recalled that if I ended up walking down a long hallway, it meant I had gone too far. So I headed back (cautiously) in exactly the way I remembered.

I passed a few sets of stairs that ascended in various directions, then came upon the first set of wooden doors. My first sign that I was heading the right way. When I reached that first set of doors, my nerves unexpectedly welled. It was as if the doors themselves stood before me to beg the question: *Are you certain of this step you are about to take?* I stopped and took a breath. As I exhaled it, I discovered a smidge of additional courage, then pushed my way through. I was one decision and one step closer to the team.

Now for door number two. I exhaled as I continued on my way.

Several steps later, I hesitated again. Not because of a physical barrier this time but, rather, the unfamiliar sounds that filled my ears. With every step I had taken since I entered the Cage, the sounds of innumerable voices had been accumulating and, with them, my thoughts. As a result, my mind was brimming with uncertainty. I was already unsure of taking this step, but now this? *Just how many girls are on this team?* I wondered.

What seemed like one hundred individual voices intensified with every step I took until I finally came to the second set of wooden doors. I had correctly remembered the way, taken every step, and made it to that second set of doors—the final decision that stood between me and officially showing up for my first day of rowing practice.

Before being all in and boldly entering, I gave myself one last chance to change my mind. I quietly stepped up to the doors without touching them, then peered through one of the small vertical windows, and without detection, I snuck a peek of what awaited me on the other side.

Up until the moment I walked into the Cage that day, I had the impression that Kevin would teach me everything I needed to know. That he would take me under his wing because I was somehow unique. However, when I peeked through that small vertical window, I saw at least fifty athletic young women, all well tanned from their recent team training trip to Florida. Every one of them tall. Many of them taller than me.

They stood gathered in clusters, chatting as they awaited their coaches. They were all wearing athletic clothes, proper rowing gear that was far better than the multicolored, metallic-bronze short tights my mom had given me. One look was all I needed to instantly assess them as confident and knowledgeable. I assumed they would be better than me, stronger than me, faster than me, more capable than me, given their experience relative to mine. I imagined they had unattainable strength, speed, and talent, like my childhood heroes. My apprehension deemed them a room full of real athletes.

I reverted. I no longer felt twenty. I may as well have been right back in the eighth grade at my varsity basketball tryout. Back to retreating behind the bleachers. Back to limiting myself. Back to questioning what I felt prepared for. Back to hiding from sight to avoid embarrassment.

When I compared myself to what I saw through the tiny window, I panicked. *How could I possibly be good enough? I have never done this before. What was I thinking?*

Everything about the scene intimidated me, so rather than flinging the doors open, finding the coaches, and introducing myself, I chose to head for safety. I quietly backed away from the doors, then turned in the direction of the parking lot, where I knew my car would be waiting.

Had it not been for two tall rower girls who pushed through the double doors right as I was about to flee, I would have escaped. A moment earlier and we would have smashed into one another. A moment later, and they would have never known I was there at all. My rowing career would have been over before it even had the chance to start. Their timing could not have been more serendipitous.

Upon making eye contact, my escape was officially thwarted. My decision was made. I had no choice but to try out for the team.

When the two girls asked if I was there for practice, I said yes (to avoid embarrassment) and followed them into the gym. Once inside, a nervous chill filled my veins. The whiteness and flickering buzz of the gym lights reminded me of my basketball days and pierced my wide-open eyes. Not a muscle in my body was relaxed. Every part of me was on full alert. I can only imagine how pale my face must have fallen.

Because I did not know anyone, I stood an awkward few feet from the group, feeling lost. A few uncomfortable moments later, one of the girls on the team must have sensed how I felt, so she came over and introduced herself. After her, several other girls wearing semisunburned grins followed suit. One by one, they welcomed me. Their collective gesture warmed my nervous chill.

Eventually, after meeting at least twenty-five new faces, I no longer doubted my presence there at that practice. By the time I met half of the girls on the team, I knew I had made the right decision. I had found my place, my purpose, my reason. For the first time in what seemed like forever, I was in exactly the right place at exactly the right time: with my team.

When the coaches finally arrived, they gathered the fifty or so of us together and explained the practice plan. Because it was January, and the NCAA rules for rowing restrict the amount of time a team can row on the water during that time of year, the coaches knew that a lot of cross-training on the rowing machines was on its way. So on my first day of practice, as a bit of snow started to fall, we were given two options: we could run or we could "erg."

When I first spoke with Kevin about joining the team, he had suggested that I start regularly going to the gym to do "some sort of physical activity." He was not specific then about what I should do. He just wanted me to get used to being active on most days of the week. He knew that it was important I become active on my own terms because it increased the likelihood that I would actually do something. So over the weeks leading up to my first day of practice, I went to the campus gym on most days just as Kevin had suggested.

On each of the days I did, I watched all sorts of people use the rowing machines there. I observed all sorts of interesting techniques too. Few of which seemed right. As a result, I had grown familiar with the machines themselves but remained clueless about proper form. That is, until the day I caught sight of a few girls wearing Virginia Rowing T-shirts.

Having finally spotted actual rowers on the rowing machines, I assumed they knew what they were doing, so I watched carefully from a distance. Once they got up to leave, I headed straight for the first open machine and diligently mimicked what I had observed. From that day forward, on each of my subsequent visits to the gym, I made a point to "row" for at least ten minutes by repeating what I had watched the rower girls do.

By the time I arrived for my first day of practice, I had learned enough from the girls I saw at the gym to understand that people who were actual rowers called the rowing machines "ergs" (short for ergometers) and that the erg is the most used machine in the sport. Rowers use them a lot. So much, in fact, that the term "erg" is also a verb. Which is probably why only two of us chose to erg on my first day of practice.

Everyone else knew something I could not, so they chose to run. Because I had not yet erged with the team, I could not understand why most of the girls preferred running then. The memory of my first 5K run and the sound of that speed-walker as he passed me still haunted me. I still hated running.

I could not have known it then, but my first rowing practice was one of the only times in my entire rowing career that I would ever choose to erg when given the option. Few people choose to erg. But on my first day, I had no idea there would be millions of meters rowed in my future.

Awaiting our erg instructions on that mid-January Wednesday, I stood alongside my one remaining teammate and looked on as the girls who had chosen to run headed out through the giant garage door on the side of the Cage. I could hear them chatting and laughing, a bundled mass of excitement. Until eventually, their voices faded as they disappeared into the foggy white of the delicately falling snow. When the last of my new team rounded the corner out of sight, the enormous room fell silent and felt chillier again.

Together, those women embraced the cold. They embraced the training. They embraced each other. And now, they embraced me.

Once the rest of the group was gone, my lone teammate and I walked back across the giant room to set up two ergs as we had been instructed. I introduced myself to her as we walked. She was a recruit. She had experience. I felt fortunate that someone like her had stayed behind to help me.

With our machines set up, we sat side by side as the novice coach explained the basics of erging. The novice coach, as I found out, would be my coach. She was in charge of those of us who were in our first year of college rowing. That meant she coached all of the new girls, the complete novices who had never rowed before, people like me. Plus, any recruited rowers who were not quite ready for the faster, varsity boats. As a result, our novice squad was a mix of girls with anywhere from six months to several years' experience. We were also a mix of girls in our first, second, and third years at UVA. Although I was the oldest among us, I had the least experience.

"The basics," as my new coach called them, were, well, pretty basic. She told me to watch my one teammate, then simply do what she did. I was lucky those girls wearing Virginia Rowing T-shirts showed up at the gym in the weeks leading up to my first day. They had unwittingly gifted me some experience with watching and mimicking. So when it came time to mimic my fellow novice teammate, I knew it was something I could do. As instructed, I watched for a minute, then began to erg for the first time under the eye of a coach.

"Not bad," my new coach said. "Really. Take today and just play with the erg. If you have any questions, ask your teammate." She walked away and left us alone after that.

Having even one teammate by my side warmed my inner chill until it completely melted. I finally felt comfortable there.

On my first day as part of UVA's rowing team, I learned two things. The first of which was to watch my teammate. To do whatever she did. That was the only advice I was given that day, and it was enough. The second thing I learned was that I would be given my first official test five days later. In five days, we would undergo an exhausting erg test, where we would row, nonstop, for two thousand meters to gauge our rowing fitness.

I have since learned that the 2,000-meter (two-kilometer), or "2K test" as it is called in rowing, is the most used measurement of raw rowing fitness. You sit at a dead stop on the erg and set the machine's little computer monitor for two thousand meters. That is about a mile and a quarter. Five laps on a track if you are running. Then, upon a start command, you take off and go as hard as you possibly can without stopping until you reach the very end of those two thousand meters. When you finish (and have had time to recover from your complete physical and mental exhaustion), you check the little monitor that is attached to the erg and then write down the details displayed on its screen.

The screen shows many details. The most important, though, are the average number of strokes you took per minute of the test, your "stroke rate"; the average time it took you to complete the 500-meter segments of the test, your "average split"; the actual time it took you to complete *each* 500-meter segment, your "500-meter splits" ("splits" for short); and how long it took you to complete the test from start to finish, your total time or "2K time."

Once you have a 2K time, you can compare yourself to literally anyone in the world who has ever taken a 2K test. It is a test so infamous that if you ask rowers, "What's your 2K?" they will know exactly what you mean.

A grueling test like that never gets easier, you just go faster. A grueling test like that is also not something people typically do within their first five days on a team. Then again, picking up a Division I varsity sport as a complete novice at the age of twenty with just three semesters left in college is not all that typical either.

On my fifth day as a rower, I met a couple of my new teammates at the Cage to take my first 2K test. We were told we could take the test without coaches, but preferably in small groups. My small group was four. Setting up four whole rowing machines side by side in a perfectly aligned row inside the massive metal-walled Cage was a stark contrast to being with the entire team. It highlighted an obvious shift in energy that made me even more aware of how much I had missed being a teammate.

Because I was so new, our novice coach had given me the same advice about the 2K test that she had given me on my first day. So as I sat down on the erg at the very end of our four-person row next to one of my fellow novice teammates, I planned to do exactly what she did. She was a little smaller than me, but since she had rowed when she was in high school, I felt I was upping my game by sitting with and attempting to match her.

When she warmed up in preparation for the test, I matched her exactly. When she set her little erg monitor, I matched her exactly. When she sat ready, holding the erg handle in her hands, poised on her seat, knees bent up in front of her, eyes affixed closely on her monitor, I again matched her exactly. And when she took one last deep breath, I matched her once more.

Having mimicked her every step of the way, when she finally announced, "Attention…Go," I aimed to match her during the test too.

Two-thousand meters later, I hopped up, invigorated, breathing a little. My teammate next to me was slumped over, wiped out. It was the best she had done on a 2K test in all her years of rowing. When I compared how quickly I recovered from my test to how she appeared, I realized that maybe I had more effort to give.

When I took my first ever 2K, my time was 7:58. Had I been a high school novice, it would have been an incredible feat. Indeed, a 2K completed in under eight minutes is an early benchmark for many young women. However, I was a college novice in the second semester of my junior year. I also had teammates who were setting higher standards by reaching for faster benchmarks. Benchmarks like 7:30 or 7:00. Some even faster than that. Seven minutes or faster, I would soon learn, is a significant benchmark for women at every level.

I finished my first week as a novice by taking it one day at a time with one simple piece of advice: to do what my teammates did. It had gotten me through my first week and my first 2K. Though incredibly simple, the advice was revelatory. So revelatory that I kept it at the front of my mind with every step I took with my new team.

February 2002,

I have found parts of what I don't want to be like. I have now also found parts of what I do. I guess some things do have to happen to allow others to be realized…Everything serves some purpose. Even if I don't always understand it.

NINE

THERE IS MORE.

THE ASTRONOMY DEPARTMENT AT THE UNIVERSITY OF VIR-
ginia has an observatory that sits at the top of the steepest, tallest
hill on campus. So steep that the effort it takes just to walk up
it used to make me cringe. I went there all of two times before
I started rowing. Once for each of the two astronomy classes I
took. After I picked up rowing though, I visited "Observatory
Hill" more often.

The first time I ran "O-Hill" with my new team, the clouds
were thick above. They blotted out the sun, giving everything a
greyish hue. The gravel. The trees. The air itself on account of the
fine mist that also fell from those thick clouds. As the air around
me condensed on my eyelashes, my shirt and shoes grew heavy.
At first, this was from the dewy moisture they absorbed from the
atmosphere with each passing minute. Eventually, it was from
my sweat.

All fifty of us UVA rowers jogged up the road away from the
Cage, then up over the little bridge over the train tracks before
we crossed the street. From there, we knew to head toward the
foot of O-Hill. After that, all we knew was that we should take
a turn at some random point, then run until we found a gravel

path where cars could not go. The restricted gravel road would lead us up the back side of O-Hill, which meant we could run up and down its switchback multiple times without having to worry about traffic.

The only advice I had up until then was to do what my teammates did. It had helped me on the erg, which made me think it could not hurt to do so there on that hill run too. So, as I huffed and puffed my way upward, with a few girls behind me and most up ahead of me, I aimed to keep up with the leaders for as long as I could.

Those are the fast girls. I wonder how it feels to be that fast? Maybe one day I'll keep up. Those were my thoughts with every piece of loose gravel that rolled backward as my feet pushed me slowly but surely up the long, grey and misty hill one step at a time.

As our indefinitely long run grew longer, the lead runners stretched out farther with their every stride until they reached the top. Where they then spun with ease and savored their lope back toward the bottom, pleased to be done with the hill.

By the time they made it down, our head coach Kevin appeared. He too was short of breath. His grey T-shirt soaked in dewy moisture and sweat just like ours. Much to the leaders' dismay, Kevin also had an idea. Instead of heading back to the Cage, he told them to spin, then head up the slope again. He then hollered to the entire hillside that we were to do continuous loops until further notice. Kevin included.

Instantly, our fifty faces dropped, and our run continued just as Kevin instructed. Loops up to the top of the switchback, then back down, then back up, then back down for an undetermined amount of time. Gradually, with every round trip of O-Hill, our frowns softened into smiles. Our smiles gave way to cheers. Until eventually, we high-fived one another as we passed.

By the end of it, our run lasted long enough for the leaders to lap me. Multiple times. But with the way Kevin changed the rules midrun, every time they lapped me, it meant a new smile shot my way because we all kept running. That was what mattered. We all struggled on that hill together for the same amount of time until Kevin told us to head back to the Cage…together.

When I decided to join the rowing team, it did not occur to me that I would have to run so much. Kevin did not mention it in our first meeting. But that is on me. I could have asked him more questions. Come to think of it, maybe it was my slow running that made him tell a local news reporter at one point that I "wasn't that good in the beginning." When I watched a recording of the interview many years later, I could not help but laugh. It was a very "Kevin" comment to make.

He was not wrong though. I was not that good in the beginning. No one is immediately great at something. That is not how it works. Some people might get better a little faster than others, but no one is great on day one. It takes guts to show up on day one knowing you have no idea what might happen. Then, because you find some hope in what is possible, you come back for day two. When you are a complete novice, it takes a willingness to get it wrong in order to discover what is right and the guts to keep coming back for more no matter how many times you get it wrong…one day, one step at a time.

On my first day of rowing, I was the new girl. Nearly every person on the team had at least six months', if not six years', worth of experience. They had a giant head start on me. They had put in a lot of time, so it made complete sense for them to be faster than me then. It also meant that if I had questions, I could at the very least ask the girl next to me. Which is exactly what I continued to do.

There were so many of us and so few coaches. We far outnumbered them, so even if they ran around making themselves crazy to help every one of us every day, it would have been impossible for them to coach each of us individually all the time. We *had* to learn from ourselves and from each other too.

During the early part of that first winter, we cross-trained a lot. Just as our coaches predicted. And given that we only had so many options for cross-training, they knew they had to be creative. That kept us focused on what we were doing. Indeed, if you are on a rowing team but cannot row for a while, periodically changing up the routine is critical.

On one such occasion during my first few months as a rower, our coaches gathered us at the Cage and broke us up into three-person teams. They mixed everyone, varsity and novice alike, so that we could compete against one another in a relay race on the ergs. Because every team had a cross-section of experience, that relay race became my first opportunity to witness real rowing speed with my own (still very novice) eyes.

After our coaches brought us together, they called out the list of three-person teams, and we gathered in our respective triplets as they read. When they were done reading, my two partners set about selecting which erg the three of us would share for the relay. Once every team had its erg selected and arranged into one of two parallel rows, Kevin finally revealed the rules.

"Fifteen kilometers, 15K," he said. "Every person on each team must do the same number of meters. You may choose who goes first, second, and third within your team, but you must switch every five hundred meters."

Kevin continued. "Help each other. Be creative. Other than those, there are no rules except first team to 15K wins."

My team consisted of me, one of the top girls on the varsity squad, and one of my fellow novice teammates. While Kevin finished his explanation, we three decided the varsity girl should go first, my novice teammate second, and me last.

A few moments later when everyone was ready, Kevin declared in his deep voice, "Attention...Go!" Instantly, his words sent our 15K relay into motion in a crescendo of cheers and the whirring buzz from nearly twenty ergs all aimed at being the first to 15K.

As we two novices cheered on our varsity hero, my eyes were glued to the numbers on the erg monitor that reflected her speed. I had never seen anything like them before. With her every push she made the meters on the tiny screen tick by faster than ever, and before I knew it, she finished her first five hundred meters. So we followed the rules and rotated as fast as possible.

Up next, my novice teammate took off before the erg's fan even had the chance to slow. My eyes again glued to the numbers on the monitor. Though a novice, I was astounded to see that she could push numbers on par with those of our varsity teammate. Only her speed did not last quite as long—her numbers petered out as the meters ticked by. Even so, she generated speed that I did not know a novice could produce.

With five hundred more meters gone, it was my turn.

In a blur, I traded places with my fellow novice teammate. With every stroke, I pushed and watched the numbers, my tiny 500-meter splits, as they got faster and faster. *Hit their numbers*, I thought as I pushed for more. Attempting to match my partners' numbers, I pushed for more yet again. My teammates cheered. The erg fan whirred. As I came in and out of focus from the strain of my effort, I felt the air inside the Cage grow warmer. More humid with every push from every girl on every erg, and every cheer that goaded our collective effort.

Five hundred more meters down. Time to rotate back to our varsity teammate.

With every 500-meter partner rotation, our 15K continued to tick by, until it disappeared as a whirlwind of effort accompanied by sweat, spit, warm breathing, cheers, and light-headedness. Before I knew it, we finished...first.

By the end of that relay, just under an hour had passed, and we each had completed ten 500-meter segments of that 15K. Never before had I pushed that many pieces. Never before had I seen numbers like the ones my teammates pushed. Even though I did not match my teammates, I had never before produced numbers like the ones I did that day.

Maybe one day I will be that fast, I thought. *One day.*

After the relay, there were donuts and bagels. With the effort I poured into every stroke, the thought of a donut made my stomach turn. As for a bagel, I had eaten so many of them back when I worked at the bagel shop. I knew where they had put me then, and I was not about to risk going back there. I preferred to keep moving forward, so I opted to eat neither.

Day by day, week by week, that was how it went. I watched my teammates, pictured myself doing what they did, then mimicked and attempted to keep up for as long as I could. Eventually, that one and only piece of advice—to do what my teammates did—enabled me to gradually work my way toward the front of the novice team.

At least once a week, we did "stadium runs," where we ran sets of stairs inside the old basketball arena. The very same University Hall where I watched the Virginia women's basketball team play all those years earlier. I felt honored just to be inside that building again, let alone drip sweat inside the very gym where I had once been a starry-eyed spectator.

At the start of every stadium run, we each picked our own flight of stairs. Every flight ran from the basketball court up to the highest row at the very back of the arena before it dead-ended at the back wall. For safety reasons, we were not allowed to share flights, so we filled every aisle that vertically split every row of bleachers that encircled University Hall.

Upon every start, we each placed one foot on the bottom stair, then gazed up our own long stairwell at the wall that seemed a million steps away. Once set, and on our coach's call, we sprinted upward as fast as possible from the court level to the very top, battling both gravity and fatigue with every step. Having started with our backs to one another, we had no way of knowing how fast we were relative to our teammates until we reached the top. Once there, we would brush the wall with one hand, then carefully turn to head back down even more carefully.

It usually took me a little extra time to descend the stairs because the individual steps did not accommodate my size twelve shoes. To be safe, I would turn my feet on a diagonal. Even when slightly turned though, a safe grip on the stairs became increasingly unattainable on account of the sweat that poured down my legs and dripped from my elbows with every flight I ran. The stairs' brown polished concrete was downright treacherous by the time my sweat was done with them.

One day, after at least three weeks of stair runs, I wiped the sweat from my eyes as it streamed down my forehead, soaking my shirt. When my sweat-stung vision became clear enough to survey the arena, I could see that I, the girl who had once professed she would never be a runner, had miraculously made it to the top in second place. I briefly savored the moment, then carefully made my way back to the bottom where I awaited the running of our next flight.

One week later, after nearly one month of erging and stadium runs, my novice teammates and I finally got to go to the boathouse to row on the water.

By the time I arrived at the boathouse for my first row, I presumed I had an idea of the rowing basics. I had nearly a month's training, and because I had taken nearly 100,000 strokes on the erg, I figured rowing in a real boat would not be a complete surprise. On my first day though, I realized how much more there is to rowing than what I could ever learn from an erg.

On my first day at the boathouse, I was the only one who had never rowed before. So, to acquaint me, our coach had my teammates show me the ropes. They took me around the boathouse, pointed out our equipment, and explained who did what. As we wandered, they talked, while I followed, listened, and realized that the kind of rowing we would be doing was different from what I expected.

As it turned out, what I had watched on NBC when I was a kid—where each rower rowed with two oars in her own one-person boat—is called "sculling" and is not what college rowers spend most of their time doing. Instead, college rowers predominantly "sweep," which means they row with one oar. One long oar of about twelve feet rather than two ten-foot oars like those used in sculling. Ultimately, if you sweep, you are called a "sweeper." If you "scull," you are called a "sculler." In both cases, you are a rower who rows.

Something else college rowers spend most of their time doing is rowing "team boats," boats that hold more than one person. More specifically, of the six or so team boats that exist in the sport of rowing, "eights" and "coxed fours" are the ones most often raced in college. So rather than rowing "singles" like what I had seen when I was a kid, my teammates and I would spend most of our time rowing eights and coxed fours.

The eight is the biggest boat in rowing. It holds eight sweep rowers who do the actual rowing. Because of its length and speed, it requires a ninth person, the "coxswain," who, instead of an oar, has a rudder for steering and a speaker system for "coxing." So the coxswain guides the rowers not only by steering, but also by speaking to them through a microphone and series of speakers affixed within the boat itself. This allows the coxswain to act as the eyes and logic of the operation (both on and off the water) so that the rowers can focus on being an effective physical driving force.

The coxed four shares many similarities with the eight. It is just smaller given that four sweep rowers row it, while one cox-swain coxes it. So even though it is called a coxed four, it holds five people.

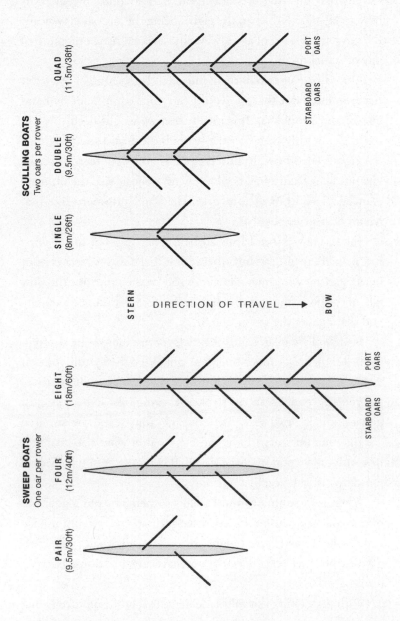

The most common boat classes in rowing (not to scale).

On my first day, we rowed an eight. Why? Because bigger boats tend to be more stable. So the eight, being the largest, is typically the most stable boat of all. A welcome characteristic on your first day of actual rowing.

Once I had a grasp of the equipment basics, one of my teammates pointed out that we would carry our equipment by hand and on our shoulders. This meant that we would need to work together not only when on the water but on land too. Factor in the eight's nearly two hundred pounds and sixty feet of length, and one better understands why rowing is considered the ultimate team sport. Without teamwork, wielding equipment like that would be near impossible.

The last few things I learned before heading out for my first row helped me understand where to sit. Each rower's seat is numbered starting with one, and every seat counts up from the bow end of the boat (the end that points in the direction of travel, the end that crosses the finish line first).

So, if you are in an eight, the seats are numbered one through eight. If you are number one, you can alternatively call yourself "bow seat" or "bow." If you are number eight, you can alternatively call yourself "stroke seat" or "stroke." Everyone else in between just gets a number: "two-seat," "three-seat," "four-seat," and so on...

The rules for seats are the same no matter what size boat you row with the exception of the single. If you row the single, people typically just call you by your name.

When my teammates and I finally gathered by our eight, one of our coaches told me to "sit three-seat" in "the second novice eight" (the second-fastest eight for the novice squad). She then gave me one piece of advice. "If you have any questions, ask your teammates."

With that, our coxswain made her calls, and I mimicked what everyone else did. As we lifted the boat off its rack, rested it on our shoulders, then carried it down the long hill from the Virginia boathouse to the water, I was relieved to be the only one with absolutely zero rowing experience. I can only imagine what it would have been like had everyone had as little knowledge as I did that day.

When we arrived at the dock, we walked our boat toward the water. We then placed our feet to the very tippy edge of the dock as our coxswain called, "Toes to the edge." By putting our toes to the literal edge of the dock, we made sure we did not accidentally hit the boat on anything when we rolled it down to the water together.

After "toes to the edge," our coxswain called, "Ready. Up and over heads." When she did, the eight of us moved our hands to the boat's gunnels, then pushed all two hundred pounds of it upward and held it directly overhead. From there, when we heard, "Ready...and down," we rolled that sixty-foot-long eight in one controlled yet swift motion from overhead, then placed it delicately upon the water with a soft *shushing* splash. Four of us then held the boat a few inches off the dock while the other four went to get our oars.

When my teammate who was assigned to sit in front of me returned with both my and her oars, she handed mine to me, then showed me how to set it up.

In any given boat, every spot has a setup that includes a wheeled seat that glides on two tracks attached to the inner part of the boat. A pair of shoes is also attached to the boat just below a rigger. The rigger itself is affixed to the gunnel (the long edge of the boat), and it allows each rower's oar to "attach" to the boat. (If you are a sculler, because of your two oars, you have riggers on both sides of the boat.)

Once my oar was ready, I reached down into the boat and played with my tiny twelve-inch-wide seat. I rolled it back and forth on its two tracks that were mounted on the interior deck of the boat. I listened to the slight grinding sound the seat's four wheels made as it rolled back and forth on its tracks. From there, all that remained was to get in.

When our coxswain called, "Ready. One foot in and down."

I took my oar handle in hand, stepped into the boat, then sat down on my wheeled seat. I then slid my feet into my shoes (which happened to be one half-size-too-small) and carefully closed their Velcro. My seat was hard, so I readjusted my butt on it a time or two to get a feel for it. I then rolled back and forth by bending and straightening my legs. My seat's wheels resumed their soft grinding sound.

As our coxswain made more calls, I was transfixed on the newness of it all. The way it felt. The way it sounded. The way the boat sank a little when we all sat down in it.

At last, our coxswain called through her microphone and speakers, "One hand on the dock. Ready and...shove."

When we did exactly as she said, we officially launched for my first row.

The air was cold but not frozen. It was still February, but because the reservoir where we rowed did not completely freeze that year, we were able to get on the water and into boats earlier than usual. For my inexperience, I welcomed the extra time on the water no matter how chilly it was.

When we docked at the end of our row on that February day of my third year at UVA, we had been on the water for more than an hour, and I was thankful for the girl behind me who had given me advice throughout the row. She helped me stay in time with my teammates. She explained the strange rowing lingo that our coach and coxswain used. She embraced being my personal translator (and cheerleader). Without a doubt, she got me through my first row.

As soon as the boat stopped next to the dock, and I turned to thank her, I discovered she was sopping wet and shivering. A shell of ice covered her oar and seat. She was frozen through her coat.

It was well below forty degrees Fahrenheit (about four degrees Celsius), and my completely novice rowing style had drenched her with every stroke I had taken during our previous sixty minutes of rowing. Despite the weather and her predicament, my teammate was smiling.

"Happy to help," she squeaked out with her shoulders hunched and teeth chattering.

Immediately after our row, I went to our coach to ask how I could get better. I did not want my inexperience to hold the team back nor did I want it to be the reason any of my teammates froze to death.

A few weeks and a few pieces of basic rowing advice later, I was switched from the second novice eight to the first novice eight. A shift that meant I had improved from places nine through sixteen on the novice team, to top eight.

By March, all of two months after I had joined the team, our coaches organized a team-wide 2K test. After the dozens of hills we had run, thousands of meters we had erged, countless weight circuits we had performed, and innumerable sets of stairs we had climbed by then, they felt it was high time to evaluate our improvement.

On the day of our 2K test, we arranged the ergs into two long, parallel rows. One front row and one back row. We were then separated into "heats" according to our predicted speeds. In doing so, anyone who was not in the current heat could cheer for those who were. At the completion of each heat, we were told we would take a break to allow those who had just tested to recover, then the next heat would get underway.

When it was my turn, I found my assigned erg. The front row was for the fast girls, while the back row was for the slower ones. Because I was a novice and I had only taken two erg tests by then, I was assigned to the back row. My location made sense given my inexperience at that point. I did not mind. It provided me a better view of the whole team, which motivated me to push myself even harder.

As I settled into my heat with about thirty other girls, I set my erg monitor for two thousand meters, took a breath, then sat ready. The Cage bubbled with anxious energy.

Then, when, "Attention…Go!" suddenly echoed across the room, we took off.

A few hundred meters into my test, I heard the voice of one of the varsity girls behind me, "Yes. Here we go, " she said.

The positive demand in her voice told me that I must have been doing something right. It was as if she was reading my mind and so was better able to push me through every single stroke of that 2K. She provided exactly the encouragement I needed. For while her voice demanded more from me, I too demanded more from myself.

When my monitor finally ticked to zero, I felt I had rowed every stroke of those two thousand meters as hard as I could. When I looked up at my time, breathing heavier than ever before, I realized how much all the training and chasing of my teammates was worth. I went more than twenty seconds faster than I had two months earlier—7:34. Not Olympic speed by any means, but I could not believe my improvement. I was within striking distance of a new 2K benchmark, and I was gradually reeling in some of the fastest rowers on our team.

Delighted with my result, I stood up and got off the erg, recovered a moment, then ventured off to find Kevin, who had disappeared. For every hill he ran with us, every meter he erged with us, every stair he climbed with us, and for the confidence and conviction with which he spoke when he addressed our entire team, I respected all he stood for. Even though he was not yet technically my coach, I could not wait to tell him my result.

As I scanned the room, I heard someone say he was in the hallway, so I made my way toward the exit. Still a little foggy from my 2K effort, I came within an inch of crashing into his chest right as he was reentering the gym.

"Seven thirty-four!" I blurted.

His reply, in his quintessentially Kevin sort of way, was simply, "There is more…"

At first, I wilted. *Does he not know how much faster I just went?* my mind insisted. But then I realized what he meant and thought, *He knows a lot. There must be more.*

By April, when I had three months of rowing to my name, I stepped onto the rusty old scale at the boathouse to check my weight. I only did it because I saw one of my teammates weighing herself, so I thought I should too. She had been a rower for many years, so I thought maybe weighing yourself was a typical part of the rowing process.

Once she was done, I stepped up, adjusted the scale, and could not believe what I saw. I was twenty-five pounds lighter than when I started rowing.

For the first time since I entered college, I weighed less than when I was in high school. And according to my parents, I seemed taller too. I no longer hunched but stood straighter since most of my new friends were as tall as or taller than me. I was, without a doubt, trimming down, walking taller, and discovering an unfamiliar bit of confidence.

If you were to ask my parents about my time in college before rowing, they would tell you that they knew I was not in the right place. However, they also knew they had to be patient and allow me to figure things out for myself.

Considering how unfit I was back when Kevin and I bumped into each other at the AFC, it did not take long for me to realize that rowing was helping me improve in nearly every possible way. During my first spring season on the team, we had spent every practice focused on fitness and pushing one another, and it had made us all faster. It was exactly what we needed, because being more fit and working together as a team were undeniably our best chances at earning speed when it came time to race.

At first, I thought it would be a miracle if I got to race at all. But once I began to improve, I moved up from the "second novice eight" to the "first novice eight" within a matter of weeks—where I remained from there forward. It was not varsity yet, but it was leaps and bounds ahead of where I thought I would be when I showed up on day one.

As for my first race, I sat three-seat in the first novice eight, and we raced on our home water. That made the newness of racing a tad less intimidating to me. Not only that, my parents, grandmother, and several friends were there to watch as my teammates and I won our races that day. Even though my family and friends understood next to nothing about rowing then, they fully supported what I was taking steps toward becoming.

By May, when both my junior year and novice season ended, my teammates and I finished with wins and losses all over the country, including a win for our team at the conference championship. A few weeks after that, we raced our last race of the season which ended with a loss. Although it was disappointing not to end on a win, I had enough mental wins to keep me hungry for the future and the chance to keep rowing for another year.

At twenty years old, I could already see that rowing was helping me. I no longer missed classes, so my grades were on the mend, which helped my GPA climb. I was learning to eat better, and I slept more. I had a whole team filled with friends who were focused and dedicated. I was also discovering that what I did each day was making me better, little by little improving me in some way. Once I realized this, I had no intention of turning back. My desire to simply be better was a place to start.

When I considered how far I had come during my first season, I no longer wondered if I might be as fast as the fast girls one day.

I realized that I could be. Without a doubt, I had made the right choice. I had found my place: with my team.

February 2002,

I finally got some of my act together and here I am. I feel a bit better, smarter, organized, and most of all, healthier. In my head I feel healthier too.

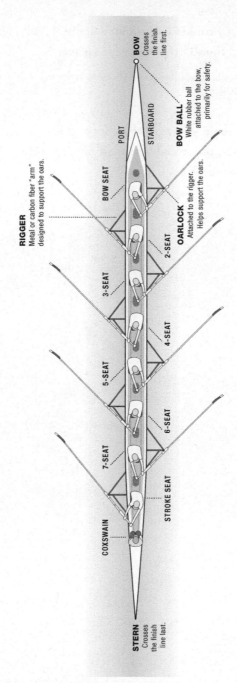

BOW
Crosses the finish line first.

BOW BALL
White rubber ball attached to the bow, primarily for safety.

OARLOCK
Attached to the rigger. Helps support the oars.

RIGGER
Metal or carbon fiber "arm" designed to support the oars.

PORT

STARBOARD

BOW SEAT

2-SEAT

3-SEAT

4-SEAT

5-SEAT

6-SEAT

7-SEAT

STROKE SEAT

COXSWAIN

STERN
Crosses the finish line last.

A port-rigged eight when viewed from above.

TEN

WE'RE GONNA DO THIS.

AT THE END OF EVERY SPRING, THE SAME CYCLE HAPPENS. People graduate and summer starts. That is when you, your coaches, and your teammates go your separate ways for a while. As soon as that happens, one can all but guarantee that your coaches sincerely hope that you and your teammates choose to do some training, anything at all, during your time apart.

Because I decided to start rowing midacademic year, I had already made summer plans to study abroad in Spain long before I decided to become a rower. This meant that I spent my first summer after I started rowing studying a lot and training very little. If I had to guess, I ran no more than three times while gone that summer, and I never once saw an erg nor set foot in a weight room. As a result, I did not exactly keep the fitness I gained before I went overseas.

When I returned from Spain, only a few weeks remained until team practices resumed. Luckily, one of my more ambitious teammates was in town for an internship. Unlike me, she stayed in touch with the erg over that summer, so I called her shortly after I got home. Because training is always easier with an accountability buddy.

We knew we were going to have an erg test to start the fall season. No matter what kind of shape I was in, I knew that even a little preparation would be better than the nothing I had done so far. With that in mind, I chose to meet my friend on most days until time ran out, school started, and our erg test arrived.

On the day of our erg test, my friend, now roommate, picked me up on her way to the Cage. We chatted the whole way, subconsciously distracting ourselves from what we were about to do. Despite the fact that I forgot my shoes and had to borrow a pair (which coincidentally, were a size-and-a-half too small also), we both tested our way into the upper half of the varsity team. Our two weeks of crunch time were better than nothing. I can only imagine how fast I would have been had I actually trained all summer.

After that first test of the season was officially in the books, Kevin gathered the whole team for a meeting. During his talks, we typically reviewed our big-picture goals—that every person was critical to the team's overall success, and that we were again setting our sights on the national championship as a team, the ultimate achievement in college rowing. Virginia Rowing had yet to win an overall national title by then, but that did not stop the team from pursuing it year after year.

Kevin began our meeting by telling us how we did as a group on our erg test. He also reminded us that a lot of strong athletes had graduated the previous spring. Considering this change in personnel, along with our new erg average, it was clear to him that we had lost size and power. Noticeable obstacles, at least on paper, to our big-picture pursuit of the team title at the NCAA Rowing Championship.

With each piece of information he shared, it seemed as though Kevin was mustering the nerve to admit something he hoped he would never have to say aloud.

Finally, he proposed two scenarios. "We can treat this as a building year. Or we go for it."

Taking a building year would mean setting our sights not on that year's national championship but on the following year's. It meant he considered that we might not be strong enough, at least not yet, to pursue the team's perennial goal.

As I quietly took in what he said, I wondered if we were, in fact, facing insurmountable hurdles. *Kevin can't mean that we should change our goal of winning NCAAs?* Although I did not have enough experience then to know for sure, I figured I was not the only one wondering.

Right when a slightly longer than normal silence fell over us, one of my more experienced teammates finally spoke up. "No. We're gonna do this. No matter what," Molly stated.

The room fell silent again. Her words set the tone. Her conviction made it easy for me to be on board. She did that a lot. We were the same year in school. She was a few weeks younger than me. She had walked onto the team when she was a freshman, and over her previous three years as a rower, she had worked her way up from the very bottom of the novice team to the very top boat for the varsity team—the "first varsity eight," the "1V" or "V8" for short.

Molly was an inspiration for what can happen when you take things one day at a time. When you are willing to get it wrong in order to discover what is right. She relentlessly had the guts to keep coming back for more no matter how long it took. Like I said, an inspiration.

Shortly after our team meeting, a few of us got together and mulled over what Kevin had said, which led to a conversation about our upcoming season. For me and Molly, it was our senior year, and though it was only my first full year on the team, it was our only chance to achieve a national championship together. Because we had become friends by then, it was something we looked forward to sharing.

We talked about what was possible. We admitted what winning NCAAs would require of us, and by the end, our intent was clear. We all agreed. In full support of one another's ideas, we knew without a doubt that we really did want to "do this." So we committed to it right there in my living room on a giant piece of cardboard in permanent red marker.

We made a sign that read, *I want an NCAA Championship every day*, as large as the cardboard could hold. We signed it, then duct-taped it to the brick wall inside the apartment I shared with my roommate. Whenever anyone came over, they signed it if they, too, were truly all in.

That was us. We committed to being champions in every aspect of our lives in order to make things happen. So we also put that concept to paper. Then signed that too. And just like the cardboard sign, anyone else fully on board was welcome to sign their names there as well. We meant every word of what we thought, wrote, said, and invited others to share.

Our red-marker-and-cardboard commitment to training for NCAAs.

A month or two after we told Kevin of our commitment despite what odds he presented, a stranger showed up at the boathouse. After our row, we found out that it was the head coach for the US National Women's Rowing Team. He had come to watch one of our teammates who had, in the past, been involved in the national team system. The very system that selects the Olympic team.

During his visit, he watched my one teammate but apparently had questions about a few others too. Molly, Beth (who had been one of my novice teammates), and as it turned out, me.

His visit planted a seed.

I understood why he noticed Molly and Beth. It was pretty obvious to me by then that whatever boats they were in went fast. I noticed things like that. It works the same as how you learn who runs fast. The only difference is that instead of being farther up a hill, their boats are the ones in the lead. Paying attention to things like this was important. I knew that if I ever had the chance to row with the fast people, I would do whatever they were doing even if I did not understand it.

I say this because there are obvious factors that contribute to boat speed, like strength and size. However, there are many factors that are not so obvious. Things like technical nuances or being adaptable and resilient. Being gutsy and naively optimistic. Being a good teammate and a relentless racer to name a few. With the more I learn about rowing, the more I realize that the multitude of obscure elements may very well be the most important.

This was a good thing for my teammates and me, because we were not in the position to rely solely on our strength and size. We did not have enough of either. We had some height, but on average, we were not tall. We had some strength, but on average, we were not strong. We were, by typical rowing standards, nothing exceptional.

We instead focused on addressing our weaknesses, getting stronger, and leveraging whatever it was that we were good at. The way we saw it, our strength was in our ability to enjoy what we were building together, both in the boat and out. The more we pushed each other, while enjoying our efforts, the more competitive we were able to become. It was our ability to be competitive while having fun that guided us and built trust.

Each week, we worked to find more from within ourselves and

one another. My basketball background elicited friendly trash talk. We played pranks and wore ridiculous outfits. We dressed up for Halloween and attempted to row in costume. We raced every set of stairs, every weight circuit, every erg. We knew exactly how fast each of us was going, right down to the tenth of a second.

Every small thing we did made our competition all the fiercer and also more sustainable. This made something great, like pursuing a national championship, not necessarily certain but certainly possible. This was the foundation of our team. Our identity.

In time, we were able to push ourselves further. Not all at once but little by little. Gradually asking more of our hearts, lungs, legs, minds, and selves. By pushing harder to find more, not for minutes or hours more in a given practice, but rather for a few seconds at a time, it made our improvement manageable. You do that long enough week after week, and it can amount to a lot of speed gained. Interestingly enough, when you break it down like that, you might not even recognize it when you end up quite a bit better. Your coaches, though? They might.

On one random afternoon of land training, Kevin told me to move my erg and position it directly behind the two fastest ergers on our team. By moving there, I could see their erg monitors and read the numbers they were pushing, which would help me execute his one directive.

"Do what they do for as long as you can," he said.

At first, I did not understand why he picked me to sit behind the two fastest ergers. I definitely did not beat them that day. I did, however, keep up for part of that practice, which opened my eyes to what I was capable of.

The hardest days of the week for me that winter of senior year were when we had to do one hour on the erg broken into twenty-minute chunks of time. We were supposed to start moderately, then finish by going as hard as we could. Every time I did that, it made me sick to my stomach to the point that I could not eat anything for the rest of the day. I only needed a few experiences like those to learn to take Pepto-Bismol preemptively—a habit that stuck for the rest of my competitive career.

I was learning and adapting alongside my teammates. Becoming better at being the best I had ever been. My grades improved from low C's and B's to nearly all A's again. I attended all of my classes unless we had a race. I even started doing all my assigned reading. Even the stuff I had to go all the way to the library for.

I was enjoying the process of discovering new things about myself. The process that was helping me become the person I was proud to be. The process that rowing itself was providing. I was hooked—more than anything, I wanted to row for as long as possible. And whatever that might take, I was willing to do. Trouble was, time with my team was running out. Senior year was flying by.

Before we broke for the winter holiday that year, everyone on the team was supposed to have an individual meeting with our head coach Kevin. We were told each meeting would last about fifteen minutes, provided we came prepared with our goals for the upcoming spring. To make it easy on us, instead of having us traipse across campus to his office, we met at one of the dining facilities instead. Kevin came to us.

When I arrived for my meeting, Kevin had been sitting for so long that he needed to take a quick break to hit the restroom. While he was gone, he left his notebook sitting on the table in front of me. Though upside down from where I sat, I could see the list of my teammates' names in meeting order, plus the notes he had taken about each person. Things like 2K test benchmarks, boats they wanted to race in, and any other goals they had.

My goals? Number one: I wanted to race in the "second varsity eight," the second fastest boat for the varsity team, the "2V." It was the boat I had rowed in all fall. Not exactly a stretch. Number two: Finish my next 2K test in 7:10 or faster. I had gone 7:34 back during my novice spring and had hit 7:11 already that fall. So my goal of 7:10 was also not exactly a stretch.

No one had asked me about goals before that, nor did anyone explain the true meaning of the word when used properly. So when it came to what I planned to tell Kevin, I guessed.

Shortly before Kevin returned from the restroom, I unintentionally caught the name on the line above mine. Her goals: 6:50 and 1V. They were far loftier than what I planned to say, so I amended mine on the spot.

"What is your next 2K goal?" Kevin asked me, getting right to the point.

"Seven minutes, I guess."

"Okay, seven. What else?"

"I want to be in the 1V," I suggested hesitantly, as if to retract it as soon as I said it.

The 1V is the highest-scoring boat for a rowing team at the NCAA Championship. It was the only boat above the 2V, the boat I came into my meeting planning to say. Given the circumstances, 1V was my only loftier option.

When I suggested making the 1V, Kevin accidentally let a chuckle slip. Then, catching himself, he reeled it back.

"If you'd said that a few months ago, I would've told you no. But now that your 2K is getting better, I'll put 1V/2V. How about that?"

I nodded. It made sense. Although I was technically no longer a novice, I was still relatively new. It also made sense that going faster on my 2K meant I could earn more opportunities to row in better boats. Numbers did not guarantee things, but they did open doors.

As my meeting wound down, Kevin broached one last topic: if I enrolled in one year of graduate school, would I want to row one more year for the team? Caught off guard by his question, I felt my face flush as I stammered over some long-winded reply about how it would be a dream to keep rowing. That I undoubtedly wanted to row for as long as I could and at the highest level possible. Despite my confused, circular response, we concluded by the end of our conversation that if the option were there, I would stay the extra year.

After Kevin noted my interest, we shelved the graduate school topic for a later time. Though I was excited by the idea, I also knew not to take anything for granted. I was not about to miss one minute of what time I knew I had, thinking about the time I might have.

A few months later, when I went 6:59, I officially had the second fastest 2K on our team.

On the day I "broke seven" on my 2K, right about one year after I started rowing, I had the worst heartburn of my life. Imagine exercising as hard as you can with the feeling you need to relieve the most acidic burp your chest has ever created, but you cannot stop to ease it. Despite my discomfort, breaking seven was easier than I thought. Maybe I would have gone faster if not for the heartburn. I made a mental note immediately after the test: *Pay attention to what I eat before hard ergs so I can go as fast as possible.*

"Subseven" turned out to be a big deal. It was a significant target for female rowers then. A benchmark made even more significant by the fact that I had only rowed for one year. It was a benchmark on paper that got me noticed in person.

Shortly after my milestone 2K, I got a shot in the 1V, a chance to row with the fastest girls on our team. I was pleased that my subseven 2K had earned me an opportunity to race my way into that boat, but I was barely prepared for what happened next. It was not long after my first race in the 1V (which we managed to win on our home water) that Kevin pulled me aside with yet another shot, another step.

After practice one day, Kevin told me, Molly, and two others that we had been invited to New Jersey for one of two national team rowing camps that were to be held later that summer. Of all the women rowing in college that year, the national rowing team coaches had selected twenty female athletes in total to attend their camps. For whatever reason, me, Molly, and two of our other teammates were among the select twenty.

Having thought about it ever since the head coach of the national team came to practice earlier in the year, I considered the invitation another dream—my chance to row for as long as possible and at the highest level. Apparently, the national team coach's visit had planted a seed. *Was it possible that I had national team potential?*

As Kevin explained, after our college season was over, and if we accepted our invitations, we could train for four weeks in the same place as the US national team—on a small lake in New Jersey. We would get to see what life was like as a national team athlete. New location, new teammates, new challenges, no racing that we knew of, just training. If we chose to attend the camp, we would be a sort of novice squad for the national team. We would be the new girls who needed to focus on fitness and skill development. We would be there on a trial basis to see how well we might fit with the team in the future.

It seemed as though the US coaches were scouting athletes who might have the potential to help the team down the line. If so, once we finished school, we might have the chance to train full time in New Jersey until we were either fast enough to make the national team or…we were cut.

Kevin reiterated that it was ultimately our choice to attend camp. Because, contrary to what you might think, full-time training does not appeal to everyone, especially when such a lifestyle comes with so much uncertainty. Me? It was an opportunity to take another step toward becoming better. Toward rowing for as long as possible and at the highest level. I smiled and savored the honor. Of course, I wanted to attend.

I did not get ahead of myself though. My teammates and I still had a lot of work to do. We meant what we told Kevin during our first team meeting at the start of the season. We had committed to going after the NCAA championship, no matter what. So we acted like it.

Just as we wrote and hung on my apartment wall, we behaved as if we wanted an NCAA Championship every day. As if we were champions in every aspect of our lives. In the boat, out of the boat, as individuals, and as a team.

March 2003,

I had a dream last night that I raced sprints against the guys. Funny thing. I won every time. Easily. After twenty tries no one beat me. Afterward, all the coaches came over to me. They wanted to know who I was and what my plans were for next year. National Team Camp, they said. I nodded because it was the most fun I'd had in years.

ELEVEN

FIND A WAY.

SIMPLE AS THAT, RIGHT? YOU PICK YOUR PURSUIT. GATHER a group of people who want that same thing. Put in the work individually and as a team. Then get a little better each day. You do those things, and the magic takes care of itself. You go on to win the national championship.

Well, not quite.

The first time I went mountain biking, I set off on a difficult course because it was what my friends were doing. I figured that if the pace or obstacles got too challenging for me, I could easily dismount to walk, then remount later, pedaling faster to catch up. That was how I kept up even though I was not as skilled yet.

On that first outing, I remember the first hill I climbed. One of my friends briefly explained that the best way to climb was to keep an eye on the ground right in front of me and also a short distance up ahead. Only every now and again should I glance all the way to the top. Because, as she told me, if I fixated on the peak, I would easily become disheartened. When you climb challenging inclines like that, progress can be slow. And often, it gets slower the higher up you go.

Her advice was sound. Whenever I focused out ahead too

long, the rocks, holes, roots, and various other immediate obstacles went dangerously overlooked. Whenever that happened, I would lose my balance and have to put a foot down. Sometimes I fell off completely. And getting back on track midclimb was quite difficult.

By the end of our ride, I learned that the best way to ascend a craggy climb was to manage my immediate needs one at a time while not getting so stuck on one thing that I could not see what was up next. And although I should spend most of my time focused on what was in front of me, periodic glances to the top ensured that I was still headed in the right direction and making progress. Any advancement, no matter how slight, would keep me optimistic when things were not going exactly as I had hoped.

That is rowing. It requires you to compartmentalize things in your mind. At any given moment, you must be optimistic about your future while also being aware of and managing the reality of what is immediately happening to you. If you hesitate for even an instant, if your mind drifts to someone or something else, then you crack the door for doubt. And doubt is the last thing you want when you need every last fragment of yourself in order to move forward, considering that your distress is both physical and mental.

My Virginia teammates and me, we were naive optimists. We had to be during my first season in the 1V. We had committed to doing this—to going after the national championship with every ounce of ourselves—yet what was happening every day told us we were, in fact, not.

No matter what we did, we lost nearly every race early on in the spring season of my senior year. We were the 1V, supposedly the flagship, our team's top boat. The boat that represented how fast our whole team was. The boat that could score the most points at the national championship. However, as we struggled week after week to bring home even one single win, we jeopardized the entire team's chance to race at nationals at all.

Among the nine of us who earned our way into the 1V that spring, we were four experienced athletes and five "walk-ons," meaning that most of us in the 1V learned how to row there at Virginia. Two of us with as little as one year's experience. So, if you compared us by typical rowing measures to our competitors, it was just as Kevin told us back in the fall at our team meeting: we were not as tall, not as fast on our 2Ks, and were less experienced than most teams that aspired to win the national championship.

The nine of us, though, were the fastest our team had when we rowed together on the water. Which meant that, despite our limitations in size, strength, and experience, our only option was to find a way or make one.

Week after week, loss after loss, Kevin did not give up on us. He simply scratched his head and reorganized us into different lineups. We would try it one way. Race. Lose. Try it another way. Race. Lose. By the time our season neared its end, Kevin had tried so many different lineups that we all had the chance to sit in nearly every single seat in the 1V. Though I did not understand it at that time, he had good reason for moving us around so much.

I have since learned that there is more to where people sit in a boat than simply filling seats with fast rowers. Coaches have to factor in how those rowers work together, not just as friends or teammates but also in terms of their technical and physical strengths. Each seat within a boat allows certain rower's strengths to shine. So even if you have the same people in the boat, the speed those people produce can vary dramatically depending on where they each sit.

When Kevin moved us within the 1V, he considered many things. For instance, the two rowers who sit in the bow of the boat (the "bow pair," or bow seat and two-seat) are typically smaller and more technically proficient. Because the bow of a boat is narrow, the bow pair's being smaller helps a boat sit higher out of the water (rather than sinking). And when a boat floats properly, it goes faster.

As for the bow pair's technical efficiency, because the bow pair is closest to the bow, they greatly impact a boat's overall stability. When a bow pair has consistently good technique, they can make an entire boat more stable, which helps everyone in the boat be more effective. And when everyone is more effective, a boat goes faster than it would have otherwise.

Directly in front of the bow pair sit three and four. These two are strong and often tall. They primarily focus on pushing hard and following five-seat and six-seat, the two who sit in front of them. Five and six are typically the two strongest rowers of all. They must have the wherewithal to push incredibly hard but also to pay attention to the boat's rhythm. This is because they sit toward the middle of the boat. By sitting in the middle, five and six have great potential for making or breaking how synchronized (and therefore effective) a rowing lineup is. When they are on, they reinforce a strong rhythm and increase boat speed. When they are off, they cause a breakdown in rhythm, which decreases boat speed.

The "stern pair" sits in front of five and six. They are seven-seat and stroke seat. These two set the rhythm for the entire eight. Much like when you watch an incredibly fast swimmer swim, an efficient rhythm can make an incredible difference in speed, so a strong, efficient rhythm is important to find.

An efficient rhythm is a mysterious thing though. Some rowers have a natural gift for setting rhythm and sitting in stern pair. It is a gift that is oftentimes inexplicable no matter how much a coach or teammate tries to understand it. But whether you understand it or not, when a stern pair's rhythm is effective, every rower in the boat stands to become more effective as long as they trust enough to follow it and back it up.

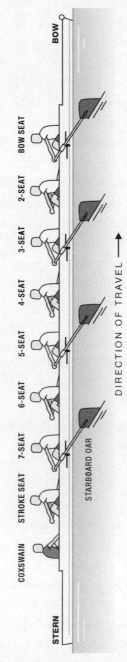

Seat rules for an eight in caricature form.

It was with each seat's role and the need for an efficient rhythm in mind that Kevin shuffled us from seat to seat with every week and race we lost. He knew because of his years of experience that once he discovered the right combination (by having us sit where we were each optimally efficient), it could unlock more speed. That is, if he found it in time.

After at least six weeks of losing and shuffling, and with our final and most important races of the season upon us, our hope for a chance to race at the national championship was running out. Until finally, Kevin tried one last possible lineup: relentlessly gutsy Molly at stroke seat and Julie, another relentlessly gutsy senior, at seven-seat.

It took Kevin that entire spring season to try those two at stern pair because they were not your usual stroke and seven-seat. At least not for a 1V. They were skinny. Built more like runners. Not particularly strong in the weight room nor on the erg. They were also walk-ons. They did not have strength, size, and experience by typical standards. What they did have were guts and naive optimism. Two factors that I now know are critical yet often underestimated.

Molly and Julie may have been lanky, but they were fierce competitors who set a new tone for our 1V. A tone that worked.

April 13, 2003,

Butts handed to us on our first races. Started figuring it out after that. Last race a success but taking it back to the garage. Good thing. I want to do a good job and win because of it. No more losing. Don't let it get to me. We're gonna do this! No regrets. No forgets.

In late April, we brought home a win at our conference championship. But because it was a race the team had not lost since its inception, and the conference consisted of only four teams at the time, the win itself was not an indication of the speed we would need to win nationals. We had to find more.

Once classes ended and exams had passed, we began training twice per day until the regional championship arrived. When it did, it meant our time to prepare was officially up. So we headed to Tennessee to race for our final chance to guarantee a qualifying spot for nationals—a bid we could earn if we won the regional championship. We had to win.

For us seniors, it was truly our last chance together. It was a chance so important that we chose to race at the regional championship over walking in our own college graduation. If we had skipped the race, we would have let our entire team down by foregoing our chance to qualify for nationals. Skipping graduation was an easy decision.

Our first regional championship race came on a Saturday morning in late May. When we went to the line for our heat, our first race of the weekend, we had no idea of how fast we were. We knew we would be up against teams that had beaten us earlier in the season. A few of them had beaten us by a lot too. We also knew that we could not do anything about the past nor our competitors. If we focused on someone or something else, it would open the door for doubt. So we did the only thing we could: we focused on ourselves and our speed.

When we crossed the finish line in our heat, we posted the fastest time of any boat in any of the heats by nearly two seconds. A large margin in rowing. A margin of about forty feet when it comes to racing an eight. A margin that proved we had gotten faster.

With the heats behind us, of the twenty-one teams that started the weekend in pursuit of the regional championship, twelve remained, and we were among them. We had taken another step, but we did not get ahead of ourselves. We had two more races before we could celebrate.

In our semifinal, the next step, we again posted the fastest time. This time, of the remaining twelve boats, we were one second and half faster than the next closest. But again, we did not get ahead of ourselves. We had one more race before we could celebrate.

Despite every race we lost throughout that spring, we kept coming back for more. In doing so, we eventually worked our way to the middle lanes of the final of the regional championship. The lanes typically reserved for only the fastest teams, those most likely to win. If you had looked at us even a few weeks prior to regionals, no one would have imagined our UVA 1V would be in the middle lanes. It is quite possible that not even Kevin did. But that is the thing with rowing. Some factors to boat speed are obvious. Others are not. That means the miraculous can happen when you least expect it.

On the morning of Sunday, May eighteenth of my senior spring, instead of walking in my college graduation, I sat with my teammates on a river in Tennessee, ready to race five other teams for the regional championship title. Two of those teams had beaten us earlier in the year. But again, we could not do anything about them. Our only option was to focus on us, one stroke at a time, until we crossed the finish line.

Just over six minutes passed from the time the race announcer's voice rang out, "Attention...Go!" to the time we crossed the finish in a commotion of splashes and confusion. As we sat there in the boat, recovering after the closest race we had all year, we looked around awaiting the result. It was too close for us to call on our own. Only when we saw people waving from shore were we certain.

A narrow half-second margin (about ten feet) over second place. The race is a mile and a quarter, and we won by all of ten feet. Not only did we take down teams who had beaten us previously, but we won both our region and the overall championship.

Following months of uncertainty, months of coming back

for more no matter how many times we were knocked down, we finally earned our team's bid to the NCAA championship. Finally, we could celebrate (a little).

Taking home that win made missing graduation all the easier.

Just over a week after we won regionals, we flew to Indiana for our chance to go after what we had committed to during our first team meeting back in the fall: the NCAA Rowing Championship.

The three-day national competition was met with so much wind that the conditions on the racecourse were rougher and choppier than anything I had ever experienced. It was the kind of choppy that caused water to shoot up my nose midrace. The kind of rough that caused many teams to fall apart and to perform worse than expected. As for us in our UVA 1V, it went exactly the opposite. We advanced through every race, making every step from heats to semifinals to finals. We surpassed teams that spent the entire season ranked higher than us. We found more speed together even though we were presented with ever increasing challenges.

By the time my first trip to the national championship came to a close, we placed fifth in the country as a 1V and sixth as a team. Far better than expected. Especially considering how many races we lost throughout the season. In the end, we were able to make it happen because rather than giving up, we kept coming back with a willingness to find a way or make one. With Molly and Julie at the helm in stern pair, I am fairly certain we made one.

The naively optimistic 1V. (Second, third, fourth from the left: Julie, me, Molly)

On our plane ride home from Indiana, Kevin sat down next to me holding his glasses in his mouth by one of the stems as he buckled his seat belt. For the next few hours, we talked about how the year had gone, how far I had come, and how he thought I could play a role as a team leader in the future.

In NCAA sports, you are generally only eligible to compete for four years. So typically, if you start as a freshman, you are allowed to compete your freshman, sophomore, junior, and senior years. After that, you are considered ineligible. But when I graduated, I still had eligibility because I had started rowing so late. So just as Kevin suggested in my goals meeting earlier that year, if I stayed at UVA as a graduate student, I could compete for one more year. After that, my remaining eligibility would expire, and I would have to move on.

Like missing graduation, my decision to enroll in one year of graduate school so I could keep rowing with my team was an easy one. The sport was making me better in every aspect of my life. I was healthier, both physically and mentally. I was being presented with opportunities that empowered me to improve myself. Whatever I had to do to keep that going, I was all in. I was certain of that. Something else I was certain of? Attending that national team camp I had been invited to.

We flew home from Indiana on June first, and the official national team camp lists were posted on June fourth. Although I had wanted to attend camp all spring, I was never completely certain it would happen for me until I saw my name on that list.

The pre-elite group, the month-long camp I was invited to, consisted of eleven names. The development group, the week-long camp Molly was invited to, consisted of nine. Of all the female college rowers in the country, just twenty were invited to New Jersey to get a peek at what life could be like as a national team rower. I felt fortunate when my teammate and good friend Molly and I had made the cut.

Nine days after returning home from NCAAs, I packed my things and prepared for my six-hour drive to New Jersey, where the US National Rowing Team trains. I knew where I had to show up and when. I also knew I would spend the better part of the summer rowing with a group of strangers. All I knew about them were their names and their respective schools. Other than that, I had no idea what I was in for.

With less than a year and a half of rowing to my name, not only was I going to be the new kid again but also the least experienced. Again.

TWELVE

A LOT TO LEARN.

DURING THE NINE DAYS BETWEEN THE NCAA CHAMPIONSHIP and the day I left for my first pre-elite camp in New Jersey, I barely slept a wink in anticipation of my next step. It was a truly exciting step because it would enable me to row for as long as possible and at the highest level. It was also a daunting step because it meant I would be rowing alongside some of the best in the country.

I drove the 307 miles from my parents' house to New Jersey completely alone. It was the longest solo drive I had ever made. Although I had driven to New Jersey once before, it had been a road trip with friends. Now, making that trip all alone was an entirely different experience.

As I headed northward through the rolling, green hills of Virginia, I glanced in the rearview mirror and caught sight of my hometown—the town where I had spent all my life up until then—as it grew smaller and smaller, and then it disappeared. When it was completely gone from view and I saw nothing but the unfamiliar open road up ahead of me, I became both nervous and invigorated. Nervous because I was heading off alone for something completely unknown. Invigorated because I was heading off alone for something completely unknown.

With every mile that passed, turn I made, and song that blared through the speakers of my dad's car, a million possibilities ran through my mind about what the summer might hold. Particularly since I knew I was about to spend the next four weeks with complete strangers. Molly's camp was separate from mine. So although she would supposedly be in New Jersey too, for all we knew, we would not be seeing one another.

When I arrived at the boathouse in New Jersey for the first meeting of camp, there were seven us. Not one of whom I had met before. Of the eleven college women from all over the country who were invited to attend the pre-elite camp, just seven showed up. One had been bumped up to the senior national team, the top group that was training for the World Championships and eventually the Olympics. While three others opted not to come to camp at all. Which left us—the remaining seven.

We had no promise of travel nor international competition that summer. We were not there to officially try out for the US team. We were instead there to get our feet wet. To see if we might have the potential to help the national team in the future. As a result, all we were guaranteed to do that summer was to train.

The idea of only training might have been what deterred the three who did not accept their pre-elite camp invitations. We seven though, we were up for anything that meant we might get to train with the national team in any way. The simple prospect of being involved with the national team system in any capacity was incentive enough.

Before camp, I had rowed mostly eights, sometimes a coxed four, which meant we almost always had a coxswain who took care of the steering and logistics. I could count on one hand the number of times I had rowed a boat smaller than a coxed four, let alone made my way out on the water without a coxswain at all.

In college, not only do you spend most of your time rowing eights or fours, you sweep. You row with just one oar. This means that sweep boats always carry an even number of rowers unless your equipment breaks or the unexpected happens, like if someone falls out of the boat (which has been known to happen from time to time).

Me? I am a starboard. Always have been. To this day, I have rowed the opposite side of the boat, the port side, less than a handful of times.

Port and starboard carry the same meanings in rowing as they do for any boat. So, if you are the coxswain, port oars are to your left, while starboard oars are to your right. It only gets confusing because rowers sit facing in the opposite direction than that of the coxswain, what one might call backward. Because of this backward-facing position, rowers cannot see where they are going unless they turn around to look. This means that from a rower's perspective, starboard oars are thought of as being to the left, while port oars are thought of as to the right.

As for deciding whether you row port or starboard, people have all sorts of random reasons for why they might choose one or the other, like being right- or left-handed. For me, it was simple. Our college team needed starboards when I began. Nothing more complex than that. So Kevin had deemed me a starboard from day one.

On the early evening of our first pre-elite camp meeting, the seven of us gathered awkwardly, standing a few feet apart. This was oddly reminiscent of my first day of rowing practice back in college. Instead of fifty girls though, we were seven, and no one knew each other.

While we stood awkwardly sizing each other up, our camp coach, Chris, arrived. When she did, she introduced herself as the assistant coach for the senior national team—the group that trains for and competes at World Cups, World Championships, and the Olympic Games. They are the tippy top. Literally some of the best in the world. And there I was, standing with six other naive, fresh-from-college rowers, being addressed by a woman who coached some of the world's best. How could I not hang on her every word?

After Chris finished with her introductory comments, she requested we introduce ourselves—our hometowns, colleges, and the like. Once the formalities were over, she got right to the point.

The senior team was apparently overseas, so Chris would be with us for only a few days. After that, we learned someone else would take over for the rest of camp. As for the head coach of the senior team, Tom, he too was overseas. So we would maybe get to meet him at some point down the line. But only once the senior team was back in town and if the schedule suited it.

Other than that, Chris did not have much else to say, so she finished by telling us where we should meet the following morning for our first official practice. Plus, one more thing.

"Seven is obviously an odd number," she said as she took a quick survey of which sides we each rowed—three ports, four starboards. Which brought her to her last question. "Who here has sculling experience?" She grinned as she glanced around our small circle of seven.

Six hands raised, indicating that, yes, they had sculling experience. Experience rowing with two oars like the women I had watched on NBC when I was a kid. Because we were seven, Chris told us we would have to row three pairs (two rowers with one oar each, no coxswain) and one single (one person with two oars in the smallest, most unstable boat of all). That was the only way to make camp work with seven.

With seven, we could not row an eight. Without a coxswain, we could not row a coxed boat. Which left us with a focus on developing our skills by rowing small boats. We were the future. We needed fitness and skill. Things we would earn the quickest by focusing on small boats. So three pairs and one single it was.

I was a sweeper who had never rowed a single before. And

of the seven of us, I was the odd woman out—the fourth starboard and the only one at pre-elite camp who had never sculled. So although I wished for anything but the single, I also knew that being the first to row it was the best way to get over my apprehension.

Our first meeting was short. By the end, I had a vague impression of what each of the next twenty-six days might entail. I learned we would run, row, then take a break before rowing again each afternoon. I also learned that I, the only one without sculling experience, would be the first to row the single. I was nervous. But I had gone to camp intending to do whatever they asked of me. That was my best shot at improving and my best shot at rowing for as long as possible.

The next morning, we went for a thirty-minute run along the dirt path that traced the shoreline by the lake. It gave me a chance to survey our new body of water—Lake Carnegie. It also gave me the chance to see how good at running I was compared to the others. Following our thirty-minute run, I was glad to see that although I was not the fastest, I was not the slowest either.

After our run, we took a short break, then got on the water to row our small boats. The three pairs and my single.

On day one of rowing the single, I felt like a novice all over again. I knew nothing other than what a single looked like. I had never carried one, let alone sat in one. So on my first day, I learned the basics.

One of our new coaches led me across the parking lot to the trailer where my boat was stored. As we approached, my nerves welled as I took in the sight of it. It was all of twenty-five, maybe twenty-six, feet long but only a matter of inches wide. My new coach told me that singles are so lightweight that people usually carry them by themselves. But since I was new, he said he would help me.

We walked to opposite ends of the long, skinny boat, then

carefully picked it up together. When we lifted it, I discovered how right he was. It was lightweight. Perhaps thirty pounds split between the two of us.

As I familiarized myself with the weight of the boat, I mimicked what my coach did by resting the end I carried on my right shoulder. I then carefully stepped in perfect timing with him as we strolled together toward a small dock. It was an old wooden one at the edge of the parking lot. So old, in fact, that it was covered in what appeared to be several years' worth of goose poop.

When we made it to the dock and he called, "Way 'nough," we stopped where we stood. He then called for us to roll the boat down to the water by simply saying, "Ready and down." Just like that, we delicately placed the boat upon the surface of the water with a soft *shushing* splash.

While my new coach walked back to grab my oars, I stood watch over my single as it floated on the glassy, greenish-brown water below. Lake Carnegie was so flat. I could see every tiny bug that landed on the lake's pristine surface, broke it into minute ringed ripples, then subsequently flew away. The longer I stared down at the water and my boat, I realized just how small that single seemed compared to any other boat I had ever rowed. So narrow. So unstable. Barely as wide as I was.

As I surveyed it, I hoped I would not embarrass myself by flipping over before I even pushed away from the dock. It was not a training single after all. It was designed for racing. Intentionally long and skinny. Made for speed.

The boat itself had a silver hull and a bright red interior, with a star and stripe that stared back at me as I reflected on how far I had come in such a short period of time. That very American paint job, the one that shone back at me from the narrowest boat I had ever been told to row, made me realize I still had a lot to learn.

With oars secure in its oarlocks, a single floats upon Lake Carnegie at dawn. (Image courtesy of Allison Mueller)

When my new coach returned with my oars, he showed me how to secure them in their oarlocks the correct way. He then explained how to step into the boat without flipping off the dock, how to control my oars while I secured my feet into the Velcro closure of my shoes (which I nervously triple checked), and how I should hold my two sculling oars when the time came for me to row.

At long last, with no more instructions to give, he helped me shove away from the dock. Once I was safely off, he headed for his coaching launch, the motorboat from which he would follow and coach me. As he walked away, he instructed me to start conservatively by rowing with just my arms instead of taking full strokes with my legs, trunk, and arms. I trusted he knew more than I did, so I did as he said and rowed with just my arms (very slowly) to the other side of a little rock bridge. The closer I stayed to the boathouse, the safer I was on that first day.

For the next hour, I rowed with only one arm at a time to practice how each one felt alone. As a result, I rowed in circles.

After several circles in one direction with one arm, I turned the boat around and rowed several circles in the opposite direction with the other arm. With every circle I made, my new coach drove his motorboat in circles along with me.

By the end of my dizzying first hour in the single, my teammates, who had spent their first hour in pairs, passed me as they made their way back to the boathouse. With each passing pair, they watched me row my circles, then continued on their way. It was only when the last pair passed that one of the girls finally shouted something.

"Hey! Did ya flip yet?" I could hear the humor in her voice as she further shouted that she had flipped during her first row in a single.

Shortly after that last pair passed, I spun and rowed arms only back toward the dock. I could not help but grin. Not only was my new teammate's comment funny, but I had made it through sixty minutes of countless circles and had yet to flip.

The single, being the smallest boat in rowing, is without a doubt the most unstable and slowest of the sport. The beauty of it, though, is that it lets you learn at your own pace. One that was for me, on my first day, circles. One arm at a time. Never out of sight of the boathouse.

Sitting there in my single alongside the old wooden dock, I undid the Velcro of my shoes, then carefully pulled my feet from them. Then, as I controlled my oars to keep from flipping, I put one foot delicately down on the dock and attempted to stand. As I did, I put my other foot down, then pulled my two oars across the tiny boat. Only once both my feet were firmly planted on the dock and I was standing upright and out of that single could I say that row one was complete.

Success, I thought. I had managed to make it through sixty whole minutes of rowing…arms only, in circles, without flipping.

With gnats, humidity, and my sweat accumulating at the

crease in my elbow, I stood staring down at that single. As its red interior, star, and stripes stared back at me, it gave me a new appreciation for rowing. I had come a long way in a year and a half, as I had gotten to my 6:59 2K quickly. However, the other girls at camp had more experience, more height, or a faster 2K, if not all of those things. And while, yes, I had spent thousands of meters rowing eights, the biggest, most stable boats of all, I was about to spend the summer doing the opposite—rowing the smallest, least stable boat of all because that is what it would take to earn the fitness and skill required at the next level. To become better, I had to step away from the familiar, aim for new benchmarks, and be willing to learn something new.

When I compared what I had learned in college to even one day of rowing at the next level, it became obvious that I had so much more to learn before I was anywhere near ready to try out for the national team. But I was enjoying rowing's developmental process. So I was willing to learn in order to keep taking steps. Steps I looked forward to, no matter what they entailed.

One week after that first row in the single, an unexpected change came. Because the development camp had nine rowers and our pre-elite camp had just seven, the coaches decided to balance the groups. To my delight, that meant my good friend Molly would join us as part of the pre-elite camp. Also to my delight, with our group now eight through the addition of Molly, it meant I would get to row a pair rather than a single all summer.

At first, we all traded partners nearly every row. But in time, the coaches realized that Molly and I matched by working well together, so they left us together for the remainder of the camp. Given every unfamiliar thing I encountered before then, it was nice to have one thing I was used to.

During the third week of camp, as we gradually adjusted to and improved in our routine of rowing small boats, both the senior team and its head coach, Tom, returned from overseas.

When they did, we learned of another exciting change: over the course of that week, two of us at a time, selected from the pre-elite camp, would have the chance to row in an eight with the women on the actual senior team.

On the day that Molly and I got to row in that eight, Tom jokingly called us "Virginia." Molly and I were exactly the same height. We both had brown hair and were lanky. The major difference from afar was that Molly was a port, and I was a starboard. We were, by all accounts, "Virginia." I took Tom's nickname for us to mean that he must have seen something he liked. His joking did not bother me.

During the row, we, "Virginia," got a few pointers from Tom. Mostly though, our job was to listen, follow, and push. I wanted to make a good impression, so I was intent on every stroke. Tom was watching.

At the end of those maybe ten kilometers of rowing, as we made our way back to the dock, I savored how fast that eight glided along. How powerful it felt. How stable it was. How exhilarating it was. It was the most exciting row I had ever experienced. I felt honored and lucky to be sitting in that seat in that boat among those elite women. They were real athletes. Some of the best in the world.

Once we landed back at the dock and just before I stepped up and out of the boat, one of the senior team women nonchalantly commented on the row. "Guys…I think we need to work on the set next time we go out."[1]

Her words burst my bubble. The most stable row, the most set boat I had ever experienced, was, to her, not set at all. She considered it unstable. I really did have a lot to learn.

For the duration of camp, we had started nearly every day with a run, followed by a row. Then a long break before finishing each

---

1   "Set" is synonymous with stability. A set boat is a balanced, stable boat that does not rock around or sway side to side when rowed.

day with an afternoon row. On some afternoons, we got to rest, so rather than training three times per day, we would train just twice. Either way, that was more than what I was used to doing.

In college, there is a time limit to how much you can train each week. The NCAA rules for college rowing make sure of that. But after college, like say when you attend a pre-elite camp, those rules do not apply. The limit is up to your own body and mind. Which I discovered firsthand a few weeks into camp as the larger amount of training began to wear on me.

At first, it was my lower back. It got achy. But because I was still not much of a runner then, I attributed my low-back discomfort to my worn-out running shoes.

After my back, a few strange red spots appeared. On the day I noticed the first red spot on my back, one slightly larger than a quarter, I bought anti-itch cream. The day after that, I showed it to a local doctor, all the coaches, and my teammates. By then, it looked like a comet. One big red dot with a trail of smaller red dots streaming from it. Their conclusion: contact dermatitis. Poison ivy from our morning runs along the lake they said.

It was a strange place to get poison ivy though. Under my shirt, on my low back, wrapping around my side. A place that never saw the sun, let alone potential poison ivy. But who was I to know? After my comet developed, headaches followed.

It was summer in New Jersey. Late June and early July. Because it was hot and I knew dehydration caused headaches, I assumed it was that. So I hydrated and took headache medicine. A few days of overdoing these solutions, and I was so hydrated that I woke up at least twice every night from then forward to pee. Still, the headaches persisted.

Finally, as if my back, spots, and headaches were not enough, chills arrived. Also in the middle of the night. Considering how much we were training, plus the fact that I was waking up in the middle of the night to pee and with chills, I attributed my daily fatigue to lack of sleep. Until at some point during the final week of camp, I called my mom.

When I told her how I felt, it took her a mere thirty seconds to diagnose the truth. "Honey, you have shingles," she said. "I'll make you an appointment for the day after you get home."

How could I possibly have shingles? I wondered. I was twenty-one. Young people do not get shingles. That only happens to people over fifty or those with weak immune systems.

I was in a new place with new coaches and new teammates, and everything we did was more mentally and physically challenging than anything I had ever experienced before. Compared to the previous summer when I had traveled to Spain and done zero training, I was in the midst of the exact opposite. I had trained two to three times daily until my body had enough and forced me to take a break.

As camp neared its end, Tom, the head coach, took time to meet with each of us pre-elites. Though he had come to watch practice back in the fall of my senior year at UVA, it was my first chance to speak with him one on one. I had no idea what to expect nor what to say. I was nervous. But meeting with Tom was indeed another step.

On the day I met with Tom, we stood near the entryway of one of the boat bays at the boathouse. He leaned back on a big wooden box. I stood next to him patiently (and awkwardly) waiting, wondering what he was thinking. Finally, he smirked to indicate that I was not in trouble nor did he have bad news. Instead, he asked about my plans for the following year. With our conversation centered around my chance to row at Virginia for another year, I excitedly explained my remaining eligibility and that I had enrolled in graduate school.

Right as I finished speaking those words about graduate school, Tom picked up and finished my sentence as if it was his own. "Good," he said. "That's perfect. More race experience is what you need."

Simple as that. He liked my plan. He had nothing bad nor more to say. I smiled. He smiled. I laughed nervously. He simply laughed. Then I walked away.

With no races all summer, I had no idea how the coaches evaluated us or if they had even evaluated us at all. All I knew was that we ran, rowed pairs, trained two or three times each day, and slept. All the while, our little group of strangers became friends.

Our camp was an experiment. Never before had there been one like it. A camp designed without the intention of preparing for a race. A camp designed to expose us to what life was like as a full-time training rower. There was no real plan or purpose for it other than that. At least not one that I knew of. Perhaps the coaches wanted to see if we were ready for full-time training. Perhaps they wanted to see if we were mature enough to train without the prospect of a race on the horizon. Perhaps there was more to why they chose the eight of us in particular. If there was, they did not share it with me.

I was home by mid-July, and within two days of my return, I went to the doctor. My mom was right. I did have shingles. The doctor suggested that it likely developed because of everything I had put myself through that summer, physically and mentally. He went on to explain that once you have chicken pox, the virus stays with you, dormant in your nerve tissue near your spinal cord and brain until your immune system weakens. Once it weakens enough, shingles can appear.

Apparently, all that training in the hottest heat of summer had taken its toll on me.

"Two weeks of nothing," the doctor said. "You need to rest."

Instead of continuing with two to three training sessions per day, I continued with absolutely nothing for two straight weeks, following doctor's orders. Though I wanted more than anything to be ready to train with the US national team, shingles made it clear that my body was simply not ready for that next step. I had the desire but was not there. Yet.

After two weeks of complete rest, I recovered, then rounded out what was left of summer by finding a new place to live and preparing for my one year of graduate school. My final year with my college team. The last year I was guaranteed a chance to row with any team at all.

For every bit of the short year and half that I had been a rower, I enjoyed the developmental process the sport revealed to me daily, so I was elated by my chance to row in graduate school. By then, rowing had taught me many things. Not the least of which was that before I could construct a solid house, I first needed a solid foundation. One built through the basics, trust, and patience. Which is why when the process entailed tasks like one-armed circles in a single, I embraced such tedium as if it was the most important thing I could do. My bout with shingles certainly reiterated the fact that I could not rush things.

When summer ended, and I prepared to start my last year of school, I was certain of one thing: I enjoyed rowing more than anything, so I wanted to row for as long as possible. Graduate school was that chance. It bought me one more year. After that, I would have to move on.

Hopefully, graduate school would also buy me the additional race experience Tom said I needed. If so, maybe I would be invited to another camp. Or maybe I would be invited to train full time. But again, I did not get ahead of myself. I still had a lot to learn.

Molly and me sitting stern pair during our first pre-elite camp together.

THIRTEEN

I DREAM TO GO.

DURING MY FINAL YEAR AT THE UNIVERSITY OF VIRGINIA, my year of graduate school, I enrolled in a class called Emotional Intelligence. It was a small discussion-based class with only about ten students, each one of us a fifth-year athlete. Almost all of us among the top five in the country for our respective sports. Three even went on to play professionally after college. All highly accomplished to say the least.

Emotional intelligence was a new concept for me at the time, especially since the subject was in its early stages of development then. It appealed to me as an athlete because of its supposed role in team dynamics. It appealed to me personally because of my desire to enjoy what I did. It appealed to me as a student because it fulfilled one of my graduate school requirements.

The class itself involved a significant amount of reading on psychology and the anatomy of the human brain, but by then, I had become a conscientious student who savored every word of what I studied. Although it was a lot of work, I committed as much to memory as I could. Of course, I cannot sit here and tell you that I remember everything we discussed during each of our lectures nor everything I read in the thousands of pages it felt like we covered. I can, however, tell you that I have yet to forget two very important things.

"How do you want to feel at the end of this day?" our professor asked. She continued by explaining the science behind that concept. That all human action stems from how we want to feel.

In reflection of how strongly I felt about enjoying what I did, I appreciated that there may have been science behind the notion that feelings fuel action. If so, it meant that the more I enjoyed rowing's developmental process, the more deeply meaningful it would become, and so the more I would be willing to commit to it, whether I intended to or not.

Following our first few weeks of study, our professor asked us each to take a personality test. She knew the results would add value to our course material by providing real-world application to what we were studying.

The test we took—the Myers-Briggs Type Indicator—is one of the most, if not the most, respected and widely used personality tests of all time. It has been highly regarded for longer than even my parents have been alive. Given its history, almost all personality tests these days are based on it in some way.

After we took the assessment, we went around the room reviewing the common characteristics and career paths for each of our specific types. One by one, as we discussed each result, I saw just how closely each of my classmates' assessments aligned with what they were interested in and good at.

When my turn finally came, I discovered that I shared my type with just one other athlete in the room. He was an ACC (Atlantic Coast Conference) champion wrestler. I was instantly proud to know that I had something in common with someone like him. But as our professor continued, and the tone in her voice changed, I learned something even more incredible.

What I know is that extraversion (E) and intuition (N) were my first two preferences. As for the other two, I cannot recall exactly which they were. What I do recall, is how our professor went on to describe my type.

"One of the rarest of all." I instantly felt special, so my face flushed a little as she said it. "People with this type tend to be natural leaders who have a gift for working through adverse situations. They are often optimists."

Those details alone would have been enough. However, my professor's description did not stop there. Instead, she concluded by suggesting one last thing. That my type, the one I shared with just one other person in my class, had been found in—of all people—Olympic athletes.

I beamed internally at the mere thought of having something in common with an Olympian. *What an honor.*

Later that fall, as I delved further into the concept that feelings drive action, Kevin called a team meeting down at the boathouse. After the one he had called the previous fall where we debated our team's perennial goal, I was not sure where this meeting would go. I did, however, think it might have something to do with our plan for the season.

We had an entirely new crop of athletes as, yet again, more than a dozen seniors had graduated. Including both Julie and Molly. So on the day of this meeting, as I looked around the boathouse from where I sat on its greyish-brown concrete floor, I realized that although I was still relatively new to this whole rowing thing, I was suddenly one of the most experienced and, clearly, oldest on my college team.

When Kevin was done with his usual welcome, rather than talking about the year's plan or something technical as I thought he might, he instead pulled out a stack of paper. While he stood fanning the stack, he explained a new activity. One we had never before done as a group. We were not there to talk about our perennial team goal of chasing the national championship. No, we would be exploring individual goals instead.

As Kevin spoke, he handed the white stack to my teammate sitting closest to him. She took a piece of paper for herself, then passed the rest along. One by one, we each took a piece of paper, then passed the stack until we each had a sheet.

Sitting there cross-legged on the cool, moist concrete floor of the boathouse, sheet in hand, I did a quick inspection. It read "Virginia Rowing" at the top with a line for my name directly below it. After that came seven questions.

Once we all had both a worksheet and pen in hand, Kevin began reading. As he read in his low, slow, deep voice, I stared at the sheet's black typeface and followed along.

"Number one." He said. "Dream goal. Long term. What is your long-term dream goal with rowing? What is possible in the long term if you stretch all your limits? I mean truly stretch them." He made certain to reiterate that it was a sky's-the-limit type of question. No judgment. Dream it. It was a dream goal for a reason.

Kevin then paused to allow us time to write our thoughts before he moved on. The room fell silent except for the sound of scribbling pens.

While I thought about what to write, I played back Kevin's words, then glanced around the boathouse. As I scanned the boat bay, I saw my teammates either feverishly scribbling or smirking quizzically as they, too, considered what to write. A moment later, I redirected my attention to my paper, where I fixated on the last sentence of question one. "What is possible in the long term if you stretch all your limits?"

Because I trusted Kevin's words and felt safe since it was just an exercise on a piece of paper, I took a breath, then wrote,

I ~~want~~ dream to go to the 2008 Olympics and win a medal (even more of a dream would be to pick one person to be in that boat with me).

When I was done, I looked up and instantly made eye contact with Kevin as if he was waiting for me and me alone to finish.

On that day, as I sat on the boathouse floor surrounded by my Virginia teammates, even though the sheet was my own and my thoughts were my own, I hesitated when Kevin suggested we write our dream goal. Having grown up playing all sorts of sports, the thought of jinxing something had crossed my mind on numerous occasions. As if the mere thought could prevent it from happening. If I dared write it, well, that would 100 percent jinx it.

But with what I was learning about myself through rowing, and with what I was reading about in graduate school, I had started to rethink my concept of jinxing things. It also helped that I trusted Kevin. I figured that if he said it was okay to not only think it but to write it, then maybe I could. So I did. Partially.

Because it was the first time anyone had asked about my dream goal, I hesitated for fear that someone might judge me or make fun of my dream. Had I not hesitated and instead written my true stretch-my-limits dream goal, I would have written, *Win the pair at the 2008 Beijing Olympics with my friend Molly.*

Molly had taught me so much about being a gutsy racer, defying the odds, pouring your heart into all you do, being a champion in every aspect of life, and enjoying every bit of that process. For as long as I had known her, every time I sat behind her, then listened, followed, and pushed, the boat went fast. I trusted her as she and Julie led us from repeated losses senior year to fifth in the country. I trusted her every stroke of the way, every step of the way, both in the boat and out. When we rowed the pair together during our first pre-elite camp, it was no different. In fact, it made me trust her more. So to imagine the two of us racing our pair all the way to Olympic gold truly would have been the ultimate stretch.

When we finished the exercise by answering all seven of Kevin's questions, we handed in our goals sheets (which I would later learn Kevin kept for years to come). We then carried on with practice.

On the surface, our moment to consider what was possible if we dreamed was just the start of another practice. A seemingly trivial part of practice. One small exercise on a single piece of paper with seven simple questions. In reality, it ended up being more than that to me. It was, with Kevin's encouragement and a single piece of paper, the first time I considered what was possible, not just within my college team but beyond it.

During the two and half years that I was able to row for UVA, I learned many things. I learned to strive to be a champion in every aspect of life. Not necessarily perfect but to become the best I could possibly be. I learned to be relentless and to give my all. I learned there is always more when you believe in possibility and reach for it. I also learned that when you give all you have and have done everything within your control, no matter the outcome, you cannot lose. Because reaching for possibility despite uncertainty (and the odds) is the only way to become your best.

By the end of my final year at UVA, my teammates and I had trained harder than ever (yet again) which helped us win some races and qualify for another NCAA championship. Where, for my second year in a row, we did not win despite training as if we could. We did, however, win in other ways. Because of the way we trained during my two and a half years as a Virginia rower, the way we behaved day in and day out, we learned (among other things) trust. Which is how I learned to race my heart out for more than just me.

Once June hit, because I had been invited to a second pre-elite camp, I packed my bags and prepared for another summer of training. Another summer in New Jersey to get a feel for life at the next level of rowing.

Our small pre-elite group was still at the bottom of the national team priority list. Still somewhat of a national team novice squad. People in our group, we were for the future, the next Olympics, the one that was yet another four years away. The 2008 Games at the earliest. But unlike my first pre-elite camp, instead of eight athletes, we would be thirteen. And instead of no prospect for racing, we learned we might get to race. That meant, by the end of my second pre-elite camp, I might earn the chance to become part of the senior women's national team.

FOURTEEN

THE HIERARCHY.

DRIVING THE 307 MILES FROM MY HOMETOWN TO NEW Jersey for camp was different the second time around. I was another year older and had a little more experience. But because my eligibility had expired, I no longer had the option to go back to my college team in the fall.

As far as I knew then, the only way for me to keep rowing once my second pre-elite camp would end was to be invited to train full time in New Jersey. Molly had been invited the year before to do just that, so I hoped I might be extended a similar invite by the end of summer. All I had to do was show the national team coaches I had something special. If I did not, I would be sent home. And if that happened, I had no idea what options existed for me to keep rowing after that.

As I drove northward, I was alone in my thoughts. Thoughts of uncertainty because I could not know the future. Thoughts of possibility because I could not know the future. Both of which made me increasingly sure of one thing with every passing mile. I would, without a doubt, do everything I could to show something special by summer's end.

On day one of camp, I stood alongside twelve other eager

athletes on the asphalt landing outside the Lake Mercer boathouse (just across town from where we had spent the previous summer). The summer sun shone brightly above. The humid New Jersey morning enveloped me in a sticky warmth. My body absorbed the season's heat as it radiated from the blacktop up through the soles of my shoes. Every sensation I felt from above, below, and within intensified my thoughts of both uncertainty and possibility.

For year two, rather than rowing on Lake Carnegie, we met at Lake Mercer, the official training lake for the US national team. And rather than eight athletes, like my first camp, we were thirteen. Of all the rowers in the country who hoped to attend that year's camp, we were the select group. And for the second year in a row, I felt fortunate to be part of it.

While we awaited our first meeting with our pre-elite camp coach, I surveyed our group of thirteen. At first glance, we were a range of ages. Rather than only college athletes as we had been the year before, we were instead a mix. Nine still in college or recently graduated, like me, and four who had graduated at least a year earlier. So, while most of us had spent the year with our respective college teams, four (one of whom was Molly) had trained full time with the national team coaches.

Even though those four had not become fast enough to vie for Olympic Team spots and were thus shifted to our group, those four did have a head start on the other nine of us. Because of their countless hours of more training and rowing experience, how could they not have a head start? Their presence alone marked a step up from my first pre-elite camp.

After our ages, I noticed a range of physiques. Some were tall and lean with long limbs. Others were not as tall but were muscular and clearly fit. As for me, I was simply within the range. Neither the tallest nor the smallest, nor the most nor least fit among us.

Just before our camp coach arrived, I recognized one last

thing: eight of us had been at camp together the year before. So, although this second camp was a step up from my first and would likely present unfamiliar challenges, it did include the familiarity of a few friends—six new ones, plus an old one in Molly.

When our pre-elite camp coach finally arrived, she introduced herself, had us do the same, then quickly shifted to the summer's plan. She explained that we would train two or three times a day (like the previous year), but rather than not having a race to train toward, she said that four of us would indeed get to race. Moreover, because the race itself was the Non-Olympic World Championships, those four would officially be on the national team by summer's end. Another step up from my first pre-elite camp.

Typically, major international rowing events culminate with the World Championships each year. But because that year was an Olympic year, the Olympic Games and an event called the Non-Olympic World Championships were held. As the names suggest, the Olympics host the highest priority rowing events, the fourteen Olympic events, while Non-Olympic Worlds host the nine or so non-Olympic events. A unique situation that happens only in Olympic years.

The last key piece of information our coach shared during our first meeting was in which boat we would all vie for seats. A boat called the "straight four." I had never rowed a straight four before. Unlike the coxed fours I had rowed in college, a straight four does not have a coxswain. No spare set of eyes. No one to steer for you. No one to take care of logistics for you. Just four sweep rowers. So if I wanted to earn a place on the national team that summer, I would have to do it in a boat I had never rowed before then.

Sure, I had practiced some of the necessary skills during our time in pairs at camp the summer before. But the kind of rowing, steering, speaking, and navigating that a straight four requires can be more demanding than that of a pair. The straight four is quite tippy and has twice as many bodies to coordinate (when compared to a pair). So, although it is technically bigger than a pair, it can be just as unstable but moves a whole lot faster.

When you combine instability with greater speed like that, teamwork becomes increasingly essential. But teamwork does not exactly come easily when you have a matter of weeks to get used to twelve new teammates who row twelve different ways.

Every day of the two and half years I spent rowing in college, I learned many things. Not the least of which was that continuous development comes with the territory. But even through everything I had learned by then, my two pre-elite camps showed me that I had so much more to learn. Being trial-by-fired in a single, challenged in a pair, my bout with shingles, and now this straight-four business proved that.

Needless to say, by the time our meeting ended, and I found out that I would have to learn yet another new skill, I considered our straight-four challenge par for the course and yet another step. A step toward becoming more self-sufficient than ever and toward pushing myself more than ever. All because it was a step that might help me earn a spot on the senior women's national team.

From that first meeting forward, each day entailed a schedule not unlike camp the year before. Two or three training sessions per day that consisted of rowing or running, with as much sleep as possible otherwise. But because we had a race this time, rather than regularly rotating partners and focusing on skills, we immediately focused on figuring out who were the fastest among us.

To do this, our camp coach created a hierarchy as quickly as she knew how. With Non-Olympic Worlds less than two months away, she did not have the typical months or years to determine our hierarchy. Instead, every decision had to happen in a matter of weeks to ensure whichever lineup (combination of rowers) she chose had time to practice before the actual event. If determining a hierarchy took too long, those chosen to race at Non-Olympic

Worlds might be left underprepared. So we wasted no time. Nearly as soon as camp started, seat-racing began.

The aim in seat-racing is to make the boat go as fast as possible as often as possible. It entails testing different combinations of rowers, then racing those combinations against one another. Boat against boat (or many boats at once).

After racing those boats one or more times, one rower gets swapped out for a rower in a different boat. Once swapped, those slightly different combinations race again. The coach then looks for any speed changes not otherwise due to the wind or water's current. If one boat becomes faster after the swap, it might mean that the rower who was swapped in is faster, thereby "winning" his or her seat-race. This is not a one-and-done scenario though. It is merely a way to narrow things down.

What makes seat-racing even more interesting is that sometimes the person with a faster erg or more experience wins. Sometimes though, he or she does not. This causes a coach to scratch her head and double (or triple) check. In these cases, depending on the day, the coach, and the race distance, you might race and swap combinations (make switches) upward of ten or more times. Sometimes you know exactly how many times and how far you might race. Oftentimes, you do not. Whether you do or do not, exhausted is an understatement for how you feel at the end of seat-racing days.

One last but critically important thing to understand is that everyone in the boat impacts speed at all times. So whether swapped or not, everyone must be consistent, both in technique and effort. If not, the results skew, which wastes time. And time was something we were short on.

Because of our shortened timeline that summer, much of the racing we did was based on our 2K times, our size, and our years' experience. Because I was not the top in any of those elements, I spent most days rowing in our camp's bottom boats.

At the start of every day, I pulled into the gravel parking lot that traced the Lake Mercer shoreline. I arrived dressed in my favorite, most comfortable, most ready-for-speed rowing gear, and hoped for my turn to seat-race. For my chance to prove my skill. To work my way into the boat that might get to race at Non-Olympic Worlds, thereby making the national team.

But with every practice I finished without a seat-race, I drove back to the dorm we called home that summer with disappointment and confusion in my heart. Until in time, it became clear that my turn to race, my chance to prove my skill, would never come.

Within two weeks' time, our coach was satisfied with what she deemed the fastest straight four combination. One that included three of the four who had trained full time that year (which included Molly) and one fresh-from-college rower. After that four, we who remained were sorted into two other fours where we stayed for the rest of camp, and until Worlds Trials arrived.

In order to officially determine which straight four would compete at Non-Olympic Worlds, we had to race a qualifying event called Worlds Trials. Whichever lineup won there through a best-two-out-of-three race format would officially become part of the senior national team.

As for me, though I was delighted to survive my second pre-elite camp without shingles, I headed into Worlds Trials sitting stroke seat of our camp's lowest-ranked lineup. The veritable basement of the national team hierarchy that year.

Look at it this way, in that 2004 Olympic year, the women picked to race at the Olympics comprised the tippy top of the hierarchy, while their spares sat just below them.[2] After those twenty-three top athletes came the dozen or so women who made it to the final phase of Olympic team selection but were ultimately

---

2   "Spares" are additional rowers who travel with the team and fill in should a racer be unable to race due to illness, injury, or some other unforeseen circumstance.

not picked. And since that final phase of selection occurs just one month before leaving for the Games, by the time those women found out they did not make the Olympic team, they had missed the opportunity to try for Non-Olympic Worlds. So even though those dozen women did not make any team that year, they still sat above the thirteen of us pre-elites.

As for our pre-elite camp hierarchy, the fastest lineup was at the top, followed by the second fastest. Then, because the rules of Worlds Trials allow anyone to race, a straight four from outside of camp entered the event. When that outside boat raced and beat our camp's lowest-ranked lineup, those rowers inserted themselves into the hierarchy above my boatmates and me.

That was where I sat by the end of my second pre-elite camp. Somewhere between forty-seventh and fifty-first among the hierarchy. At best.

When my boatmates and I lost on day one of Worlds Trials, it knocked us out of the competition from there forward. So instead of occupying my final days of camp that July with racing, I had no choice but to watch. Watch as nine rowers from camp kept racing. Watch as four rowers from outside of camp kept racing. And watch as my chance to show the coaches something special all but disappeared. Given that being knocked out on day one of Worlds Trials is a less than stellar showing, I was convinced I would be sent home soon thereafter.

On the final day of racing out at Lake Mercer, I arrived early to watch my teammates close out Worlds Trials. Then, when racing ended nearly as quickly as it began that morning, I tramped through the brush along the little muddy path back toward the boathouse to congratulate them. It was on my way back, just as I was pushing one last skinny, leafless branch up away from my forehead that the head coach, Tom, as if on a whim, unexpectedly pulled me aside.

"Shoop. You have a second?" Tom asked, quite simply.

In that moment, I was more nervous than ever for what he thought of me. I had failed to make our camp's fastest lineup. I had failed to advance past day one of Trials. I could not go back to college to gain more race experience. So I could only imagine what he might say.

"The plan isn't clear yet, but if you like, you are welcome to stick around to row a single." He said (again) quite simply.

I was both shocked and elated to discover that one incredibly brief and impromptu meeting was all Tom wanted. Just long enough to broach the topic of my sticking around a little longer. His words instantly faded my fear for being sent home that day. I wanted to hug him. I also wanted to cry. But instead of doing either, I listened and felt my heart pound in my throat until, finally, my grin emerged.

For whatever reason, Tom had the mind to suggest that I could row a single if I wanted. I would not be training for anything in particular. I would not receive any coaching in particular. But I would gain experience in the single. Given that my Trials boatmates went home shortly after our loss, I had no idea why he offered me the chance to stay. Maybe he had offered them the same, but they had turned him down (of that, I cannot be certain). Whatever the case, I did not question his reasons and wholeheartedly accepted his offer. I wanted to keep rowing and to keep developing more than anything, and the single was my opportunity.

When Tom finished speaking, I had no sense of how long I would get to row the single. Nor any sense of a training plan. Nor a purpose other than working on my rowing skills. What mattered to me most that day was that I was not going home.

Later that afternoon, I called my family to tell them I would be in New Jersey a little while longer. I then took the rest of the day off. A lot had happened. And with no idea of what might occur in the days ahead, I figured a little rest could not hurt.

Camp ended in mid-July. By then, the women who had made the Olympic Team were busy with their final preparations for the Olympics, while those who had made our camp's straight four were busy with their final preparations for Non-Olympic Worlds.

As for the rest of us, our camp's second fastest lineup was combined into an eight with the four women who had beaten my boatmates and me at Worlds Trials. Apparently, they too had been invited to stay in New Jersey for the rest of summer. Rather than staying simply to row, as was my directive, I found out they would be busy preparing for a race—one set to take place in Canada a few weeks later. Although I was grateful I had not been sent home after Worlds Trials, I could not help but be a tad envious of my camp teammates' opportunities to race.

From mid-July onward, they practiced together, every day, toward a common purpose: to race. Whereas I came to practice to row the single for the sole purpose of…rowing a single. So, from mid-July onward, I arrived at the Lake Mercer boathouse, then watched as everyone else launched their team boats in preparation for their respective races. Only once they were on the water would I launch with my one instruction to "get a feel for the single." Becoming faster was completely up to me otherwise.

It was following my first few days of getting a feel for the single that Tom approached me again and with another offer. One that shed light on the competition in Canada for which the other girls were preparing.

Though the Royal Canadian Henley was not the caliber of Non-Olympic Worlds and was nowhere near Olympic caliber, it was a race with more than a century of tradition behind it and one that drew competitors from all over the world. As Tom explained, the others would each be racing at least two events there, and when he considered the demands of such racing, he figured they should have a spare. That was his offer—that I go to Canada to be my teammates' spare.

As their spare, I would fill in should anyone become sick or injured. No matter what seat. No matter which side of the boat. No matter which event. I was to be ready for anything. Once he explained my role as the spare, Tom further suggested that since I was going all the way to Canada, I may as well have a race to call my own.

Because I had been rowing the single, Tom proposed that I race it in Canada—which was off-putting at first. For although I had been enjoying my time in the single, I had only just started rowing it consistently. I had never actually raced the single. In fact, I had only minimal practice in it, having never once completed more than one thousand meters at race speed. And one thousand meters? That was only half the distance of an actual race.

Tom continued by suggesting that the race would provide valuable experience. One thing I knew I needed should I hope to keep rowing well into the future. So I warmed to the idea of racing the single and agreed to everything he suggested.

As soon as I agreed, Tom's expression broke into a slight side grin as if he was about to share an inside joke. "There's just one more thing...You can only race championship-level events."

Because we were technically heading to the Royal Canadian Henley as part of a national team camp, I could only race at the highest level for any given event. For the single, that meant the Champ Single, the level that actual national team athletes raced. Despite my completely novice sculling skills, I stood by my decision. The Champ Single may have been a significant step up from my level of experience, but it was my option, and I knew enough by then to take Tom up on whatever he offered.

After everything I had gone through during my second pre-elite camp—racing among athletes stronger and more experienced than me, racing (and losing) at Worlds Trials, learning how to row the single with little other than intuition as my guide—I was thrilled to pop out at the end of that second camp still in New Jersey, still rowing, still on the radar, and with a race to prepare for.

On the last day of July, instead of heading home to Virginia to aimlessly search for a way to keep rowing, I was in the back seat of a friend's car on my way to Canada, well on my way to my first international race. I may have been at the bottom of the national team hierarchy then, but I felt fortunate because at least I was on it.

FIFTEEN

NOT AS FAST AS YOU THINK.

I FIGURED DORM LIFE HAD ENDED FOR ME BACK WHEN I finished my freshman year at UVA. But considering I had just spent two consecutive pre-elite camps living in college dorms, I realized how wrong I was. Then on July 31, 2004, when my friends and I pulled into the parking lot of yet another dorm, this time in Ontario, Canada, I began to think that if I wanted to keep rowing after college, I might have to get used to the whole sharing rooms and sleeping in twin beds thing again.

Here I was, two months past graduate school, and when I showed up for my first international race—the Royal Canadian Henley—it was back to a dorm for me.

Because our dorm room lacked air-conditioning, my room-mate and I opted to leave our windows open at night while we slept. This left me stirring at every unexpected and unidentified sound that crept in through them. And so, on the night before my Champ Single race, it was no different.

All of six nights after we arrived in Canada, my nervousness for my first 2,000-meter race in a single kept me awake later than I would have liked. Whenever I awoke, I noticed things I had not before. Things like how short and narrow my twin-sized bed felt.

How flat and unsupportive my pillow was. And how I wished I could trade in my scratchy blanket for something softer.

During my search for comfort that night, I repeatedly readjusted my pillow, then inadvertently untucked my sheets, which exposed my toes. With my every subsequent shift, my nerves mounted. Until my mind fixated less on my bed and more on my big race.

By morning, I found I must have fallen asleep somehow because I felt (slightly) rested.

Because my race was not until later in the day, I had time to eat breakfast and run through some of my standard race-day thoughts. My thoughts were both nervous and excited as I attempted to convince myself that everything would be okay. Eventually, after I ran through nearly every possible scenario for how I hoped the day would go, I breathed to calm myself, then made my way to the course.

When I arrived at the racecourse for my Champ Single race, the conditions were the polar opposite of what I had pictured while I ran through my race-day thoughts. The course was a complete mess. A significant wind had developed overnight, and as a result, the conditions were worse than subpar. They verged on dangerous.

It was with this in mind that the race organizers had no choice but to suspend the entire regatta—all rowing races, not just the Champ Single—until the weather calmed.[3] A little relieved, I waited.

When it became apparent that the weather had no intention of improving, the race organizers weighed their two options: cancel everything or race with the conditions as they were. Bearing in mind how far people had traveled, rather than canceling, they opted to resume the regatta with what else? The Champ Single.

---

3   "Regatta" in the sport of rowing is another name for a series of races.

James, the coach who had accompanied us to Canada, informed me of the race organizers' decision as soon as he heard it. While I listened, my cheeks dropped, and my stomach turned. I then stared past him and down the racecourse to take in the whole scene. It was nothing but a sea of whitecapped waves.

Why they chose to resume racing on such precarious, washing-machine-like conditions with the smallest, most unstable boat of all, I will never know. But I had gone all that way, so I headed in the direction of my equipment and prepared to launch.

Understanding my apprehension, James helped me carry my equipment to the dock. He then held my boat steady while I sat down in it, then adjusted my butt on its tiny, wheeled seat. For as narrow as an eight had once seemed to me, it may as well have been a barge compared to where I sat in my barely-as-wide-as-I-was single that day.

While I carefully put on my socks and secured my feet in my shoes, my boat bobbed beneath me. Once I had my feet set, I then gripped my oars with my visibly trembling hands and looked up at James.

With every passing second that I tentatively bobbed there by the dock, water splashed over my boat's gunnels, steadily filling it. As it filled, James and I both knew I had to shove, or I would sink. Upon recognizing this, James carefully lifted the scoop-like blade end of my dockside oar, then guided me off the dock. As he walked slowly, bent over to keep me stable, he looked me in the eye once more, and in his Irish accent, gave me one final piece of advice.

"You know, you'll get out there and realize they aren't as fast as you think they are."

When he smiled, I smiled back. It was exactly what I needed to hear. With his one final push, I was off the dock and on my own.

From there, I cautiously rowed my way toward the start line. With my every stroke, I ran five aims through my head. The five things that would allow me to consider my first ever all-out 2K in a single a success. First, make it to the start without flipping. Second, lock onto the start bridge (similar to the starting blocks for a swimming race) without flipping. Third, leave the start line without flipping. Fourth, cross the finish line without flipping. And fifth, make it back to the dock. Without flipping.

I repeated these five aims to myself as I slowly but surely bumped my way to the start. All the while, water washed over the bow of my long, skinny single, submerging its bow ball. Every so often, a slightly larger wave rolled far enough up the boat to splash me in the back. Whenever that happened, my hands gripped my oars all the tighter.

Still, I pressed on. Until eventually, I made it to the start line, then carefully rowed into my assigned lane. When I did, I completed aim one. I then turned the stern of my boat (the end I stared at as I rowed) toward the start bridge, where a kind volunteer attempted to help me. He steadied my boat in place until the other racers and the race announcer were ready. Aim two complete.

It was just as I completed aim two that the race announcer chimed in with a change. "This will be a countdown start," the announcer said.

This meant the start command would happen faster than usual due to the rough conditions on the racecourse that day. The last-minute warning was the official way of preparing us for the change. Even though I knew the start would happen faster than normal, because this was my first race in the single, I could not guess just how fast.

Until one brief moment later, "Attention…Go!" rang out across the whitecaps toward me.

In an instant, we six racers took off, and I completed aim three.

Over every stroke I took, my boat bobbled in nearly every direction upon the inconsistent surface of the water. With each successive wave and consequent bobble, my hands tightened, and my knuckles whitened as I hung on for dear life. I knew even the slightest bobble could unexpectedly flip me into the choppy water below. I had no choice but to take it one stroke at a time.

At barely 250 meters into the race, having taken about thirty whole strokes, James's words flashed across my mind. *They are not as fast as you think they are.*

Upon that fleeting flash of a curiously hopeful thought, I—against my better judgement—turned my focus away from just me and cut my eyes to the right then left across the lanes to see how I was progressing. The instant my eyes darted, I could not believe what I saw. James was right. The other more experienced racers were not as fast as I thought. I was winning.

With my confidence bolstered by my being in the lead, I pushed my legs harder. Instantly, the wind blew more as if it to laugh at my gumption. The waves then rolled more. And in a few strokes more, I was breathing more. Meanwhile, my heart pounded more, while my boat rocked uncontrollably upon the tumultuous water.

Suddenly, one of my oars clipped the top of the very next wave that rolled past me. When it did, my oar handle nearly flew from my hand, which caused my grip to reflexively clench. In that moment, I could no longer think of taking strokes. Not even one at a time. Instead, my entire being focused on one thing—not letting go of my oars.

As my fingers attempted to clench further, my boat reacted by lurching right, then left in a frenzy of confusion and disastrous strokes. Then, on the very next stroke, my boat pitched to the left again, causing not my oar this time but my left leg to graze the top of another wave as it rolled past. While my boat flopped and collected more water, I felt like a rag doll and was certain it was all over for me. My heart pounded further, not from exertion this time, but from the surge of adrenaline that washed over me as I anticipated the inevitable. I was about to flip!

But no. I miraculously recovered. Somehow, I did not flip.

As a result of my near disaster, two things followed. First, I was no longer anywhere near the lead. Second, upon seeing my first of several catastrophic strokes, the crew in charge of athlete safety zipped across the whitecaps in its inflatable rescue boat to my lane, then followed me for every stroke of the race from there forward.

When I finally crossed the finish line, I was two lanes away from my own due to the diagonal direction of the wind, and…I placed dead last. Two minutes behind the winner. Since two *seconds* is considered a large gap over the typical 2,000-meter race, dead last barely scratches the surface of just how badly I lost that day.

As soon as I had crossed the finish line, I stopped rowing and instead let myself drift. The wind blew me even more diagonally, while my boat rocked in a circular motion over the waves that continued to mercilessly roll. As I drifted, I attempted to unfurl the white-knuckled death grip I had on my oars. Between the wind, waves, and misty rain that began falling midway through the race, I had no choice but to focus less on taking strokes and more on hanging on. But with the more I hung on, my grip tightened until my left hand went numb. Now that the race was over, I finally felt I could return my focus to taking strokes.

It was overcast, windy, drizzling, and I had lost the race by more than a lot. But because I technically achieved aim number four, I grinned at my small win, then caught my breath, and rowed back to the dock without flipping. In doing so, I accomplished the fifth of my aims.

When James asked me later what I thought of the race, I told him that it was going okay until I almost fell out of the boat and that it was otherwise not all that bad. Especially if I took out all the "crabs," those times when my oars unexpectedly got stuck underwater and caused me to bobble.

In the end, my time was at least two minutes slower than a

typical time. The conditions really were that rough. But despite my dead-last finish, I could not be disappointed because I crossed the finish line without flipping. After all, I had never completed more than one thousand meters at race speed before then. I had to start somewhere. Even if that meant dead last.

Back in college, I had been voted an NCAA All-American— twice. That meant a majority of college coaches considered me one of the fastest female college rowers at the time. Yet, for all the speed I gained in college, I did not row the single except on occasion at pre-elite camp. As a result, I had yet to develop sculling skills. So when it came to my first big race after college, especially in rough conditions, like what I braved in the Champ Single, I felt less like an All-American and more like a complete novice, whose main measure of success was to make it from one end of the racecourse to the other without flipping.

During our seven-hour drive back to New Jersey, my friends and I laughed and talked about how much fun we had in Canada, both racing and otherwise. I found humor in my experience in the single and eventually came to be proud of it for one simple reason: it helped me grow more confident because I overcame something incredibly intimidating. Which I was pleased to discover made me even hungrier to keep rowing.

For the duration of our seven-hour drive, I thought about how much I had learned during my first two and half years as a rower, and I imagined what the next level in rowing might bring. Based on my Champ Single race, I figured it would likely require me to be even more open, adaptable, and brave because the competition and conditions would undoubtedly be tougher and the days longer. At the next level, everyone would be more experienced, stronger, taller, and have faster erg times. So I was sure that far more unpredictable and challenging circumstances would lie ahead.

These were all things I imagined I would experience if Tom

invited me to train full time. But because he had not extended me such an invitation before he headed to Athens for the 2004 Olympics, my future was still uncertain.

By late August that year, all I knew was that the Canadian Henley was over and that Tom wanted to meet with those of us who had raced in Canada and at Non-Olympic Worlds upon his return. With that meeting still a few weeks away, I had no choice but to wait (again) and to hope for an invitation from Tom to move to New Jersey to train full time.

August 2004,

It ought to be interesting where I end up...In New Jersey? Training? Who knows? I hope I get invited. We shall see how it all plays out. Big changes are coming in one way or another!

A few weeks later, when we finally met with Tom, rather than another impromptu individual meeting, we instead met as a group in a tiny back room at the Lake Mercer boathouse.

Lake Mercer is technically an official Olympic training site. One that the national rowing team shares with four high school rowing programs. The name might sound majestic, but I can assure you, it is a no-frills place. Just a simple cinderblock building with not much inside. Even less outside. Only the basics of what you need to train for rowing. It can be bone-chillingly cold in the winter there due to its inefficient electric baseboard heaters. The kind of cold that makes sweatpants and a stocking cap a must for weightlifting. Definitely not the kind of luxury accommodation you might picture for a national team.

When we met, Tom walked us through the boathouse's cubicle maze of an office area to a conference table that hid in a tiny, one-windowed back room. Because the table itself nearly filled the entire closet of a meeting space, the less than ten of us (nine or so rowers, plus Tom) filed in one by one, then shimmied along the wall until we each found our own empty seat.

The only thing missing from making it exactly like your typical morning office meeting was the coffee and donuts or bagels, and someone sitting awkwardly at a tiny side desk taking down the meeting minutes.

It was our first sit-down group meeting. We had no idea what we were in for. But when coaches like Tom invite you somewhere, you go.

As I settled into my seat and thought of what Tom might say, I became a little uneasy.

Just two years prior to our meeting that day, Tom had been the assistant national team coach. But in a turn of events, he took over the team as head coach in the middle of an Olympic cycle (the four-year time span between each Olympic Games). So, on the day of our awkward, backroom meeting, though he was already two years into being the head coach, he was only just starting his first full Olympic cycle in that role. As it turned out, it was not just us rowers who were on the cusp of something uncharted.

Tom began our meeting by explaining that things would proceed differently than they had in the past. He told us the training would be nothing short of "hard," and that the core training group would be "small," no longer thirty or so athletes. He also told us the rowing itself would be mostly in singles because rowing the single is an incredibly effective way to gain fitness and to learn how to row efficiently. The two things our little group needed to focus on.

The single helps with fitness because until you become technically efficient (better at the actual rowing part), the only thing you can do to make the boat go faster is push yourself as hard as humanly possible.

As for how the single helps with efficiency, well, when you are the only person in the boat, you and you alone create or destroy speed. As a result, the boat itself teaches you technique. It allows you to slow down to your own pace because you do not have to account for working with others. You can simply focus on yourself and the water. And because the water is always changing, you learn to pay attention to everything you do. As long as you pay attention to what you are doing when the boat goes faster or slower, then keep doing whatever helps you go faster, you will likely become more efficient at the actual rowing part.

Following his overview of the new training scenario, Tom told us that anyone who hoped to earn a spot on the next summer's national team would need to become fast in the single and improve on the erg. Not just on 2Ks like in college, but on erg tests as short as ten seconds and as long as thirty minutes. Neither of which I had ever done before.

Tom rounded out his description of how things would operate by stating that those who were the fastest on the erg would earn more chances to row in the team's most important boats. And though erg times did not guarantee spots on the team, Tom did say they would increase one's chances. This all made sense to me. How could becoming faster in the single and also on the erg not prove beneficial?

Once he finished describing the grand experiment that the United States' main rowing training center was about to become, the moment of truth finally arrived. The answer to whether I would be invited to train full time.

One by one, Tom rounded the table asking exactly three questions. "Do you have a place to live? Do you have a job? Do you have something here in New Jersey other than rowing?" As each of us answered in our own way, he took note of each response without judgment.

While Tom worked his way around the table, and I thought of how incredibly talented each woman sitting there was, I glanced over at Molly and thought of something she had once said. It held true so often that I came to trust it: "You cannot count on something until you are in the process of doing it."

As Molly's wise words ran through my mind, my thoughts worked their way through anticipation and worry, with waves of excitement. *Would Tom ask me the same three questions?* I wondered. Finally, Tom turned to me.

More than anything, I hoped Tom would ask me the same three questions he had just asked every other woman sitting at that table. But because I knew it was not guaranteed until he actually asked, I did not take that moment for granted. For all I knew, he could still change his mind.

"Shoop." Tom paused, with a gaze that pierced every layer of my confidence. "Do you have a place to live?"

With one question, just seven words, Tom broke eight months' worth of tension.

"I'm working on that." I replied.

As my anxious chill melted, I could feel my grin attempting to burst forth in gratitude. I wanted to jump up and hug Tom right there. But instead, I restrained myself as I answered simply, then listened as Tom continued.

Susan, another starboard who had been at both pre-elite camps with me, had been asking me all summer to live with her. Tom had asked her at the start of summer to move to New Jersey to train full time. As she considered Tom's early offer, she attempted to plan ahead by asking me to be her roommate. Trouble was, I had not been invited when she had been. Her 2K time was more than ten seconds faster than mine (a significant amount faster at that level), and she was two inches taller than me. Her early invite made complete sense.

Because I had not yet been invited when Susan first asked me to live with her, I could not tell her yes. But given the questions Tom was finally asking me, I planned to take Susan up on her offer to live together immediately after our meeting that day.

Susan and me during our first fall of full-time training.

Tom continued. "Do you have a job? Do you have something other than rowing? This is going to be hard, so you need to have something else going on. You need to be sure you can afford to be here…I want you to be able to go out for Chinese food or whatever it is you do for fun every now and again if you want."

That was how Tom always said things. While seriously explaining one concept, he drops something that seems like a complete joke. It was his way of making sure we were listening. It also made things clear and honest. His "Chinese food" comment was a small thing, but it hammered home his point.

Once Tom officially extended me the offer to train full time, I considered it to be my one and only chance, so I fudged it a little. In my typical nervously enthusiastic Shoop fashion, I fumbled over an awkwardly long response about how my parents knew some people who could help me with a job. I then fumbled over having "something else" going on. In reality, I was not sure I would be invited, so I had not solidified anything. So no, I did not actually have a job nor a place to live. But I had options. I would simply find a way to make it work.

I was excited by everything I learned from our meeting. I was going to be part of a team again, albeit a small one. One that would start with just seven rowers. Five from our pre-elite camp and two from that outside club we had raced against at Worlds Trials. Plus, two coaches—Tom and Laurel.

Laurel was one of the women from that year's Olympic eight who, after taking silver at the 2004 Athens Games, retired and planned to start coaching alongside Tom. After some time to herself, of course. Once she joined us though, our group would be seven singles and two coaches on one small lake in New Jersey.

Within a few days of our meeting, I was back in Virginia ecstatic to be packing my things to officially move to New Jersey to train full time with the national team coaches. Because the internet was slow back then and there were no really efficient search engines, I spent a good deal of time going back and forth over the phone in search of a place to live. Once Susan and I finally agreed on a place, we achieved the first of Tom's three stipulations. We had a home.

After that, I just needed to find a job. Hopefully, that would happen before mid-September, when our first practice of the new Olympic cycle was scheduled to take place.

Three whole weeks after the 2004 Olympic Games ended, the next Olympic cycle, the one aimed at building toward the 2008 Beijing Games, began. When it did, it marked an opportunity to take yet another step.

SIXTEEN

TIME TO ADJUST.

TWO THINGS DO NOT HAPPEN WHEN YOU TRANSITION FROM college to full-time training. You do not become rich, and you do not become famous. At least not the vast majority. This happens for lots of reasons. For one, many athletes go on to be coaches. Not because it is all they know, but because they realize that coaching, when done right, can positively impact countless lives. Another reason is that rowing is a relatively misunderstood sport. And that makes sponsorships for even the national team hard to come by. But if you want to know the biggest reason, it is time. You simply cannot spare it.

When you focus on becoming your absolute best, it literally takes all of your time. I mean all of it. You do not have time to go around telling people what you are doing. You do not have time to split your attention among many things. At most, you might have time for two, possibly three, things. But even then, that cuts into how well you can do even those few things.

As for training with the hope of making the national team someday, the two, possibly three, things you focus on are training, recovering, and working. Training and recovering so you can gradually improve. And working so you can afford to train and recover...so you can gradually improve.

This is why it helps to have a genuine desire to become your best. When you genuinely aim to become your best, you are far more willing to focus every last bit of your energy on what truly needs your attention. And you do it without question.

Once I was invited to step up from college to train with the national team coaches, I knew my life would change. Particularly because I knew training at the next level would require many new things.

For starters, I had to leave Virginia, the only place I had ever called home, for "Jersey." I knew little about New Jersey except for what I had experienced during my two pre-elite camp summers there. I knew the summers were hot, muggy, and mosquito-filled—not unlike the Virginia summers I grew up with. I knew it was a 307-mile drive from my parents' house, which meant the familiarity of home was within a six-hour drive. I also knew that I would have some new friends (plus an old one in Molly) who would be there with me in New Jersey. And that was comforting.

But compared to what I knew, there was far more that I did not know. Like how it would feel to be surrounded by fewer teammates and coaches than in college. Or how it would feel to spend most of my time in a single rather than in team boats. Or how it would feel to hold a job while also training two or three times a day for many hours a day, full time, year-round.

On top of these unknowns, I would also be held to significantly higher standards for erg times, strength in the weight room, and running speed. Not to mention an ever-increasing expectation for improvement. Basically, I had to improve, or I would be sent home.

No matter what you may or may not know, though, when you make the step up to row at the "elite" level, you train under complete uncertainty. This is because you cannot know whether anything you do will actually result in your making the national team one day. You train as if you might, but you simply cannot be certain until the day it happens. And that—the not knowing when or if my next race would come—was something I had never experienced before. Sure, for a month at camp. But never indefinitely.

On the day I wholeheartedly accepted Tom's invitation to train, I was motivated by the opportunity because it meant taking another step toward becoming my best through the sport I had grown to love. Rowing had become my outlet for continual growth and learning, so it had become more important to me than anything else. And that, I would come to learn, would be a critical asset as I continued taking steps and facing greater challenges. For although I had taken on and overcome many things, the toughest challenges were yet to come.

Despite all the unknowns, on September 5, 2004, with just over two and a half years of rowing experience to my name, I uprooted my life and moved to New Jersey to train full time with the national team coaches. For as far as I knew then, that is what it would take to become my best.

Because my parents supported my decision, they helped me pack a small trailer with hand-me-down furniture and supplies, then accompanied me on my 307-mile drive to New Jersey. When we arrived, it was ten days before Tom had told our training group to meet him at the Lake Mercer boathouse for our first official day of practice. Ten days early might seem like a lot, but I had several things to take care of before practice started.

My move-in process and ten-day countdown began with my parents helping me settle into the little white duplex that Susan and I had agreed on. While my dad and I moved various pieces of mismatched furniture into the living room, my mom busied herself in the kitchen unpacking, washing, and organizing an old set of dishes. When the three of us were finished downstairs, we headed upstairs to organize my bedroom.

My new bedroom was too small for any two people to stand

inside it at the same time. That is, if they wanted to move their arms. It was at most nine feet by eight feet and just large enough to fit my secondhand bed and antique nightstand. A puzzle made all the more challenging by the large radiator that ran halfway across my tiny bedroom's far wall. Though the room did not have a closet, it did have two windows. And because it was the farthest from the street, on the rare days I could sleep in, it was quiet. While my room was the smallest in our little duplex, it was the one I wanted, because it meant I paid the least rent.

Following just two days in my new town, my parents had done all they could to help me adjust to my new home, so we said our goodbyes, and they drove the 307 miles back to Virginia. Apart from one quick trip a few weeks later, that was the last I would see of them until the holidays rolled around.

After my family left, I spent what remained of my ten-day countdown with Susan and Molly. Susan, of course, lived down the hall from me, while Molly had moved into a house less than two blocks away. So close that if I stepped out onto my bluish-grey front stoop, I could see her porch light. Having an old friend like Molly just down the street was, again, comforting.

When I was not with Susan and Molly during those days leading up to our first day of practice, I looked for a job. A search that began with the classified ads in the newspaper, then proceeded with me uncomfortably making cold calls.

On the day my search began, I sat down in our living room on our hand-me-down couch and flipped open the local newspaper to the page that read, "Employment Opportunities." As I took in the advertisement-filled page, I pulled out my black pen and started circling…everything. Nannying, house-sitting, tutoring, telemarketing. I even wondered if I was qualified to drive a bus, deliver mail, or be a fencing coach. I was open to anything that would allow me the flexibility to train because training was, without question, my priority.

After the classifieds, I moved to searching local businesses, making calls, then going office to office dropping off my resume. In my cover letters, I carefully explained my unique situation. That I was "training with the national rowing team coaches." That I was a full-time training athlete but not yet on the national team. It was an explanation that I hoped might sway someone to hire me, despite my not being able to prioritize the work I would do for them.

After all, no matter how qualified you are, it is not exactly easy to find a job when you follow up your introduction by telling potential employers you need to work irregular hours that would likely change last minute.

That was where I found myself the day before practice began. A college graduate, driven, capable of many things. Yet after nine days of searching, the only job I could get was one with a temporary staffing agency as "a temp." A job that meant sitting alone in an overly air-conditioned, white-walled room under the flickering buzz of office lights. No windows. I would get paid to trifold an endless stack of letters and stuff each one into its own business-sized envelope for ten dollars an hour for several hours at a time.

Thankfully, I did not have to lick and seal the envelopes. And at least I could sit—a critical element of the job given the highly challenging training that lie ahead. Though entertaining yourself by seeing how quickly you can make large stacks of paper disappear can become mind-numbing after the first five hours, the job was ideal because it provided what mattered most: flexibility.

The day after I found that job, we started practice.

On the morning of our first practice, Susan and I woke up, grabbed a snack, hopped into her silver Pontiac Grand Prix, then drove slowly down our narrow one-way street. At the bottom of our street's little hill, we took a left. Then three turns later, we were cruising down a much larger hill.

When we made it to the bottom of that much larger hill and

stopped at the red light there, even though it was early, and my eyes and ears had not yet adjusted to being awake, Susan felt compelled to crank up her favorite rap station. She then took a bite of her apple, glanced over at me, and laughed in her characteristically Susan way. Comedic yet menacing.

As soon as the stoplight turned from red to green, Susan looked ahead, opened her eyes wide, then laughed again as she floored it across the little rock bridge and into the direction of Lake Mercer where we knew Tom and our teammates would be waiting. It was a Wednesday and still dark.

With each passing mile, we sped ever nearer to our first official day with Tom as our coach, and Susan danced along to the music that blared as she drove. I could not help but smile. Over the course of the two summers that she and I had spent together at pre-elite camps, I found her comedic demeanor to be oddly calming. That morning was no different. Her touch of humor was exactly what I needed to ease my nerves on that first day.

Seven miles of car dancing later, and we went from speeding along to creeping down a dead-end gravel road. One that led us between two corn fields and into the direction of what appeared to be nowhere. But rather than nowhere, it was the final bit of the way to the boathouse.

As we made our way toward the foot of that dead-end road, Lake Mercer emerged through the early morning light like a mirage. Just before we reached the tall grasses that lined the lake's edge, we curved left, then bumped the final few hundred feet through the potholeladen parking lot and parked as close to the boathouse as we could. At last, following a drive that seemed eternal yet instant, we arrived.

Only a few cars were in sight. The whole of Lake Mercer and most of the 2,500-acre park that surrounded it was empty, silent, and calm. That is, except for the eight of us who were there for our first day of practice together. Me, Susan, Molly, four others, and Tom.

We were it on that mid-September morning. Laurel, our new assistant coach, was set to join us a few weeks later. Having just raced in her third Olympics, she was taking some well-deserved rest before joining Tom to help coach us. Laurel, like Tom, made sense.

Being there at Lake Mercer was a privilege. And since it would soon be our home away from home, Tom made sure we understood how to treat it right. So when the eight of us finally gathered in the boat bay on that quiet September morning, rather than receiving practice instructions and rowing like I thought we might, we instead spent nearly the entire morning…cleaning.

As Tom doled out instructions, the seven of us hustled to fulfill his every request. We first cleared space by moving the biggest boats to the highest racks. Our plan was to row singles, so it made sense to move the fours and eights as far up and out of the way as possible. With the lower racks cleared, we then pushed the wheeled rolling racks toward the front of the boathouse. Having those racks toward the front of the bay provided even greater access to our singles.

With every piece of equipment we repositioned, it became clear that rowing singles would be our only focus for the foreseeable future.

A little over an hour's worth of instructions and rearranging later, and we had fulfilled each of Tom's requests. We had moved, rolled, lifted, and swept nearly everything in sight. And for everything we did, Tom was right there with us every step of the way as if he too were part of the team. When we climbed racks, he climbed. When we swept the boathouse, he swept. When we moved things, he moved things. When we hustled and became sweaty, he did too.

Once we had nothing left to rearrange, Tom surveyed the short supply of boats that remained on the low racks, then surveyed the seven of us while he thought quietly. Within a few moments, satisfied with his decisions, he entrusted us each with a single and a set of oars, then proceeded to teach us how to properly carry, wash, and store each piece of our newly loaned equipment.

After that, rather than finally going for a row, Tom went on to explain a few more things first. Like how we would each be personally responsible for anything that happened to "our" boats. And that if we wanted to go fast and be allowed to continue to train there, that we should treat "our" equipment right.

It was clear that if we wanted to be part of that team, we would have to be accountable for literally everything, each other included. Only once we agreed to that did we finally get on the water that morning. When we did, it came with one directive. One I knew well by then.

"Go for a quick spin to get a feel for your boats," Tom said simply. "Just row."

Upon his words, we all moved in the direction of our respective equipment. I collected my boat and oars, then headed toward the dock to launch for my first official row at the US national team's training center. With Tom, the head coach of the US national team, as *my* coach…

All totaled, we spent less than thirty minutes on actual rowing that first day. Tom instead prioritized accountability. He knew we first needed to be accountable to ourselves and to one another; otherwise, we would never find maximum speed.

That was the plan for our little experiment. To begin slowly, one step at a time. Because in order to build a strong house, we first needed a strong foundation. Had we moved too quickly on day one, we could have easily damaged what little equipment we had by taking it for granted and being careless. Similarly, had we trained too aggressively during our earliest stages together, we could have become sick or injured.

Though I did not realize it on day one, by starting with the basics of cleaning and going for one very short row, we took our first step together toward a much larger plan. A plan that would eventually consist of two or three practices per day and millions upon millions of meters of rowing. A plan that would eventually consist of three or four training sessions in the weight room each week and running nearly daily. A plan that would eventually involve countless other demands and challenges that we could never have predicted on day one. But like I said, our plan began with the basics. Very intentionally placed. To provide us time to adjust to our life of full-time training.

During our first two months of training, although we practiced together each morning, we ran or trained on our own on the rowing machine or in the single nearly every afternoon. Which for me, meant more time to stuff envelopes for ten dollars an hour as a temp. A tiny yet critical part of my life then.

On afternoons when I worked longer hours, I had no choice but to erg on my own. When that was the case, I would hustle home, quickly change, then clear some space in our little duplex's living room by pushing our secondhand coffee table out of the way. I would then awkwardly drag my old rowing machine—the used one my mom bought for $250 two years earlier—up from the basement and through our kitchen, ultimately setting it up where the coffee table had once been. Once set, I got to work ticking down anywhere from thirty to sixty minutes of training and sweating. Alone. My makeshift training space, though neither well ventilated nor well air-conditioned, served its purpose.

On the occasional afternoon when I finished work early and could make it to Lake Mercer before dark, I rowed. Often alone. But if I was lucky, Susan or Molly would join me. I preferred that because, when it comes to training, time always goes faster with your team.

One late October afternoon, Susan met me out at Lake Mercer after work. I was already there when she raced into the parking lot just before sunset, dust flying, still dressed in her work clothes.

While she hustled to change, I put our oars on the dock so that all we had to do once she was dressed and ready to row was to grab our singles and go. Because it was October, the days were shorter and the sun was well on its way to setting by the time we were ready, so we moved faster than we would have otherwise. Once we hit the water though, our pace changed.

It was quiet out on the lake. The water was flat. Pristine. Almost black below me. An image made all the starker by the white hull of my boat as it floated delicately upon the water's surface. As I absorbed the moment, I took a breath, exhaled it, then took a stroke. As my boat began to glide along, it gradually calmed my mood. Eventually, the world fell still around me.

One stroke at a time, Susan and I quietly, steadily traced our way around the edges of the lake together. With every stroke, I listened to the sounds of my oars as they occasionally skimmed the water. The sounds of my boat as bubbles and tiny ripples peeled away from its hull as it sliced the water's mirrorlike surface. The occasional bird calling from a distance. Until finally, Susan and I broke the stillness with our periodic talking and, eventually, laughter.

When the final ten minutes of our row came at last, having navigated the entire way around our lake, the sun dropped behind the horizon, the water fell even calmer, the air even cooler, and the trees themselves even blacker. The sky pink and peach beyond them. Nothing but the sounds of nature, the light plop of our blades, and the delicate skim of our boats which was period-ically offset by Susan's maniacally comedic laughter. Laughter that echoed across the empty lake as we landed back at the docks right as the sun set.

Over every stroke we took around Lake Mercer that evening, I savored the fact that I was not alone. I was instead side by side with my new friend, roommate, and teammate, who was taking steps along with me. Though that evening out on the water might not have been the physical training Tom had in mind, it was exactly what our minds needed.

A single rowed on flat, calm water. (Image courtesy of Allison Mueller)

What Susan and I stumbled upon during our row together that evening out on Lake Mercer soon became integral to our lives. As we took on gradually greater demands during our first two months of training together, it became apparent that if we wanted to become better at the training itself, it would take more than just the training itself. Even something so simple as time together, both in the boat and out, made us better.

On certain Wednesdays (one of the two days a week when we only had morning training), a group of us would meet for dinner at a nearby restaurant that was not too expensive and spend the time bonding over how sore we were or joking about something ridiculous that had happened at practice. Probably something our coaches said or did. Sometimes it was whatever homemade invention they wanted to test on us. Or some contraption they wanted us to use during one of our "survival of the fittest" runs that sent us winding through (and often getting lost in) the woods that encircled Lake Mercer. Whatever the incident, if it made us laugh hard enough, we immortalized it as an inside joke. The kind you wait at least a decade before telling your coaches.

On one such Wednesday, as we huddled around our high-top table in the middle of the noisy restaurant, our conversation shifted from jokes to serious, then back to laughter by the time we were done.

"Here's a question for you. If you make the Olympic team, would you get *the tattoo?*" one of my teammates very seriously asked the group of us sitting there.

Together, we came to one conclusion: *If you make the Worlds Team, you probably won't get the tattoo. If you make the Olympic team, you might. But if you actually win the Olympics? That's a given. You must get the tattoo.*

As I replayed our conclusion in my mind, I imagined how incredible it would feel to become that good one day. *Good enough for the Olympic Team…*But when I also considered how I had been performing on the twice weekly race pieces we did during practice, I knew being that good was still a long way off.

Whenever we did race pieces during my first fall of full-time training, we did them twice a week, every week, most often in singles. If it was too rough for singles, we rowed bigger team boats instead. If it was downright dangerous due to cold temperatures or excessive winds—winds worse than those I experienced back in Canada during my Champ Single race—we would erg. On some days, though, days when the water was only on the verge of dangerous but not downright dangerous, we braved the elements anyway. Because, as Tom explained, if we wanted to be competitive at the World Championship or Olympic level, we had to be prepared for anything. Only rarely would races like those be postponed due to choppy water.

By their very nature, race pieces are high intensity, all out, go as fast as humanly possible pieces. Chances to practice pushing yourself to your maximum. To stretch your limits beyond what you previously thought possible. In fact, if you practice them enough, and your motivation is strong enough, you might even find yourself pushing to the point of blackout.

For these very reasons, our twice weekly race pieces served

perfectly as our regular speed gauges to see how we stacked up against one another within our training group. Given that Tom had told us back during our first team meeting that finding speed in the single would help our chances for being picked for that year's World Championships team, our twice weekly race pieces provided twice weekly opportunities to take literal steps toward making the team.

With our results posted immediately after every set of race pieces, our standings could not have been more obvious. So twice a week, every week, we all knew exactly who was progressing toward the team and...who was not.

The way it worked was you first had to show an ability to go fast in the single without help from the coaches. The very act of rowing a small boat like a single can teach you an immense amount of technical skill and develop in you an immense amount of intrinsic motivation just by rowing it. So if you were able to intuitively become faster on your own, you might then get some technical advice from the coaches. After that, if their advice helped and you became a little faster, you might have even earned yourself a better boat (which too could help you go a little faster). And getting a better boat, especially when even a millisecond of speed could mean the difference between first and...everyone else, that was a sure sign you were doing something right.

At the end of every Wednesday and Saturday that we spent racing against one another out on Lake Mercer in our singles, I would clean my equipment, head to the locker room, change, then walk back to the boat bay, where I knew Tom posted our results. And after each set of pieces we raced during my first two months of full-time training, whenever I checked the results, though I hoped my name would be at the top, it was, without fail, at the bottom every time. That was my pattern. One that marked the longest period of stalled performance I had ever experienced.

With every step I had taken before then, I had improved.

Having gone from complete novice to full-time-training athlete in less than three years' time, I had grown accustomed to steadily advancing. However, in the two months since my move to New Jersey, even though I felt I was still taking steps and so thought I would further improve, my weekly results highlighted otherwise.

Had it not been for the simple fact that I wanted to row more than anything, I would have folded. With every week that I lost and met setbacks, I would have given in and walked away from the struggle. But because rowing was helping me to become my best, I was motivated to shake off loss after loss and to return for more every single day, trusting that my results would eventually change.

October 2004,

I have started to think that if you wanted badly enough for something to happen, then it most certainly could. I mean, who knows where I will be in four years? That is longer than my whole rowing career so far...Let's not just see. Make it so.

SEVENTEEN

NOT SURE.

WHEN I MOVED TO NEW JERSEY, I DID NOT EXPECT TO instantly soar straight to the top of the team. Of course not. I knew better than that. At the same time though, I did not expect to sit at the bottom for as long as I did. At least not long enough to create a pattern of stalled performance like the one I experienced during my first few months of full-time training. No one hopes for that. But that is what it was. A pattern of stalled performance that was only interrupted by two things: a visit by my college coach and the first time I heard the words "good job."

On the day my college coach, Kevin, came to watch practice, he rode along with Tom in the coaching launch, the motorboat from which Tom coached us. And while we rowed the two-hour practice in singles, Kevin and Tom sat together, observed, and talked. Quietly. I was still struggling to figure out how to go fast in the single then, so I could only imagine what they must have said about me as I passed.

Two hours of "figuring it out" later, having completed yet another row in the single, I cleaned my boat and oars as usual, put them away, changed out of my rowing clothes, then went back outside to find Kevin. It was the first time I had seen him in many months, so I was pleasantly surprised when he appeared at practice that morning. I looked up to him. I attributed everything to him. If not for him, I would not have been there in New Jersey training full time, so I looked forward to talking to him, stealing an awkward hug, and thanking him (yet again).

Oddly, when I found him in the boat bay, he barely said hello. Instead of sharing a warm hug, it felt as if we were two strangers clumsily meeting for the first time.

It was not until four years after Kevin's visit to that practice that I learned of something Tom had said to him that day, which explained why Kevin had awkwardly kept his distance. By keeping our interaction brief and standoffish, it prevented him from letting it slip that, on the day he rode along during practice and watched me struggle in the single, Tom had told him that because of my results on our twice weekly race pieces that he was not sure if it was going to work out for me. Which meant that I would probably not be making the national team. That might be why I was rarely given coaching advice during my first three months of training, apart from the obvious answers that came in the form of my comparatively lackluster race results.

I did not receive much specific feedback from our coaches early on in my full-time training. But on the day I did, I remember it right down to the way the sleeves of my sweat-soaked T-shirt hung warm and heavy from my shoulders.

Following the equivalent of two thirty-minute race pieces in our singles, I walked toward our tiny, musty-from-sweat locker room to change in preparation for our next training session. It was there in the oddly small, windowless vestibule between the men's and women's locker rooms that Tom and I passed. I had no escape from the confusing interaction that followed.

As Tom approached, I shyly bowed my head in subconscious reverence, then glanced only my eyes diagonally toward him.

Rather than staying quiet as usual, he spoke as he neared. "Good job, Shoop."

His words stopped me where I stood. My forehead wrinkled quizzically as my mind blanked. I had not expected him to speak.

When Tom recognized that I did not understand his comment, he elaborated. "On the pieces today. They were better."

I smiled, then attempted to hide my appreciation for just how much his few words meant to me. *Good job...*

With our interaction ending nearly as soon as it began, Tom went on his way. The heavy metal door to the vestibule clanged behind him as he left.

That morning's race results had yet to be revealed, so I was not sure if Tom spoke to me out of pity or because I had earned the nod. Either way, because I was curious, I changed faster than usual, then hustled to the boat bay, where I knew I could find the answer.

When I scanned the list of names and times, I saw mine. Up three spots from my usual place near the bottom, I was fourth. A little progress and that simple "good job" from Tom refilled my store of hope. A store that helped me keep trusting that my results would improve. A store that would last another several months, if not longer.

By December, a little over a month after Kevin's visit, the cold finally pushed us off the water completely. With Lake Mercer nearly frozen from prolonged periods of subfreezing temperatures, it was no longer safe to row on the water, so we moved fully indoors into winter training. That meant every single practice session whether easy, medium, or full-bore-all-out would be on land for the foreseeable future. We would just be erging, lifting weights, running, and possibly spending some time on the indoor stationary bike. Since it was New Jersey, we knew winter training could last from December until well into March or April when the weather improved again. A bleak prognosis.

Within a week or two of this realization, as we prepared to take a break from training together during the weeks surrounding Christmas and New Year's, Tom called another team meeting.

During this meeting, we learned that some of us would be invited to travel to San Diego for a winter training trip. For those invited on the trip, it meant leaving frozen Lake Mercer behind for at least ten days in exchange for some time to row on the water in the warm sun of Southern California.

At that point in time, the United States Olympic Committee (the entity that oversees all of the Olympic teams in every sport for the United States) had three main Olympic training centers. One of which was located seven miles south of San Diego, California, not far from the Mexican border in a little place called Chula Vista. "ARCO," as we used to call that training site (so named because the Atlantic Richfield gas company was once its sponsor), hosted athletes from all sorts of sports, including track and field, kayak, archery, BMX, triathlon, and rowing, to name a few.

The training center itself had everything an athlete could possibly want. Dining hall, dorms, a track, fields, boathouse, weight room—even physical therapists on hand and exam rooms for medical appointments if needed. What puts it over the top? Because the training center faces east overlooking the San Ysidro Mountains and Otay Lake, the sunsets are awe-inspiring. The perfect backdrop from which to savor a type of training as intense and time consuming as ours.

During our meeting, Tom revealed that some within our now eight-person group had already been invited on the trip to ARCO outright. They had performed up to a certain standard by that point in the year. As for the rest of us, Tom said we would have to meet further standards before being invited. Anyone not invited to ARCO (rather than rowing on Otay Lake in the warm Southern California sun) would stay in New Jersey to train indoors. On the rowing machines. While staring out the boathouse windows at frozen Lake Mercer. Wishing for its water to miraculously thaw.

By the end of the meeting, Tom pulled aside the few of us who had yet to qualify for the California trip. He told us that our opportunity to qualify would come in the form of an erg test after we returned from our two-week holiday at home. But not to worry, he had a plan to help us perform on that erg test. Not only would we have very specific training to do during the holiday break, we would also have very specific targets to meet on that erg test upon our return. Targets faster than any times we had shown by that point in our training. Targets we had to hit if we wanted to go to ARCO.

As far as Tom saw it, the decision was in our hands. If we hit our targets, we would get to go on the trip.

The general expectation for earning the privilege of going on a trip like that was that we needed to show progress. But over the course of my first three months in New Jersey, I had yet to improve my times on any of the monthly erg tests we had performed. During that time frame, our standard series of tests consisted of a ten-second test, a one-minute test, and a thirty-minute test. All were designed to measure very different elements of fitness. All were wildly different from anything I had done in college. And for whatever reason, despite hard training, I had generated nearly identical results on all three of the thirty-minute tests I had taken that fall—1:54.9, 1:54.8, and 1:54.9 were my exact average splits.

When Tom broke the news of what I would have to do to earn the privilege of going to ARCO, I was taken aback. My average time per 500 meters (my 500-meter split, that is) would have to be more than one second faster than I had ever gone before. From the 1:54.9 average that I pushed on my last test to 1:53.7. If you were to compare that kind of improvement to running a four-mile race, it would be like running it twenty seconds faster than you had ever run it before. No small feat.

My new standard was daunting. Improving my 500-meter split average by even one second on an already all-out test is a big ask when you train *with* your team. So if you take into account the fact that I had just two weeks to find a significant amount of additional speed while also being away from my teammates and coaches, calling my new target a leap would have been an understatement.

As our time wound down before break, and we were completely off the water, our little training group made it a point to meet in the evenings to cross-train together. Those evenings were our last few times to train as a team rather than solo for a while. And because we had grown closer over the course of our first three months of training together, we aimed to savor whatever time we had left as a team.

At exactly 6:31 p.m. on one of the last Friday nights before our two weeks apart, I sat in the boathouse pedaling on a stationary bike. As I pedaled, I glanced left and stared out the window at the dark December sky. I could tell that a light flurry had started to fall, as its tiny snowflakes shimmered in the floodlights outside. All the while, the few of us sitting there side by side on the bikes laughed as we wondered what "other people our age" were doing on that very Friday night. Probably not one hundred minutes of cross-training on a stationary bike in the dead of winter like we were.

That was when I knew. I knew without a doubt that there on that bike was the only place in the world I wanted to be. With my new teammates by my side. Building one day at a time toward a bigger plan.

Although we were young, inexperienced, a bit silly, and most certainly naive, we were a team in the making. A team brought together through our training and through the little things that made us laugh—both within and apart from practice. Small things like those evenings on the bike or at dinner laughing about tattoos and wondering how it would feel to be good enough for the Olympic team one day. Indeed, those small moments brought us together in ways that the training alone could not.

As I sat pedaling that snowy December night and thinking about my teammates and the larger plan we were building toward, I knew, without question, that I had to find a way to hit the target Tom had given me. If I did, I would get to go on that miraculous ARCO trip. I would also take another step toward making that year's Worlds team.

On the last day we saw Tom before we broke for break, as promised, he gave us each a printed copy of our training calendar. It contained specific information about what we were to do over every single day from mid-December until early January, when we would regroup. Namely, the details of the two to three training sessions we were to complete each day. Although we would be apart and instead at home training alone, having a calendar meant we would carry on as if there was no such thing as a holiday break.

That is the national team. There are no days off. You train. You recover. You work. All of your effort is wholeheartedly focused on those few things so you can become your best because that is important to you and is what you love. So you willingly plan *everything* accordingly.

Before I headed home to Virginia for our two-week break, I reached out to Kevin to ask if I could borrow an erg while I was in town. I also asked for his advice on how to set a personal record, to "PR," on my upcoming (critical) erg test.

When we spoke, Kevin told me without hesitation that I could use an erg. He also shared a strategy that could help me PR. An instruction that meant spending some extra time on the rowing machine—time practicing the new target Tom had set for me. By pushing that very speed, I would practice (and thus gain a feel for) the level of effort I would need on the day of the actual test. Because I trusted Kevin, and what he said made sense, I added his suggestion to my training calendar. Which meant I planned for even some additional training over our holiday break.

When I arrived at my parents' house in late December with

an erg in tow, though it was new for them, my family supported my need to train rather than binge watching movies, going to holiday parties, and lounging around eating pie.

For days when cross-training was on the calendar, I set up my mom's old exercise bike in my parents' living room. If erging was on the calendar, I set up the one I borrowed from Kevin in the kitchen—the noise from which chased my parents upstairs for several hours or out of the house altogether. On days when I had to do all-out-full-bore, high-intensity pieces, I went to the University of Virginia boathouse, which Kevin also said I could use.

No matter what, during our two-week holiday break, I did not miss a single day of anything Tom put on our training calendar.

By the time we regrouped in January, my four months of patient, persistent work despite only minimal progress, plus my added sense of diligence over the holiday break finally paid off. When I took the critical thirty-minute erg test, I went an average of 1:53.5. Not only was it my fastest yet, but it was even a little faster than the target Tom had set for me.

Although only a few of us ended up hitting our targets, Tom allowed everyone to go on the training trip to ARCO. Seventeen days later, we all headed to California…together.

EIGHTEEN

TAKE IN THE VIEW.

FROM THE MOMENT WE ARRIVED AT THE ARCO OLYMPIC Training Center, Molly and I were in awe of the entire place, so we explored every square inch of its 155 acres. The Olympic rings adorned nearly every facility. Images of Olympic legends filled the center's main buildings. Meanwhile, an Olympic flame burned upon a massive pedestal at the top of the highest hill. A place of prominence to highlight that flame's historic purpose. Just being there was a dream.

For the duration of our ten days at ARCO that January, we stayed in the center's suite-style dorms, where we quadrupled up—four rowers sharing two bedrooms (two rowers in each) and two bathrooms. Each bedroom came with two extra long twin beds, two small closets, and one nightstand with a lamp to share. Although our new "homes" were no larger than typical college dorms, they were what was most important: clean, quiet, and a short walk from everything ARCO had to offer.

We took all of our meals in the dining hall just down the hill from our dorms. Also clean and quiet (most of the time), the dining hall sat central to the site and had a friendly staff that provided meals to suit every need. A welcome break from grocery shopping and cooking the same simple meals for myself every night.

The flame that ignites possibility.

Farther down the hill from the dining hall sat the track-and-field facility. Where, if you were to stand facing east, you would see the San Ysidro Mountains in the distance with Otay Lake at the foot of them. It was there by the lake that our small boathouse quietly waited.

During the trip, our training schedule carried on similarly to the way it would have had we been back in New Jersey. The main differences being that we could wake up two hours later, and (because of the warm weather) we could row at least twice a day. We otherwise kept our pattern of easy, moderate, and hard training days, days when we did race pieces, days in the weight room, afternoons off, and a little time to cross-train. For which Tom gave us an idea one afternoon.

Because we had rowed nearly 200,000 meters over the course of our first week at ARCO, Tom suggested a change-up. Of the seven of us who had trained together in New Jersey all fall, five—including me, Molly, Susan, and two others—had never been to ARCO before. So on one of the last days of our trip, Tom suggested we go for a run around Otay Lake, then jog up the mountain that overlooked it. He told us that once we reached the top, we should stop and take in the view back west. Not only would we be able to see all of ARCO and Otay Lake from there but also the sunset over the Pacific Ocean.

Tom had sent us on enough "adventure runs" around Lake Mercer by then that we knew to anticipate that this run might take longer and be more challenging than whatever he described. So as he gave us turn-by-turn instructions in his usual "you'll figure it out" sort of way for how to make it around Otay Lake to the base of the mountain, the five of us listened intently and figured we would be okay as long as we stuck together.

Later that afternoon, we five met outside the dining hall, then headed down the hill, past the track, and toward the boathouse. From there, we veered left off the boathouse's gravel driveway, then began running along the edge of Otay Lake toward the base of the mountain that overlooked it.

Because it was January and late afternoon in Southern California, I knew the temperature would only drop for what remained of the day, so I dressed accordingly. My favorite grey hooded sweatshirt over my three-sizes-too-large white dry-fit shirt, with my old Virginia sweatpants rolled up at the ankles. These were the very ones that I wore almost daily back in college. The ones I was wearing on the night that my swimmer friend's roommate mistook me for "a real athlete." They served as a regular reminder of how far I had come since then.

The five of us ran single file along the dusty trail that traced the edge of the lake. The space surrounding us was wide open, while the worn trail was quite narrow due to the tall grass that stood straight up along the sides of it. The cool air smelled of eucalyptus and dirt, with hints of something sweet. The dry leaves and strands of peeled bark from the trees crunched crisp under our feet as we ran. Through the tall trees that lined the lake's edge, I could see the mountaintop itself was a greenish-yellow, dotted with reddish-brown bald spots of dirt and grey lumps—the rocks that lived at the very top. The sky was blue behind the peak.

As we ran, we talked. Tossing jokes back and forth as was our custom. Jokes about practice. Reflections on that incredible trip to ARCO and what a privilege it was to be there. Mostly though, we talked about nonrowing things.

Within a mile or two, we had made it to the end of the lake, where we then scampered up a short slope toward the road in search of the trail Tom had mentioned. When we surveyed the horizon along the road though, not one of us could see a trailhead that would lead us up the mountain. So, keeping the mountaintop in sight, we jogged (still single file) along the white line at the road's edge in search of the trail. Any trail that remotely resembled the one Tom described.

Eventually, we came to an extra wide gate. The kind you would expect to see many times over at a cattle ranch. Figuring it for our destination, we climbed through the wide spaces between its rails, glanced up at the steep mountain, then followed the trail upward. Our lake and ARCO at our backs.

At first, we were relieved to have discovered the gate and trail. However, when the trail began to wind farther away from not only Otay Lake and ARCO but also the mountain, we recognized something was wrong and stopped. Because we were completely new to the area, we conferred there for a moment. Then, considering how long we had already run, we decided our best bet was to hang a left off the trail and trudge straight up the side of the steep mountain. Rather than simply finding our way, we instead chose to make one.

Our new route was pretty manageable for the first few minutes, so we continued to jog. But as the hill grew steeper, and ARCO and Otay Lake became smaller, we slowed under the climb's abruptness. At first, we were annoyed with ourselves for getting lost and having a tougher time on our run than expected. Before long though, we could not help but laugh. It was not the first time something like this had happened to the five of us.

We could have easily turned back as soon as it became obvious we had gone the wrong way, but we carried on because we were undeniably intent on making it to the mountaintop. Susan, Molly, and me the most. For as far as our naive persistence had taken us, there really was no turning back. As we continued upward along our abruptly steep climb, our excursion, without question, had irreversibly transformed from adventure run to full-on hike.

Still, we laughed...

Every once in a while along our vertical trudge, we lost sight of the peak due to the steep angle of the climb itself. Whenever that happened, I had no choice but to lean forward, match the grade with my body, stare only at the grass before me, and clutch it to keep from tumbling backward down the hill. While the air moved dryly around me, the grass felt cool and moist between my fingers. Its blades thick and secure.

The farther we trudged, the clearer it became that my progress was noticeably easier on all fours. So that was how I proceeded. Safely on all fours, clutching the grass.

With my newly discovered grass grips to aid my upward progress, I only every now and again took my eyes off what was in front of me to check my heartrate monitor. Once my heartrate exceeded 165 beats per minute while simply walking up the hill, I decided to stop looking at my watch. I did not need a number to reinforce just how hard of a climb it was. Instead, I focused on nothing but the grass until at least another five minutes passed. At which time, I glanced up to be sure we were still headed toward the peak.

The higher we climbed, the faster the sun seemed to set, and the cooler the grass felt. Until finally, right when I felt the peak was within our grasp, I heard a strange noise coming from above us a short distance up the slope. When I scanned the ridge, I made out the image of two people easily running along. Horizontally running along.

As we inched nearer to them, the two people I thought I saw yelled down quizzically and jokingly, "What the heck are you guys doing down there?"

It was Megan, one of our day-one-of-practice-at-Mercer teammates, and Liane, one of the spares from the previous year's Olympic team. Both were more experienced than the five of us. Both had been to ARCO in the past. Both had climbed that mountain in the past, too, and so knew where the real trail was. Neither of them, however, had wanted to join us when we originally set off on our run that day.

When we made it to the ridge where we had seen them running easily along, we discovered an extra wide trail that was flat and broad enough for a car. And on it, Liane and Megan were running in the direction of the peak, laughing as they ran. We could not help but laugh too.

Once all five of us were off the side of the mountain and finally standing on the wide road, we fell in behind Megan and Liane, then followed them the rest of the way to the top. A few minutes later, all seven of us were at the top, where we finally took in the view.

By the time we made it to the peak, the sun was well on its way to set, so we quickly made our way back down along the correct trail with Megan and Liane as our guides. A much faster trip than the route we had made on our own.

Though we had not taken the intended trail that day, we figured out a way to get to the top because we were so intent upon that view Tom had mentioned. A view that was more than worth it because we made it to the top together, laughing at our predicament, and never once giving up on ourselves. In doing so, our climb (and that view) became another small moment that brought us together even more...as a team.

As we neared the bottom of our hike, I barely made out the image of a small car as it rounded the curve of the road toward the base of the mountain. As the car neared, I recognized it was Laurel, our assistant coach, in her tiny rental car. It was nearly dark by the time we made it to the road where she was. The sky was no longer pink and orange, but rather those last remaining purples and blues before nightfall when the stars would soon take over. Because it was nearly dark, and we had been gone for a few hours, far longer than we should have been, Laurel, a little worried, came looking for us. She often looked out for us like that—in a protective mother hen sort of way.

Though I can only describe her car as nothing other than tiny, we seven piled into it on top of one another while Laurel sarcastically chuckled at our nonsense. Once we managed to squeeze the doors shut, we gave the signal, and Laurel drove us home. All of us completely tickled by our adventure.

Tom was right. The view was amazing. Made all the better because of that tough climb. The one we did *together*.

Three days later, we flew back home to New Jersey. Back to our frozen lake. Back to our routine of indoor training mixed with the occasional adventure run. Sometimes through the snow around Lake Mercer. Always together. And rather than sleeping in and eating in a dining hall, it was back to rushing to work between training sessions and going to bed exhausted.

Even though I was still toward the bottom of our training group when we left ARCO that January, I was more devoted than ever to rowing and to what our small team was building together. As a result, I became even more willing to do whatever it would take to progress. Which, at that point, meant focusing on what was right in front of me and taking it one step (or crawl on all fours) at a time with my teammates by my side and the occasional glance to the top.

January 2005,

There was a short movie about the Olympics playing at the ARCO Spirit Store, so Mols and I went to see it. It made me cry. A seven-minute film made me cry...within the first minute...

All of a sudden, I realized how much I would like to go to the Olympics, or even Worlds for that matter. There are seven months from now until Worlds. A lot can happen between now and then, for better or for worse. This is my first step toward better.

My first trip to ARCO.

NINETEEN

A BETTER BOAT.

NEW JERSEY WAS STILL FROZEN WHEN WE RETURNED FROM ARCO. So frozen that we even asked Tom if we could cross-train by speed-skating on our now thick-with-ice home lake. A proposition he half considered. Winter had made it clear it was there to stay, so Tom knew we would have plenty of time to erg.

Because the little duplex that Susan and I lived in was old, it was drafty. And because we could only afford to turn up the heat so high, we took to sleeping in sweatshirts, sweatpants, and wool socks to stay warm. But even then, on the coldest and darkest of those winter mornings when I awoke for practice—despite also having my comforter pulled up over my head and my tiny space heater next to my bed—it was virtually impossible to shake off the chill that could creep into that house overnight.

On one particularly cold, dark morning, as I carefully changed out of my sweatsuit and into my practice clothes, thoughts of what lie ahead that day occupied my mind: another erg test.

It had been nearly a month since our previous test. Two weeks since our ARCO trip. So, having logged two more weeks of winter training, it was time. Because it was now February, Tom did not have another thirty-minute test in mind. Instead, this test would be two thousand meters. The infamous 2K. Although I had not taken a 2K in a while, I appreciated that it would be considerably shorter than the thirty-minute tests we had been taking.

Later that day, when I finished my 2K in a time of 6:54, it meant I had gone four seconds faster than my previous best. Another new personal record. I know four seconds might not sound like much. Particularly when compared to the one minute by which I had improved during my first year of rowing back in college. Back when rowing was brand new and I had a steep learning curve. But ever since then, I had come to understand that progress does not stay steep. It instead begins to take far more time. The nearly one year of full-time training it had taken me to earn a new PR proved as much. So I appreciated my four-second improvement for what it was: a sign. A sign of progress that helped me to trust. To trust that staying patient and managing whatever was in front of me was working. Because of those four seconds, I trusted that I was still headed in the right direction.

My 2K PR that February was my second in two months. When compared to how the fall had passed—with next to no improvement on the erg—stacking two PRs in two months was a sign that things were looking up for me. Then, when my 6:54 2K also earned me the privilege of a second trip to ARCO, not only did it seem things were looking up, but I felt I was finally showing some real progress.

Even though spring had technically arrived, March still felt like the dead of winter in New Jersey. So I very much looked forward to our second trip to ARCO and rowing under the warm Southern California sun again. I also looked forward to another adventure run up that mountain with my teammates (though preferably up the correct trail this time).

On the day I boarded my flight to head to ARCO, I could not believe it was March. When I thought back to my first day of full-time training (when we cleaned the boathouse and rowed those thirty short minutes in singles) and compared it to what we were now doing (around five hours of actual physical training each day), I realized how far we had come in just six months. And because I was finally reaping the benefits of our gradually expanding training plan, I assumed our training would continue to progress as it had all year. Which it did, apart from a few noticeable exceptions that surfaced while we were out at ARCO this second time around.

Because it was the end of March, talk of summer selection became more common. So we spent more time discussing what specifically would increase our chances for making the 2005 World Championships team. Specific things like selection events, climbing the team hierarchy, and which veteran athletes might reappear as part of that hierarchy as summer neared. When the time came for our coaches to officially select the team, they would take into account all of these things and more.

When it comes to selection for the national rowing team, there are two main routes toward being picked. Win an official selection event (a race held with the express purpose of selecting the national team). Or make it to and stay at the top of the team hierarchy for as long as possible, which winning a selection event can help you do.

Given that my only experience with team selection consisted of my ineffective struggle to make a boat for Non-Olympic Worlds during pre-elite camp the summer before, I knew I needed to keep learning and to keep taking steps should I hope for a better result. Especially since more (very experienced) athletes were with us at ARCO this time.

Some of the women who had raced at the 2004 Olympics had gradually been rejoining the training group over the previous months. So instead of only a small core of seven rowers plus a few others, we were now more than a dozen. An eclectic blend of less experienced athletes like me, plus a few seasoned veterans who had raced internationally at events like the World Championships or the Olympics. I admired those women for their experience. I knew I stood to learn a lot by rowing with them, so I welcomed their presence.

When I realized the timing of the veterans' return to training, it appeared strategic. It was as if Tom was intentionally growing our group like a rubber-band ball. Having started with a small core (those of us who had been rowing singles on Lake Mercer since September), it seemed Tom was now gathering veterans at very specific points in time. Because the veterans' experience would help us further develop, our potential for finding additional speed could only grow.

With Worlds now just five months away, finding additional speed became our focus. So to do just that, Tom started by building our daily lineups (which of us rowed in which boats) by combining those of us who had less experience with the veteran rowers. That way, we could learn from one another and hopefully discover more speed.

Within a matter of days though, Tom's approach to our lineups changed. Rather than rowing mixed lineups, the more experienced rowers began gravitating toward one another and into stacked boats. Boats designed to pick up speed by separating the faster athletes from the relatively slower ones. A strategy that would allow Tom to test potential lineups in advance of summer. A strategy I understood because of my place on the team hierarchy.

However, when my newer teammates also began cycling through the stacked lineups as the days ticked by, I became curious as to whether my turn would come before our trip ended. *Had I not shown signs of progress too?*

By the end of our ten days at ARCO, we had rowed various mixed and stacked lineups over hundreds of thousands of meters under the warm Southern California sun. Even so, never once did I row even one single meter in a stacked lineup. Not only that, I was the only one who never did. Apparently, what progress I had made was not yet enough, which meant I was still near the bottom of the hierarchy. But since the team had expanded by then, I was even farther from the top of it.

The day after we returned to New Jersey, we got right back to our routine of training, work, and exhaustion as if we had never left. And even though our daily schedule proceeded as expected without skipping a beat, some rather unexpected things began to happen.

Because the weather warmed while we were away, Lake Mercer thawed, and we were able to row our singles immediately upon our return. So on our first morning back, as I prepared to launch for an eighteen-kilometer row, because it was the first time I had rowed a single in at least a month (if not three), I anticipated it might take me a little extra time to get used to rowing a boat as small as a single again.

I spent perhaps two hours out on Lake Mercer in my single that morning. As was Tom's plan for us that day, the main focus was to improve our technique. We did that specifically through various drills and by rowing steady state by keeping our heart rates low.[4] With our heart rates low, we could fully focus on becoming more efficient through technical improvement. Something that would only make us faster in the long run.

As I rowed along, I executed each of Tom's assigned drills. Drills like pausing, where I would take a moment to stop at a given point in my stroke to think about my specific body position.

---

4   "Steady state" is a term often used in reference to a continuous level of effort. One that relies on aerobic metabolism. Because the body's oxygen supply is enough to meet demand, one's heart rate remains regular, and one's physical effort is sustainable (as long as fuel does not run out).

Or varying my stroke rate from time to time.[5] Or even rowing at a shorter slide, where I shortened the distance that I let my seat's wheels roll along their tracks, thereby taking intentionally shorter strokes.

By the time I completed at least 16,500 meters of steady-state rowing and drills, having concentrated for nearly two hours on my technique, my mind eased knowing that I was finally in the home stretch of practice. As our first of three practices for the day neared its end, the water calmed until it was nearly as flat as glass. While my mind relaxed, the morning sun, light-blue sky, and greyish clouds reflected on the water's mirrorlike surface. As I savored what remained of my row one stroke at a time, I noticed very little sound other than those coming from my breathing, boat, and oars. With just 1,500 meters separating me from the dock, I aimed to relax and simply row.

As the dock drew nearer, I was thoroughly wrapped in what I was doing. Mentally, I was in my own world. A world that drew me in further with every stroke I took. Hence my hearing very little outside my own bubble of breathing and rowing. As I breathed and relaxed, my boat glided the final bit of the way between my efforts. I worked, then it worked. Until...

"Shoop, stop pulling with your arms." Tom's voice shattered my tiny bubble of a world.

Startled, my head shot over my right shoulder toward where he had been sitting in his motorboat. With the engine off, his boat made zero noise. Between that and my deep concentration on what I was doing, I had not noticed him watching me.

Tom continued. "Nope. Stop pulling with your arms...nope. Nope...no. No...no. How else can I explain this to you? On the

---

5   "Stroke rate" refers to the number of strokes a rower takes per minute of rowing. During steady-state rowing, stroke rates are lower (typically eighteen to twenty-two strokes per minute), while during races, stroke rates are higher (typically thirty to thirty-eight strokes per minute).

very next stroke, I want you to literally let your arms hang out in front of you. Do not pull them in at all. Just leave them there."

On the very next stroke, I exaggerated his already exaggerated advice and did not pull with my arms at all. Instead, I pushed my legs, followed through with my body once my legs were nearly done pushing, then let my arms relax until they felt like noodles. I felt more like a carpet unrolling than a door swinging open.

Because it was the first time in my life I had ever rowed in that way, I initially resisted. But once I gave in and did as Tom instructed, my hands relaxed, and the blades of my oars exited the water more smoothly than ever. Then my boat lifted higher in the water and went faster despite the fact I had not put in more effort. Technically, I put in less.

"Yes. See. Do that again," he said.

So I did.

That was Tom. Simple. Almost frustrating at just how simple he made rowing seem. He was right though. Every time. Maybe I was frustratingly simple to him. Maybe that was the real reason why he said so little to me for so long. Whatever it was, it worked.

After I got back to the dock, I washed my boat and put it away, then wrote down Tom's advice in my training log as I prepared for our second practice of the morning. Weights.

March 28, 2005,

AM1—18k in the single. Drills and steady state. I learned something in the last 1,500 meters. Don't open right away. Use a good leg push. Don't pull with the arms. Trust it. The boat goes faster.

Two days later, the time came for us to do more of those all-out-full-bore race pieces on the water. It was the first time in a while we had been able to do them in our singles given the winter weather, how windy it had been, and how little we could row a boat of any size during that time.

As I rowed toward the dock at the end of practice following those race pieces, the first we had done on Lake Mercer since the fall, I thought again of Tom's advice about my arms. As I concentrated on nothing but "not pulling with my arms," I wondered if it had helped me on the pieces that morning.

When I was in the final one thousand meters of my row back to the boathouse, rather than being fully immersed in my own mental world, I instead noticed Tom following me. He did not say anything for the first minute or two but just putted along watching me. He then eventually drove his motorboat a little closer. Once he was close enough for me to see his face, he appeared perplexed with his head cocked slightly to the side.

"Good job…Shoop?" He said in a quizzical way.

I grinned. I was not sure why he said it. But since it was only the second time I remembered hearing those words during my first six months of full-time training, I figured it was a good thing. Perhaps it was another sign that things were looking up for me.

Tom followed me for the rest of my row back to the dock after that. Silently.

When I checked our list of results from that morning's pieces, I had miraculously placed in the top three. In a matter of days, I had gone from bottom three to top three. Which made me wonder, *Maybe this is real progress?*

Stepping away from sculling had evidently helped me improve. By not sculling, and by practicing my rowing skills in other boats, I had apparently learned something. Somehow. Perhaps my improved erg score helped. Perhaps having the veterans to learn from helped. Perhaps it was simply that time was running out for me to find speed, and my body responded. I was still too inexperienced to know exactly what had helped. One thing I knew though, when I did whatever Tom told me, even if it seemed ridiculously simple or completely different from what I was used to, I went faster, so I took whatever he said to heart.

A little over a week after I had finished in the top three on those race pieces, I got a better boat. A sure sign that something was finally going not just better but right.

In rowing, physical improvements, like those on the erg or in the weight room, are hard fought. Which makes them easily discouraging when they come slowly because there are no shortcuts. You cannot fake them. You cannot rush them. And their progress is not always linear. Especially the further you choose to pursue them. Believe me when I say that it can sometimes take years of training to squeeze out even a few extra milliseconds of speed.

As for technique, though it is also hard fought, those improvements can strike like lightning from one stroke to the next. Those "aha! moments," as I still call them, are the small pieces of advice and self-discovery that I began filling my training logs with once I learned to recognize them.

Me carrying my better boat.

Three weeks after my flash of improvement in the single, I became acutely aware of how quickly March had passed when one of our first official requirements for being picked for the 2005 World Championships team arrived in the form of a USRowing selection event. One called the Spring Speed Order.

Every Olympic sport, whether rowing or swimming, soccer or track and field, triathlon or basketball, among many others, has what is called a governing body. In the very same way that USA Swimming is for the sport of swimming and US Soccer is for the sport of soccer, USRowing is the governing body that oversees the sport of rowing in the United States. And much like every other governing body, USRowing operates under the watchful eye of the United States Olympic Committee.

At the end of the day, USRowing makes the rules. At least, as far as rowing in the US goes. This means that USRowing has the final say as to who makes the national team. This also means that by racing an official USRowing event, you increase your chances for being picked for the team. That is, if you perform well.

The Spring Speed Order was one of the few times we would get to race anyone outside of our training group that spring. For that reason, the 4,000-meter race was one of our few gauges to see how we were progressing both within and outside of the training center. And since it was an official USRowing selection event, performing well was, without question, preferable.

On the morning of the event, twenty-nine singles arranged themselves into one long line and prepared to race four thousand meters. Once every racer was in place and the start time arrived, each boat took off one at a time at ten-second intervals in a time trial format upon the race announcer's calls.[6] When you race in

---

6   A "time trial" format requires racers to take off one at a time, at a predetermined, timed interval (usually ten or twenty seconds). Times are taken from each individual's start. Because no one starts at the same time, you have no idea who is winning until the very end when you view the final results.

a time trial format, there is no way for you to know how you are doing relative to anyone else. You are too far away from your competition to compare, so you have no choice but to focus on you and you alone. Absorbed in your own little world, always thinking that you can find more speed on every consecutive stroke, because you never know who might be just ahead of or behind you.

By the time that morning's 4,000-meter race ended, I placed ninth out of twenty-nine racers. Just one-tenth of a second behind eighth place over the course of what turned out to be a seventeen-minute race. An incredibly small margin from top eight.

Three hours after that 4,000-meter race, my placement toward the top of the pack earned me the privilege of racing a 2K on the water. My first since my catastrophic near flip in the single in Canada just eight months earlier. Though my Champ Single experience felt decades old on the morning of the Spring Speed Order, it had been…just eight months.

A few moments before I launched to warm up for my second race of the morning, Tom approached me. "Shoop," he said, "it seems to me that you achieve whatever goal you set. And that's great. But…you should consider taking bigger risks."

I had no reply for him other than, "Okay."

Though our conversation was brief (as usual), Tom's words instilled in me a mild sense of confidence. *Does Tom think I'm faster?*

As I sat in my single preparing to shove from the dock, I triple-checked the Velcro of my boat shoes and grinned internally at the thought of what Tom had said. I then took a breath, and with a touch of additional courage in tow, pushed away from the dock to begin warming up for my most important race of spring thus far.

I had finally started to show speed improvements, so as I warmed up in the direction of the start line, I took Tom's advice to heart and amended my race strategy. My new plan? *Take a bigger risk.*

When I arrived at the start of my second race of the Spring Speed Order, I could not help but think of how my last 2K in the single had gone. That Champ Single race in Canada just eight months earlier where I nearly flipped due to the choppy conditions and my inexperience. The race where my aims were simply to make it from start to finish without flipping. The race where I only expected so much from myself.

But eight months had passed since my Champ Single misadventure. I had put in eight months' more time in the single. I had rowed on far worse conditions. And I had become more fit. So, as I sat there at the start of my second-ever 2K in a single, because of every step I had chosen to take, I was more confident and so believed I could aim higher than not flipping. What made it even better that morning: the water was as flat as glass. The perfect conditions for me to aim higher. *Could I win?*

When the time came for the race to begin, I was lined up alongside five other boats. Each of us in our own lane. Each of us locked onto the start with our own volunteer to hold steady our respective boats' sterns. Then, once we were each ready, the race announcers made their final call.

"Attention…"

Upon "Go!" six boats took off down the racecourse, and because I aimed to take a bigger risk, I stayed completely focused and was in my own world despite my surge of adrenaline in that moment. Nothing mattered but what I was doing. My breathing. My boat. My oars. My plan. The water was dead flat, a rower's dream.

At 250 meters into the race, right about the time I found my race pace (the stroke rate and rhythm that would most efficiently carry me down the racecourse), I did not peek over my shoulder to see where I was relative to my competitors. Instead, I continued focusing on myself, my boat, my oars, my plan, and nothing else. I could not do anything about anyone else. So the best thing, the only thing, was to stay focused. Ever the more concentrated on what I was doing with every stroke I took.

I pushed my legs and breathed naturally with every stroke. I followed through with my body and did not pull with my arms, like Tom taught me. I heard the water as it bubbled along on the sides of my boat. I fell into a rhythm and forced nothing. I simply pushed my legs as hard as I could, then relaxed as much as possible so I could push them again. Over and over and over.

At the end of each stroke, I relaxed my face and feet as I breathed out. Upon every exhale, my hands felt loose and light while my face relaxed down and forward. In a matter of minutes my mind went blank…

By the time I had taken enough strokes to make it to where just four hundred meters remained—less than one-quarter of the race—my mind momentarily stirred. That was when it happened. Because my mind was no longer blank, I could tell I was moving faster than ever, and so I could not help but glance across the lanes to see how I was progressing. Instantly, I was floored by what I saw. I was vying for the lead.

With less than two minutes left to race, my confidence surged as I internally implored, *Take a bigger risk.* When Tom's words zipped across my mind, I dug in and pushed for more. Once my ears began to ring, I no longer heard the water bubbling alongside my boat. Instead, I heard nothing. Nothing but the ringing.

My hands tingled as I attempted to maintain my grip on my now sweat-soaked oar handles. My callouses ripped to blisters under the pressure I felt in my hands with every push I gave. My head shifted from relaxed and forward to a backward tilt. My eyes squinted as my jaw jutted out in one fixed, effort-filled grimace. That was when the silver-lined black spots closed in.

At first, they encircled my peripheral vision. But as I pushed for more, they encroached upon the middle and threatened to blind me. Then, as the dots merged, and I approached the point of blackout, my body weakened, and my boat started to tip. When my body sensed this imminent danger, its natural instinct for survival took over. This caused my effort to wane until I regained (some) control over my boat, and the silver-lined black spots receded. My vision returned just in time to catch sight of two boats as they passed me.

I had been in first or second place for nearly the entire race. But with less than thirty strokes to go before I crossed the finish line, because I nearly passed out, I fell off the pace. As a result, by the time all six boats crossed the line, I was fourth.

My fourth-place finish gave me mixed feelings that morning. I was excited because my finish was far better than I had performed all year. Technically, top ten in the country based on that day's racing. At the same time though, I could not help but be disappointed. I had been so close to winning.

After the race, Tom pulled me aside to ask me one question. "What happened out there?" He said in a mildly dissatisfied tone.

"You told me to take a risk." I replied. "So I did, and I almost passed out."

"Well, that's fair…" Tom's tone eased. I had done as he asked. He could not be mad.

Two days later, we were back to practice as usual. But rather than easing into training with some steady-state rowing, we met at the Lake Mercer boathouse and instead took a 6,000-meter erg test. When I finished the test with yet another personal record—my third PR in three months—then considered how I had improved in the single, I noticed a new pattern. A pattern of progress. At last, my eight months of figuring it out with little feedback other than my high heart rate and stalled numbers appeared to be paying off.

Less than an hour after our erg test, Tom gathered us together inside the makeshift weight room at the Lake Mercer boathouse. As we huddled around him, I wondered what he had planned.

After the intense few days of racing and testing we had just endured, I half-expected yet another challenge or for him to say he was displeased.

Imagine my relief when he instead jokingly pointed out that we had "trained through" the entire weekend of racing and also our erg test. That we kept working hard without resting to store energy. And even with this disadvantage, we had all managed to perform well at the Spring Speed Order and also on our erg test.

Tom went on to explain that fatigue is a natural part of training at our level. That it is common to feel "tired" most of the time. He even joked that if we wanted to make the Olympic team one day, that we could "expect to be tired for the next four years."

When Tom was done with his postpractice speech on that mid-April Tuesday morning, we all smiled and laughed together at the thought of what he said. Our gradually growing rubber-band ball of a Lake Mercer training group was finally making strides toward the larger plan and becoming a team. That pleased Tom, so he laughed with us. As for the next four years, that sounded like forever to me. I had barely been a rower for three.

TWENTY

ONE RUNG UP.

ALL OF THREE WEEKS LATER, THE CHANCE TO RACE OUR singles in another USRowing selection event arrived. Not only was it another chance to gauge our speed both within and outside of the training center, but it was also an opportunity for me to improve upon my top-ten finish from the Speed Order. Given my performance there and how my confidence had grown a little because of it, I went into this weekend of racing with high hopes that I could take another step.

But when the weather on day one of racing brought wind and waves instead of flat, calm water, it nearly caused my single to sink, which exposed my not-yet-experienced-enough sculling skills. And so, I did not perform as I hoped I might. Rather than top ten or faster, I barely finished among the top eighteen. It was as if Mother Nature herself had other plans for me. Plans that knocked me back and forced me to keep taking things one step at a time.

As soon as racing ended that weekend, Tom wasted no time. He brought together our now much larger training group and explained that some of us would be shifting focus away from rowing singles and toward a different piece of that year's plan.

With summer all but upon us, it was time to split the training group based on that year's "priority events." That is, based on which boats (and on which athletes) greater emphasis would be placed for the World Championships.

In years prior, the US team had performed decently well in the eight at both Worlds and the Olympics. But rather than continuing to emphasize the eight as in years past, the 2005 team's priority events would instead be the pair, the smallest and slowest sweep boat, and the quad, the largest and fastest sculling boat.

The reasoning behind this priority shift was not arbitrary. It was a matter of medals and resources. Emphasizing an eight would require nine athletes to vie for just one medal. Whereas, emphasizing a pair and quad, would require only six athletes to vie for two medals. By placing the team's fastest athletes, those at the top of the hierarchy, in the boats set to race the priority events, the potential for medals further increased. Given this increase, it made sense to shift priority to the pair and the quad.

When I did not perform as well on our most recent USRowing selection event, it showed that though I had worked my way toward the upper end of our training group at times, my improvement in the single was neither consistent enough nor strong enough to earn me a foothold at the top. So while practically every athlete who was training there on Lake Mercer by mid-May (nearly twenty by then) kept sculling as part of the quad group (the group that would focus on the quad), four of us left our singles behind and instead shifted focus to rowing pairs.

At first, I did not know what to make of being shifted to the much smaller pair group. Maybe it was that my improvements in the single had appeared too late. Maybe it was that I was still at the bottom of the team. Maybe it was something else entirely. Whatever it was, although the four of us in the pair group were not in consideration for the quad, we were just four rowers. Which meant we might have found ourselves with a little extra one-on-one coaching from Tom as summer neared—a considerable advantage.

On the day we four split off from the rest of the team to form the pair group, of all the partners I could have been paired with first, it was Molly. Having raced together back in college, I had cultivated a trust in her over nearly my entire rowing career. Because of the obstacles we had overcome together along the way, I wholeheartedly trusted her, so I felt fortunate to be behind her in the pair again.

When Molly and I shoved from the dock for our first pair row, we had not rowed the pair together in what seemed like forever. Not only that, neither of us had rowed a pair in almost a year. So, no, we did not instantly click and get right to speeding our way up and down the racecourse. Instead, as we progressed through our first row, rather than smoothing things out as we went, our frustration only increased upon every wobbly, slow stroke we took.

Ninety minutes of frustration and slow rowing later, when we turned in the direction of the boathouse to begin bumping our way to the dock, I noticed Tom heading our way in his motor-boat. In his typical Tom way, he followed us and watched without saying a word. He only turned his head slightly and observed. The longer he followed, the more intently he stared. The more intently he stared, the more his head cocked to the side as if we were some code he was intent upon deciphering. Until finally, he spoke.

Tom instructed us to row over to the side, away from Lake Mercer's buoyed racecourse, and toward the large open space that was a short distance from the docks. Once we were there—us in our pair and Tom in his motorboat—he explained that we would be rowing circles. That one of us would row at a time in whatever way he described, while the other would sit still, holding her oar handle to keep our boat stable by acting like a giant training wheel.

I had never rowed circles in a pair before, so I was initially hesitant. Because of the way the boat twists slightly against you rather than going straight, rowing circles feels weird. And since one of the critical keys in rowing is to go as straight as possible, rowing in circles seems wrong until you get used to the drill and trust that it can help you. Even then, when you finally relax enough to focus wholly on technique, the boat can unexpectedly tip. When it does, your body jolts into survival mode and involuntarily recoils to prevent the boat from flipping. Because your adrenaline surges in those moments, it can take a few extra strokes before you regain even the slightest sense of relaxation. Even though abruptly tipping like that momentarily hinders your progress, you cannot help but laugh off your stumbles because it is likely they will not be your last.

As I rowed my first of many giant circles out on Lake Mercer that evening, Molly stabilized our pair. With every circle I rowed, the sun drew nearer to dusk, and Tom putted in his motorboat in even larger circles around us. All the while calmly describing *exactly* what I should be feeling at every moment.

Because he was sitting in his motorboat and I had never seen him actually row, I wondered how Tom could possibly know how rowing felt. But he did. With every one of his words, it felt as though he were taking my strokes for me. Which, despite his not rowing the boat with me, encouraged me to trust his advice even more. So I listened more intently to everything he said.

As he spoke, tiny beads of sweat gently rolled down my arms into the creases at my elbows. Once enough of them collected there, they combined into larger streams that flowed down my forearms then dripped into the glassy water below. With every word, every bead of sweat, and every passing circle, the lake grew calmer. As I fell deeper into our world of circles, everything outside of it became silent. I felt nothing but the way the boat floated. I heard nothing but my breathing, the bubbles that peeled away from the sides of our pair, and occasionally Tom's calm words.

Every single thing perfectly matched the stillness of that mid-May sunset on Lake Mercer.

Somehow sensing my shift to calm, Tom told me to relax even more and to *listen* to the boat. To move with the boat. To further loosen my face, feet, and hands. To even tilt my left ear down toward the water so I could listen more intently and pay even closer attention to what I heard and to what I was doing. To exactly match the boat as it moved.

Though tilting my ear seemed an odd request, I trusted Tom, so I gave in.

Instantly, his words of precise explanation changed to, "Yes. Do that again. Do you feel how you are moving *with* the boat now?"

I did. When I felt my new sense of calm, I grinned, which tensed my face a little. So I breathed to relax it. I could delight in my discovery later. In that moment, I was feeling something new, so I wanted nothing more than to savor what I was finally learning…without interruption. For the first time in my nearly three-and-a-half years of rowing, having taken millions of strokes, I could finally hear and *feel* the boat. So rather than forcing my every stroke, I instead let the boat tell me what to do. And Tom saw it, which verified my progress.

Molly and I took turns making circles after that. Tom calmly identified when we were "getting it" and when we were not. When we relaxed. When we moved with the boat. Or when we were not. His words focused solely on guiding us toward self-discovery because that was our best way to truly learn.

When the sun finally left us with too little light to continue, Tom released us from our circles, and we headed toward the dock. During the final few strokes of our row that evening, I was mesmerized by the sounds our boat made when we matched its fluidly flowing rhythm. Then, as Lake Mercer dimmed, Molly and I, having discovered a new level of awareness, landed back at the dock…no longer frustrated.

Rowing circles in pairs was not the only thing we did that May. Of course not. We had to keep finding more speed. And technical improvements honed by rowing circles in pairs was just one part of that. While racing against each other was another. Which is why, on at least two days a week, every week, much like we had all year, race pieces became a regular part of practice again.

By the time race pieces in pairs became standard, Molly and I were two weeks of circles and thousands more strokes more experienced than we were on our first day back in the pair together. Because we had gradually discovered more speed with every stroke we took, we improved to the point of becoming the faster of the two pairs for a time. But because of how selection works, Tom eventually separated Molly and me.

Having us swap partners would help the coaches discern who were the fastest in our group by comparing speed among different sets of pairs. Once the fastest were identified (one port and one starboard in this case), those two would continue rowing their pair together until they lost during race pieces, or more rowers joined our group. A strategy that would last for years to come.

On the day we traded partners, I switched from Molly to rowing with Megan. "Dirks" as we called her then. She was one of the veterans. Relatively quiet. Two inches taller than me. She had an immense amount of experience, and Tom seemed to trust her. Not only that, she had won an Olympic silver medal less than a year before the day she and I were to begin rowing together. I was honored to be paired with her. For as much as I had learned by rowing with Molly, I could only imagine what discoveries might surface by rowing with someone as experienced as Dirks.

Before immersing us in race pieces with our new partners, Tom allowed us a few days to "figure each other out." This would allow us to make small adjustments and get used to one another before jumping into more race pieces. After a few days of figuring each other out, we raced again.

When we did, much to my surprise, instead of winning, Dirks and I broke even with Molly and her new partner, Sharon. Sharon had been training with us in New Jersey all year. She was a few years older than me and had more experience than me. However, she too had yet to make the national team at the senior level, the senior team, the highest level there is.

A few days later, rather than taking a step forward and coming out ahead, Dirks and I lost.

Such are the ebbs and flows of learning. To make boats go, you need to match. It is not about being right, no matter how much you think you know. Nor is it about giving up everything and only following. It is about working together no matter what. The subtle compromises made from one stroke to the next. And when you trade partners as often as we did, you have to compromise in order to figure things out with someone new on a regular basis. The only constant being that things will definitely change. Which means your only option is to learn and take it one step at a time.

Recognizing our need to become faster somehow, Dirks taught me as much as she could about rowing over our next three weeks of circles, drills, and race pieces. She broke things down, told me how to push and when, and just as Tom's words had exactly matched how I felt, so too did Dirks's words.

At the tail end of one of our practices in the pair together, Dirks made a call for us to stop rowing. Right where we were. Right there, in the middle of our lane, with less than five hundred meters to go on the racecourse, and before we turned to row toward the dock. When we stopped, the thick, early June growth along Lake Mercer's leftmost shore shrouded my vision in a deep green.

We drifted in silence momentarily as Dirks considered what to say. While she thought, my shirt, humid with warm sweat and bugs, clung to my chest. When I pulled it up to wipe the sweat from my eyes and neck, it made a slight sucking sound. The air I breathed grew dense with concern as I wondered just how many things she might tell me I had done wrong. All I could figure was that she was frustrated by having to row with me. We were not exactly having a great row.

When she finally collected her thoughts, she turned her head sideways toward me. As I stared at her profile, rather than the frustration I expected, Dirks simply and calmly suggested, "Don't try so hard all the time."

I blinked another pearl of sweat from my eyelids, felt the humidity as my effort-soaked shirt resuctioned to my belly button, and I took in what she said. I had long learned that the best way to make boats go fast is to push harder. So I tended to default to precisely that…all the time. But when this incredibly experienced woman suggested I do the opposite, I felt I could trust her, so I attempted to do as she said.

For the final ten minutes of our row that day, we took it one stroke at a time with Dirks instructing me every push of the way. We started with a light, lower-effort leg push. Then, as we flowed gradually better by rowing together, matching our effort and strokes, she told me exactly when to push with just a hair more effort. Every ten to twenty strokes she called for us to push a little harder, which helped our pair flow more efficiently and earned us more speed.

"Dirks!" I victoriously squeaked as our boat picked up speed. "You taught me to row."

A cold chill ran up the back of my neck and down my right leg as I said it. Whether my chills were caused by my excitement for such a significant aha moment or the amount of sweat I had produced during such a long row on a day as humid as it was, I cannot be certain. Whichever it was, I still remember the way those sparks of efficiency felt that day as Dirks passed her wisdom down to me.

I was sad our row had to end. We had just started coming

together right as we made it to the dock. It was better than never though. It had happened, and I had learned something new. Between Tom's calm words and Dirks's guidance, it was the first time I felt in control of my technique. Couple that with the tenacity I was learning from Molly, and I finally felt I was discovering real speed. Speed that was a step or two above college... just in time.

When mid-June arrived, yet another USRowing selection event arrived with it. A National Selection Regatta this time. This NSR2 was more significant than any of the previous selection events I had raced. Partly because we would race our pairs there. Partly because it was the race closest to summer. Mostly though, it was because whichever pair won could officially claim its place on the national team. The team that would race at the World Championships in Japan later that summer.

USRowing's rules stated that, immediately following the race, the winning pair would have the opportunity to sign a contract. If the two rowers in the winning pair chose to sign, they would commit to representing the US at the World Championships in the pair. The NSR2 was evidently more than a race that could simply improve our chances for making the team. It was an opportunity to *actually* make the team.

If Dirks and I won the NSR2, we would be in direct control of our 2005 national team destiny. But if practice during the weeks leading up to the event was any indicator of our chance to win, the odds were not in our favor.

In the final week before the event, it looked as though Molly and Sharon would be the ones in direct control of their 2005 national team destiny. They had beaten Dirks and me in practice nearly every single day, over piece after frustrating race piece. This confused me, given the improvements we had made together. Dirks, though, she did not seem overly concerned. If she was, she hid it well.

When Dirks and I took off down the racecourse on that muggy mid-June morning of the NSR2, with less than two weeks left until final team selection, our luck finally changed. Miraculously, having endured three weeks of doing the opposite of winning, Dirks and I finished the first race of the event with the fastest time among the pairs. A welcomed boost of confidence that we did not take for granted. Instead, we focused on finding more speed. Speed we trusted we could find before we would compete in the final the next day. The critical race that would determine which pair would take control of its national team destiny.

I cannot tell you what I thought when we left the docks on the morning of that NSR2 final. I cannot tell you what I thought as we warmed up. And I certainly cannot tell you what Dirks thought as we sat at the start line in those final moments. What I can tell you, though, is how simple we kept it, how focused we were, and how Dirks and I crossed the finish line...

In first.

Despite having lost repeatedly in practice, despite the odds being stacked against us, despite my inexperience relative to Dirks's, we pulled off the win. Which I attribute, in large part, to Dirks keeping her cool all the while.

Rather than letting the past frazzle her, Dirks chose to manage what was right in front of her. She focused on the task at hand, then took things one stroke at a time. Despite our setbacks, never once did she fold. Instead, she continued to search for ways to improve. In doing so, she showed me a confidence hard-earned over time. Something she had earned through many more ups and downs than I had faced by then. The ability to stay focused despite the odds was yet another thing Dirks helped me under-stand. Which helped me take another step.

After racing, Tom brought Molly, Sharon, Dirks, and me together to debrief as a small group. He spoke minimally and directly as usual. He told Dirks and me that, yes, we had "technically done what is necessary" to be officially named to the 2005 Worlds team. He also expressed that, though it was our right, he did not think it was in the best interest of the team for us to race the pair.

To help us better understand why, he further explained that a group of college rowers would be joining us once they finished their respective schools' season and broke for the summer. They would come from all over the country. No two of them from the same college. When he expressed that they had the potential to contribute speed to the team, he even went so far as to suggest that they may be faster than the four of us standing there before him.

By the end of his explanation, even though Dirks and I had the right to sign on the dotted line to commit to racing the pair at Worlds, it was clear that Tom preferred otherwise for the sake of the team. Although his comments may have appeared unsympathetic, and it meant giving up securing a spot for myself on the Worlds team right then and there, I understood Tom's rationale and so trusted him.

The point was to make the entire team as fast as possible. If that meant adding a few more people, so be it. I figured that if Dirks and I truly were the fastest, we could still come out on top in the end. We would just have to wait a few more weeks.

Tom concluded our meeting by reassuring Dirks that he was glad to have her back with the team. He then turned to me and said that our pair performance had put me "one rung above Sharon." For as uncertain as the year had been and for as low as I had been on the team hierarchy for nearly all of it, I had technically worked my way toward the top of it by winning the NSR2. But despite the event's significance, I had only moved one rung up from the bottom. I was still new. And Tom needed more evidence.

It may have been just one rung, but it was a rung, nonetheless. A rung that proved I could climb. A rung that moved me one step closer to making the team. A rung that showed me firsthand how every moment, no matter the odds, truly is an opportunity to turn it all around. Particularly, if I stayed focused on what was in front of me and took it one stroke at a time. Just as Dirks and I did.

TWENTY-ONE

THE MATRIX.

JUST AS TOM PROMISED, LESS THAN TEN DAYS LATER ON THE first official day of summer, the college athletes arrived, and with them came the final stages of team selection: "the matrix."

The matrix was the method Tom most often used to find the fastest lineups. For those of us in the pair group, that meant he would take our group of now twelve athletes, assemble us into six pairs, then intermix us over a series of races—allowing the cream to rise, so to speak. Not unlike the way it worked when I was switched from rowing with Molly to rowing with Dirks. Only now, Tom had twelve rowers to shuffle instead of four.

Once the matrix for final selection of the pair began, we expected the shuffling to go on until an obviously fastest combination emerged. Possibly for weeks. Once it emerged, those two rowers, one port and one starboard, would be selected to race the pair at the World Championships in Japan at the end of the summer. After the pair was identified, selection for the eight would follow.

When we started the matrix, we were assigned partners, then we had a few days (sometimes less) to figure things out. After that, we would race a series of pieces for time, then be reassigned to new partners based on those results. That is how "the cream" could rise. Those who performed well would only row with others who had also performed well, which would (theoretically) enable the fastest to become even faster.

Before diving headlong into the matrix, to help us understand the process and add validity to the results, we first did a test run. For these practice races, we lined up pairs and singles (from the quad group) in alternating lanes, time trial style, one boat at a time as we had done so many times before. That way, if any boat overtook another because it was that much faster, it would have a clear lane rather than having to go around the slower boat. Set up that way, there was no way interference from overtaking should have been an issue…

Rowing is all about working together and matching each other no matter what. My now three and a half years of rowing experience had already taught me that and more. But when my first partner of the matrix and I took off from the dock on the day of our practice race pieces, we did not match. At all. The boat instead wobbled uncontrollably. Every time I tried to take a stroke, I could not get a good enough grip on the water with my oar. This made it impossible for me to row productively. Rather than effectively pushing the boat along, I instead splashed waves of water with every stroke I took.

By the end of that morning, not only were my partner and I furiously frustrated and confused by our inefficiency, we were overtaken by another boat. And not just any boat. A single. One rower in her own boat beat us. By a significant margin too. So significant that even though we had a head start on her, she passed us before we made it halfway through that morning's first piece.

That does not happen. Although I still considered myself new to rowing, I knew enough to understand that the single is supposed to be the slowest boat. That means the only way for a single to beat a pair is if that pair is *very* slow.

I did not have to check the results that Tom posted as usual in the boat bay to know how my pair partner and I had performed that morning. Instead, after we put our boats and oars away, and Tom released us all from practice for the morning, I ducked out quickly to be sure no one realized how upset I was. With my tears already welling, I fled to the locker room, grabbed my things, and made a beeline for Susan's car. She and I had ridden to practice together that day as had become our custom. But of all days for it to be her turn to drive, it had to be that day.

As I hurried toward Susan's car, I avoided eye contact and did not speak with anyone I passed on my way there. By not stopping, I reached the car ahead of Susan, where I had no choice but to wait in horrified silence until she sauntered over. From what I could tell, she and her partner had performed just fine that morning.

Once Susan was close enough to the car, she clicked her key fob to unlock the doors from where she was. As soon as I heard the click, I lifted the handle of her silver Pontiac Grand Prix, climbed in, and buckled my seat belt. Not a moment later, the waterworks erupted.

Finally, Susan joined me inside her car. By then, I was visibly an emotional wreck. My tears were a full sob. The kind where your bottom lip sucks in and out as your gut clenches uncontrollably with every contraction of your diaphragm.

I had concealed my emotions well enough after practice that Susan had not realized anything was wrong until she sat down in the car, was also buckled in, and put her key in the ignition to speed home. Only when she was there, one foot away from me in the car, did she realize the sounds of my irregular breathing.

"My life…is over," was all I could get out.

With a look that I can only describe as confused terror, Susan turned to me: "What do you mean your life is over?"

That confirmed it. She had not noticed my results from the morning. My sobbing continued.

When Susan finally pieced together what had happened, her confused terror turned flat, then direct. "Get it together, man. We'll come back later, and everything will be fine. It's practice."

That is what teammates do. They kick your butt every day in practice to make you better. Sometimes they kick you in the gut. Sometimes they smack you on the back of the head to get you out of your own thoughts and back on track. But above all, they hold your hand when they realize it is the thing you need most. Which, in her own way, is exactly what Susan did.

Our drive home was a little quieter than usual after that. Susan was right though. It was just practice. I could not do anything about what had happened. I could only do something about what was in front of me: our next practice.

Later that afternoon, Tom so closely followed my pair partner and me that it felt as if we were the only rowers he coached during the entire ninety-minute-long practice. By the end of those sixteen kilometers of rowing, it felt like we had taken eight hundred steps back and had no idea what we were doing. At Tom's instruction, we had rowed circles and performed drills. He had asked us to do things I had never heard him say before. But as usual, because everything he had told me in the past had worked, and I trusted him enough to give up securing a spot on the Worlds team on the day Dirks and I won the NSR2, I trusted him again. So I did as he said to the best of my ability.

Another day later, we raced again. This time, our pieces officially counted toward the matrix. And rather than being slower than a single, my partner and I finished among the top three.

Rowing works in inexplicable ways sometimes. Considering the number of times my results had started to defy the odds, it seemed that not counting on things until they actually happened was a great thing. Because it turned every moment into an opportunity. Especially, when I focused on what was right in front of me and kept taking things one step at a time. When you do that, particularly in your moments of sheer and utter demoralization, your will to succeed emerges. When it does, you find more focus and, apparently, more progress.

In a matter of days, my first partner of the matrix and I went from being beaten by a single to working our way toward the top portion of the matrix. Given our steep upward progress in that short time, we could not have been more excited to give it another shot. Nevertheless, when we were assigned new partners before our next practice, we were disappointed to be separated.

Because Tom knew this, he pulled my partner and me aside to reassure us that we had made progress. That being split up was just a part of the process. While he spoke, I smiled at my old partner, genuinely happy, and hoped we both would keep learning with whomever we were each paired with next.

Day after day, new partner after new partner, race piece after race piece, it became apparent that something had changed for me. The matrix was showing patterns. Patterns of progress. Patterns that I was figuring things out more than ever before. I was intent upon finding more and giving everything I had one stroke at a time, fully focused on the task at hand. For all I knew, my new signs of progress were pure luck. I had to keep moving forward to prove it was real. Not just to the coaches but also to myself.

So every day, *Small adjustments.* Like Dirks taught me. *Match my partner. Do exactly what she does, then find more effort.* There is more. Just as Kevin, Molly, and Tom taught me. *Stay patient, positive, and determined.* Just as I had learned to do throughout my initially slow progress. One stroke, one step, one small piece of advice, and one small adjustment at a time along my quest to become the best I could possibly be. Until finally, everything I learned through each experience over my first three years of rowing earned me a seat in one of the only two boats left in contention for final pair selection.

When the cream finally rose to the top of the matrix, I was one of the final four remaining rowers. One of only two starboards, and as it turned out, the one with the least experience.

On July 2, 2005, the day we were told would be the last of pair selection, just four rowers remained. Just two boats whittled down from six. Just three 1,500-meter pieces separated us from the answer to the final question. *Who would be the two women chosen to race the pair for the United States at Worlds?*

When we took off from the docks that day to warm up for the final round of pair selection, I sat in the bow behind Caroline, one of the college rowers Tom had mentioned back at the NSR2. From where I sat, I could tell that her strawberry blonde hair was slicked perfectly into a bun. The lenses to her sunglasses, spotless. Her focus, laser sharp, as always. If there is one thing Caroline has always been, it is prepared in every way possible. Undeniably certain that nothing stands in the way of her being able to push herself to her absolute limit. Trust me, you want her *in* your boat, not lined up against you.

Following our forty-five-minute warm-up, Caroline and I pulled into position just ahead of Tom's motorboat, where he and Lori (a college coach who had joined the coaching staff for the summer) sat waiting. We always arrived on time, if not early. Yet another precaution that Caroline preferred.

While we awaited our competitors, I rubbed my hands one palm at a time down the sides of my shirt to rid them of any iota of sweat. I needed them dry for this. I did not want my hands to slip on my oar handle.

When the other pair finally approached, my heart pounded a little more. I took a breath to calm it. Our boat drifted slightly in our lane. Despite the obviously mounting tension, Caroline and I focused by concentrating on readjusting our boat's position to ensure that we raced in as straight a line as possible.

Meanwhile, the other pair—Sam (another of the college rowers and an Olympic silver medalist) and Anna G. (yet another college rower)—rowed up alongside us in their lane, then stopped when the bow of their boat pulled even with ours.

Tom was right. Several of the college rowers were fast. Just as he predicted. Three of them—Sam, Caroline, and Anna G.—were among the final four in contention for the pair with me that day. Which meant that at least one college rower was about to earn herself a seat in one of the national team's priority events.

Once Sam and Anna were in position in their lane, all four of us sat ready for the start of race piece number one. *Final selection* race piece number one.

At the start, we were four rowers sitting ready in two pairs, while Tom and Lori sat in one motorboat off to the side. Lake Mercer was devoid of activity otherwise. Just a faint lapping of tiny ripples on the sides of our boats, and the motor from Tom's launch gently idling. As my focus narrowed, all fell silent around me. I was intent upon nothing but Caroline's back, the way my oar handle felt in my hands, and the looseness of my feet in my shoes.

Upon one last deep exhale to both align and ease my nerves, Lori's raspy yet authoritative voice tolled, "Attention...Go!"

In an instant, we four went from a dead stop to full-bore fury.

From our very first stroke, I thought of nothing but matching Caroline by exactly mirroring everything she did. She was the port. I was the starboard. When she breathed and pushed, I breathed and pushed. When she sat strong and let her arms hang long so her legs and body could do the work, I did the same. Our plan: *leave no question*. To do so, we focused on us and nothing else.

Fifteen hundred meters later, we crossed the line ahead of the other pair by several seconds of open water, which meant we won by more than three seconds—a decisive victory. Winning the first of three 1,500-meter pieces by open water was a good thing to do on the final day of pair selection. A very good thing. Particularly, considering how low on the team hierarchy I had once been.

For piece number two, I was switched into the other pair to trade places with Sam. By making that kind of switch, Tom and Lori could discern which pair combination was the fastest. Depending on the results of piece two, they would either switch us back, or they would not, for piece three.

Once we made the switch and I was sitting in the other pair behind Anna G., I adjusted my shoes, seat, and oar to make myself as comfortable as possible in my new position. As soon as I was ready, we spun our boat around and made our way back toward the start line.

Anna G. was the other port in final contention for the pair. She, along with Sam, Caroline, and a few other college rowers, had arrived in mid-June. Anna and I were nearly the same height, we both had brown hair, and she too smiled a lot. And though she was two years younger than me, she had also picked up rowing in college, albeit about six months before me. All in all, when the two of us raced together that summer, despite our lack of experience, our boat exuded positive energy and speed. If I had to guess, Anna G. and I were the last two people Tom thought would be in final contention for the pair that year.

At the start of piece number two, as we floated in the next lane over from Sam and Caroline, I relaxed my face, feet, and hands as my heart fluttered up in one last bout of nervous energy. I took one last deep belly breath, then exhaled it from every pore of my body in an attempt to regain some semblance of composure.

With all quiet again except for the lapping of tiny waves on the sides of our boat and the idling motor of Tom's launch, I anticipated the start.

"Attention…"

Bleh!

Before Lori got out her "Go!" command, all I heard was the sound of Anna G. vomiting over the port side of our pair. When my eyes involuntarily reacted by shooting to the right, I got an up close look as it happened. When they did, my focus shifted from nothing but Anna's back to watching her do something completely unexpected.

Meanwhile, Lori called, "Go!" and the other pair took off, leaving Anna and me well behind and still sitting there at the start.

Tom and Lori did not stop piece number two to wait for us. Had it been the World Championships, the announcers would not have stopped, so neither did they. Instead, they let the piece play out, which gave Sam and Caroline quite the head start.

Amid a blur of nerves, distraction, and vomit, I blurted, "Go. Go. Go!"

It was the best I could come up with in my state of shock. The race had taken off without us. So, *to race* was our only option.

Because of the head start that had developed while Anna was otherwise occupied wiping vomit from her chin, we started the second race piece at a significant deficit. Despite the other pair's lead, Anna and I did not roll over and give up. Instead, we reeled in Sam and Caroline one stroke at a time and caught them before the piece was done.

When we crossed the finish line of the second 1,500-meter piece, we were nearly bow ball to bow ball, just shy of a tie with the other pair. Had it not been for their head start, Anna and I would have won outright.

Two minutes later, I was switched back into the boat behind Caroline, where I readjusted my shoes, oar, and seat in preparation for the third and final piece—the last bit of evidence Tom needed to decide who would race the pair and become two of the top priority athletes on that year's Worlds team. And also, two of the fastest rowers in the country.

By the time we finished all three race pieces that morning, we had made two switches, both of which involved me. I had witnessed how nerves and desire can lead to vomit, even at the start line. And I had learned that Caroline and I were the fastest pair of the matrix by a large margin.

Following the pieces, Caroline and I cooled down a little before rowing calmly back to the dock. We then washed our boat with smiles on our faces. All the while, though I was hopeful, I could not help but wonder what Tom would say in our post-practice debrief.

After Caroline and I had washed and put away our equipment, I slowly made my way out of the boat bay and toward the locker room to change. On my way, I noticed Laurel standing off to the side by the little whiteboard where Tom usually posted our results. When I passed her, I could tell she was discreetly attempting to get my attention. When I stopped, she turned my way, trying to withhold a smile in case anyone was nearby.

"Lindsay," she whispered. "That was *excellent*."

Like Tom, Laurel too rarely spoke. When she did, it was honest. Indispensable. She gave invaluable insight when needed most. She really was our mother hen. A three-time Olympian. A silver medalist. A sculler. A sweeper. A coach. A mentor. More experience than anyone I had ever known because she had done and seen nearly everything. If you were to meet her, you would discover how unassuming true excellence is.

So when someone like Laurel utters the word "excellent" your way, you take it to heart. Not only did her words confirm that I had done something right that day, they refilled my store of hope…for good.

After I changed out of my sweat- and humidity-soaked practice clothes, Tom confirmed that Caroline and I would be the ones to race the pair at Worlds. That is, as long as we won that year's Worlds Trials. The same series of races I had gone through during my second pre-elite camp the previous year in straight fours. Only once we won could we officially claim our spots on the senior national team. Luckily, as far as we could tell by then, when Caroline and I got into our pair together, we went significantly faster than anyone else, which boded well for Worlds Trials.

July 2, 2005,

Don't think so much. Follow. No frustrations. No question. Learn from every piece. Leave. No. Question.

Two weeks later, Caroline and I won Worlds Trials to officially claim our spots on the 2005 Worlds team. Two and half weeks after that, on August 3, 2005, following a few more rounds of selection and seat racing, not for the pair but instead for the eight, Caroline and I were also picked for that boat.

In ten months' time, I had climbed my way from the absolute bottom of the team to the very top. In doing so, I became one of the top six female rowers in the entire country for that year. Not only that, after countless setbacks, frustrations, last places, near flips, months without PRs, and innumerable rows through excruciating winds, choppy water, and subfreezing weather, all on top of being told that I needed to become stronger and more fit, I became one of just two female American rowers who had earned the opportunity to race not one but two events at the 2005 World Championships. Something only a few Americans had ever done or have done since.

All because no matter how many times I lost, I chose to learn by focusing on what was right in front of me and taking it one step at a time. Which (along with the occasional glance to the top) kept me hopeful and willing.

When the time for us to race at Worlds would arrive, it would be just Caroline and me out there in our pair. As for the eight, it would be Caroline, me, Dirks, Sam, Anna G., Susan, Liane, and Sharon, plus our coxswain, Mary, another veteran.

Each of the rowers who made the Worlds team that summer

had either trained year-round in New Jersey, arrived mid-June from college, or was a returning veteran athlete from the 2004 Olympic team. As for Mary, she had coxed the eight in Athens, so she was the expert among coxswains in my eyes.

Just two and a half weeks after the team was officially selected, the entire US national rowing team, men and women alike, scullers and sweepers alike, met at the boathouse at three o'clock in the morning to hop aboard a bus bound for Newark Airport. Where, by 7:00 a.m. on that late August morning, I was finally on my way to Japan to compete in my first World Championships as part of the US national rowing team.

TWENTY-TWO

AS LONG AS WE LEARNED.

WE WERE THE DICTIONARY DEFINITION OF UNDERDOGS when we touched down in Japan just over a week in advance of the 2005 World Championships. We had nearly zero race experience at the international level among those of us in our pair and eight, given that only three of the nine of us had ever raced an Olympic class event at the World Championships before. Our coxswain, Mary, plus Sam and Dirks. So apart from what experience those three shared, we had little understanding of what might happen while we were there in Japan. As I quickly learned though, no matter how much experience you have, things rarely go as anyone expects.

It had taken us twenty-eight and a half hours to get from our 3:00 a.m. bus back in New Jersey to the Bird Green Hotel in Ogaki-Shi. It was the longest day of travel I had ever experienced, so that alone made it exciting. But as excited as I was to explore our new town and hotel—what we would call home during our nearly three weeks in Japan—I was exhausted, it was already late, and we were not there to play tourist.

Because it was 7:30 p.m. by the time we arrived at our hotel, I forced myself to shower, grabbed a bite of dinner, then headed straight for my tiny box of a room to sleep. Our rooms were small. So small that sharing was impossible, so we each had our own. Mine consisted of a tiny bathroom separated from the main bedroom (though I should say "bed" considering how small it was) by a frosted glass door. The walls were simple. The bed was simple. Upon it rested one tiny pillow, no larger nor thicker than a box of cereal, but not nearly as cushioned. Given my exhaustion though, I did not mind how minimal it all was.

Within a matter of minutes, my fatigue overwhelmed what remained of my excitement. So I brushed my teeth, then dropped facedown onto my bed and hoped for a better night's rest than the one I had gotten on the plane. But like I said, things rarely go as expected.

First, 12:30 a.m. Next, 3:23 a.m. Finally, 7:45 a.m. Those were the exact times my eyes absorbed as I spent my first night in our new "home" by waking up every three to four hours from the time I first rested my head upon my cereal-box-sized pillow until breakfast. By 9:00 a.m., my teammates and I were on yet another bus on our way to the racecourse for our first row.

Following a meandering forty-five-minute bus ride through the lush, green Japanese countryside along a river and past rice pads, our bus pulled into the parking lot at the racecourse, then came to a halt. While I awaited my turn to file off the bus, I gazed out the window and noticed that an ominous layer of clouds had rolled in and had begun to blot out the sun. Then, once I was off the bus and cresting a little hill during my walk toward the water, I saw something even less welcomed: extreme winds and flooding—never good signs when you are about to go for your first practice row ahead of your first World Championships.

Because of the weather, we could not row. So we erged instead. We had flown all the way to Japan. I had barely slept in two days. Taken buses, planes, shuttles, and more buses over almost thirty hours. And here, we erged.

Twelve kilometers on the rowing machines inside a gigantic white temporary tent later, and we were back on another bus riding the forty-five-minutes back to the Bird Green Hotel. By 5 p.m., despite its unforgiving discomfort, I passed out hard on my bed. Again, facedown, like a starfish, my head turned to the left.

Having slept through several alarms, I awoke three hours later in my own small puddle of drool. When I realized how late it was and that I nearly missed dinner, I shot up and ran out my door.

After catching the end of dinner—where I attempted to make awkward small talk with the five coaches that I ended up sitting with—I made a quick note to myself in my training log: *No nap tomorrow or I'll never adjust to this time change.*

On day two, rather than 9:00 a.m., we left for the racecourse at 7:00 a.m. with the hope we could skirt the high winds. It worked. While at the course that morning, we were able to fit in two rows for a total of twenty kilometers. Between rows, we ate lunch. As for the afternoon, Tom gave us a little extra time to ourselves to further adjust to being there in Japan.

It was during our afternoon to ourselves that Susan, Caroline, and I decided to take a walk through the little town of Ogaki-Shi to ward off passing out from exhaustion in the early afternoon again. Our idea seemed like pure genius to the three of us. By not napping, we hoped we would finally get to bed at a normal hour and actually sleep through the night. It may have been our first trip to Worlds, but we already knew sleep was vital to our performance.

After passing the whole afternoon strolling through the little town, meeting locals, taking pictures, and exploring, Caroline, Susan, and I were proud of how clever we had been to invent a new way to adjust to the twelve-hour time change. That is, until the exact moment we walked back into our hotel and bumped into Tom.

Excited for our genius that afternoon, we proudly approached Tom and told him where we had been.

He stood quiet for a moment, blinked at us, then in his on-the-verge-of-sarcastic way, he simply said, "Rookie mistake." The three of us looked at one another, then back at Tom. He smirked, chuckled, then turned and walked away.

Though we had not fallen asleep, we *did* spend the whole day on our feet and so had not rested our legs—our most crucial asset as racing approached. The way I saw it, either we had made a mistake, or Tom was joking with us. Because I could not be sure which, I took it as yet another lesson learned and aimed to conserve as much energy as possible from there forward.

That second day in Japan was a Tuesday. August twenty-third to be exact. A full day too. We had rowed twice, taken a walk, made a rookie mistake, and by dinner, had learned that two typhoons were forecast to roll our way. So rather than carrying on as planned, we were told we would have one more chance to row before being limited to the ergs until the storms passed. Stuck on the erg with the first race of the World Championships a few days away? I never would have expected that.

On top of every bit of that unexpected information, we also learned that racing would be condensed due to the storms. Rather than spread out over the course of seven or eight days, the entire World Championships program (its full series of events and races) would instead take place over just six or seven. When our coaches told us that the storms would steal at least one day, I hoped they were right. *Let it be only one day.*

Because Caroline and I were set to race two events there at Worlds, losing even one day meant we would have less time to recover from one race to the next. Without proper recovery, our energy would wane over the course of the week and with every race we rowed. If that happened, we would be at a disadvantage by the time the finals—the most important medal-deciding races—arrived at week's end.

August 25, 2005,

Monitor fluids. Monitor sleep. Eat well. Stretch. Don't walk around too much even if you're bored. Stay calm. Let the erging begin...

By Friday, because the storms had fizzled, we were able to get back on the water two days earlier than expected. So, by Monday, exactly eight days after we arrived in Japan, racing began for Caroline and me.

When you race an international competition like the World Championships or Olympics, there is always some sort of race progression that is planned well in advance of the actual event. Never (at least not that I know of) would you show up for just one race, race it, then be done. Even if there were only a few boats entered in your particular event, you would still do some sort of exhibition race first to determine which team should be in which lane for the medal-deciding final.

The medal-deciding A-Final is the top-level final, the final that decides places one through six. The second level final, the B-Final, decides seventh through twelfth. And if the number of entries warrants it, having even a C-, D-, E-, or F-level final is not uncommon at the World Championships.

When it comes to how you get to an actual final (your specific progression), this too varies based on the number of entries in a particular event. When there are six or more entries, the progression consists of heats, reps (short for "repechage," from the French for "second chance"), and finals. In the case of twelve or more entries, you would progress through heats, possibly reps, and semifinals before your particular final. And in the much less common case of twenty-four or more entries, you might even find quarterfinals sandwiched between the heats and semifinals.

No matter how many entries your event may have, though, it is only once you race each stage that you learn how you stack up against your competition. That is what dictates your progression and which final you ultimately make.

Given these rules of racing, when Caroline and I prepared to launch for our first race in the pair, we knew we first had to manage a heat. That was all that mattered in that moment, because only after we raced the heat would we know our fate from there onward.

Shortly before we launched to warm up for our heat, Caroline and I met with Tom for our prerace meeting. Even though we had been practicing in our pair for more than one month and so had meetings with Tom before, I still was not used to it being just the three of us. During our meetings, Tom typically aimed to reinforce our race plan, impart wisdom, and instill one last bit of confidence. So in those final moments before we hoisted our pair onto our shoulders to walk it toward the dock where we would then launch for our first race at our first Worlds wearing our USA uniforms, Tom shared something that took the edge off my nervous energy.

While I ran through my race-day mental checklist—water, time check, bathroom, breathe, uniform, socks, sunglasses, time check—the look on Tom's face gave me the sense that he was somewhat proud of us. So I stood a little taller, I breathed a little deeper, my mind eased, and my confidence gradually grew. Then, when he finally spoke, my confidence grew a little more.

"Go out and find *your speed*," he said. "That's all that matters."

Not one of us could know how fast we would be nor how fast our competitors would be. How could we? Caroline and I had never raced at that level before, so we had literally nothing to go on when it came to the world stage. That meant our only option was to focus on ourselves and to take it one stroke at a time. Only once we crossed the finish line would we have some real evidence as to how we stacked up against the best in the world.

Because I trusted Tom's words, I nodded in affirmation of

every word he spoke to Caroline and me. By the end of our prerace meeting, the plan for our young USA pair was simple: blades in, breathe, push hard, sit strong, leave no question, find *our* speed, one stroke at a time, together. When Tom was done speaking, Caroline and I carried our boat toward the water, prepared to launch, then shoved and rowed our way toward the start line. Just the two of us. Off to find our speed. Against the world.

Forty minutes of warm-up later, we sat poised at the start line in lane five with the pair from France in lane six to our left. Australia in lane four to our right. Past Australia and even farther to our right, Belarus, Bulgaria, and Russia rounded out the six boats that comprised our heat. Heat one.

With no more warm-up strokes left to take, no more time left to count down, no more anticipating left to do, we at last awaited the start signal. I breathed and relaxed my face, feet, and hands just as I had practiced through all our preparation up until then. I wiggled my fingers and glared through my eyebrows as my focus narrowed. Eventually, I saw nothing but Caroline's back as the world fell still and silent around me.

Until the start command pierced my personal silence, "Attention…"

Every time you race in college, it is loud. The boats are big, and there is always a coxswain to guide you. She steers you as straight as possible, because even an inch of distance saved can mean the difference between first and everyone else. She keeps you accountable to the race plan. She interjects the right words to distract you exactly one stroke before you realize just how hard you are working. She has your back the moment before your mind starts to wander.

But this was not college. It was the pair at the World Championships, a race we had flown halfway around the world to race, and we did not have a coxswain. Instead, we did everything ourselves. So rather than loud and tumultuous, the race was quiet except for the sounds of our boat, our breathing, our thoughts, and eventually, an effort-induced internal ringing in my ears.

Midway through the race, "Go USA!" cut through my ears' internal ringing. It was Lori, who had made the trip to Japan with us. She had bellowed encouragement in her characteristic raspy coaching voice from shore, where she was watching. When I heard her words, my mind grinned, and my confidence grew, which threw a chill down my right leg. In that moment, Kevin's infamous words came to mind: "There is more."

I knew I had more. The simple fact that I could still discern actual words told me so. I pushed for more, breathed more, and followed more in order to more perfectly match what Caroline was doing in front of me.

Seven minutes, eight seconds later, we crossed the finish line in second place (behind Australia) with the third-fastest time posted by any of the twelve pair entries that day. We were also a large open-water margin faster than Russia, Belarus, Bulgaria, and France. Although we would not advance straight to the A-Final without having to race again, second place was a great showing for our first international race together. Tom was right. Finding our speed was what mattered.

Caroline and I were new to international racing, but because we had beaten teams in our heat that were more experienced than us, our confidence grew a little more. Which I welcomed since we would have to race a repechage in the pair before we would learn which final we would ultimately make.

August 29, 2005,

We had the third fastest time today! Overall, our warm-up went well, and we were happy with what we learned. We can tweak a few things before our next race...Until then, drink plenty of fluids. Take an ice bath. Sweet focus for practice in the eight before racing tomorrow.

The very next day, our result in the heat for the eight was strikingly similar to the pair's. Right down to our second-place finish. Instead of posting the third-fastest time though, our time in the eight was the second fastest of the day. Although our speed in the pair and eight was promising, and so increased our confidence, it did not take away the fact that we would have to race both boats again before learning which finals we would ultimately make. It was a more challenging progression than the one we would have followed had we instead won both our heats. A progression that meant Caroline and I would be racing six 2Ks over seven days rather than four 2Ks over eight days. A tall order for two rookie athletes like us.

August 30, 2005,

Day two of racing. A pretty good start. We led much of the way and pushed well. Anticipate, commit, and push together. Go together when we need to. Focus on Mary's calls...Time to get plenty of rest and water.

Day three of racing brought both of our repechages—our second-chance races. First in the pair. Then in the eight, three hours later.

In our pair rep, when Caroline and I flew across the finish line in a time of 6:56, we were barely two seconds off what was world-record speed then. Possibly faster than any two American women had ever gone in a pair before and significantly faster than any of the other nine boats that also raced through a pair rep that day. Not only was ours a speed that earned us a spot in the A-Final, it was a speed that made it seem like we might be among the three fastest women's pairs racing there in Japan. To put this speed in perspective, we were faster in our pair than some of the eights I had raced as a college novice just three years earlier.

Ahead by open water at the halfway point, the 1,000-meter mark. (Image courtesy of Row2K, Row2K.com)

Later that same day, we took first place by nearly sixty feet in the eight rep. A very large margin. And much like the pair, we were the fastest of all the eights that raced through the reps that day. Based on how each of our races had unfolded by the end of day three of racing, it seemed we were gaining momentum as a young team. Poised among the top three in both the pair and the eight was indeed a strong start. Particularly, since it was (for most of us anyway) our first World Championships. Thankfully, we had two days to rest, recover, and practice before we would race the A-Finals.

The night before our pair final, two coaches stopped Caroline and me in the hallway of our hotel. In passing, they semijokingly threw a question our way that caught me off guard.

"How does it feel to know that you are going to take home two medals from your first World Championships?" one of them rhetorically suggested as if it were fact.

I turned toward them quizzically, laughed nervously, then grinned at the thought of even one medal, let alone two. It was a nice thought. Imagine two rookies like us earning two medals at our first Worlds. What a far cry from my near flip into the choppy waters of the Canadian Henley just one year before. A testament to how far you can go with a little hope and by taking things one step at a time.

To the coaches we bumped into in the hallway that night, the evidence was mounting in a positive way. Based on the times from our first four races and our performances relative to our competitors' speeds, people had apparently begun to assume we would medal in two events—which is rare in rowing. Rare because the sport itself is so strenuous that athletes seldom enter more than one event at a given race. At least not at the World Championship or Olympic levels. In the rare case they do, it is not often that they medal in either event, let alone both.

I cannot say that I did not wish for what the two coaches had said to us to come true. But the World Championships was not a time to get ahead of myself. I knew better than to take things for granted, so I knew not to expect even one medal until we were in the process of earning it.

After the two coaches turned to continue toward their rooms that night, I took their words as a compliment and smiled at Caroline. Then, as I headed toward my own room and my cereal-box-sized pillow, I returned my focus to what I could do to turn my hopes into reality: rest and prepare for our last two races. The two biggest races of my life by then.

What Caroline and I endured during that week required that I pour out every ounce of my being until I had absolutely nothing left. It was more effort than I had ever put forth in such a short time in my whole life, and it caught up to me by the end of Worlds. Six maximal effort 2Ks against the toughest competition in the world in less than one week will do that to you.

On the morning of the A-Final of the pair, Caroline and I lined up at the start along with Australia, Belarus, New Zealand, Russia, and Romania. Rather than relatively flat, calm conditions as they had been all week, the racecourse was instead a wavy mess. On account of the heightened challenge that the conditions presented, as soon as Caroline and I took off from the start line, something went wrong. From our very first stroke, our timing was off. We did not match at all. As a result, over every single stroke of the race from there, what speed we produced required more effort than usual.

Surprisingly, despite our early inefficiency, we managed to keep ourselves among the leaders for the first 1,500 meters of the 2K race—top three with less than two minutes to go. However, because we had not matched perfectly from the very start of the race, our rowing was less effective than it would have otherwise been. When that happens, every bit of speed you create requires more effort and so drains your energy. Quickly.

By the time we crossed into the final three hundred meters of the race, our inefficiency caught up with me. My energy drained, I was no longer able to match Caroline in any way, so we fell apart. From one stroke to the next, Caroline and I disconnected from one another completely. Rather than moving fluidly, like we had all week, our boat bobbled uncontrollably and slowed down considerably. With no extra energy to spare, it was all downhill from there.

Whether it was our fatigue, the tumultuous race conditions, or the pressure to perform, not only did we lose our near-front-of-the-pack position, we fell behind. By a lot.

When we finally crossed the finish line, we were well outside the medals and in an incredibly disappointing sixth place. This did not happen because our competitors found new speed. No. It happened because we went significantly slower. Having raced our rep with close to world-record speed in a time of 6:56, we finished the A-Final in 8:01. Behind the pairs from New Zealand, Australia, Russia, Romania, and Belarus. Three of which we had beaten a matter of days earlier.

The very next day following our disappointing pair finish, we raced the A-Final of the eight, where not only were we among the leaders in the closing 250 meters of the race; we were *the* leaders with less than sixty seconds to go. But over every stroke as we neared the finish line, our competitors reeled us in faster and so gained on us.

As we hurried toward the finish line, and our fatigue and nerves grew, our inexperience showed. Once exposed, the entire field, every country, every other team in the race, boat by boat, began to pass us. It was then when we fell out of first, then out of second, and were barely holding on to third that I knew I had to find more. With the world bearing down on us, I opened my eyes wide, breathed, sat back a little on my seat, then pushed for more on the very next stroke. But rather than propelling all two hundred pounds of our eight, plus our nine bodies within it, forward under my own additional effort, it felt as if someone punched me in the right side of my ribcage, just below my armpit, as hard as humanly possible.

In an instant, I gasped.

Even though my body instantly recoiled into survival mode on that frighteningly painful stroke, I forced myself to keep pushing. However, because I could no longer sit strong, I slumped, still breathing, confused, and a little afraid.

When we crossed the finish line of our last race of Worlds, the heft of the week's six-race effort came crashing down in one final blow. Not only did it feel as though I had broken something in my side, but just 0.38 seconds separated us in our fourth-place finish from second place and the silver medal.

The race is a mile and a quarter long, two thousand meters, somewhere around 220 strokes, and only one single foot came between us in fourth place and a medal. So, no, Caroline and I did not know how it felt to take home two medals from our first World Championships because we took home none.

That first Worlds experience was our first test of being gold-medal worthy. Medal worthy at all. We were poised, and it looked as though we were there, but the level of competition got away from us, which exposed our need for more preparation. We may have been on our way. We may have improved a lot in an incredibly short time. We were just not there yet. So we needed to stay patient.

On our flight home from Japan, I thought about how far we had come in one year as a gradually growing team. From seven singles to a team just shy of two medals at the World Championships. I also thought about what it had taken to push us that far. More training than I had ever before endured. More running, more erging, more lifting, more rowing. I could only imagine how much more it would take to come away with better results. Though I had no way of knowing what that *more* might be, I knew what mattered most was how we chose to respond from Worlds forward.

We had to stay patient. As long as we learned, Worlds would not be a total loss.

September 4, 2005,

Unfortunate events, but we did our best. Trust that the race is 2,000 meters from start to finish whether you're in front or behind. Don't wait for the hand of God to come. Keep going, keep it together, and pull your butt off...

How do people get to do this year after year? Most fun I remember having in a very long time. I want to do this for as long as I possibly can...September nineteenth is the first day back to get ready for a shot at next year!

TWENTY-THREE

CONTROL WHAT YOU CAN.

CONFIDENCE IS SOMETHING THAT PRACTICE GROWS AND tests gradually, one fine detail, one small step at a time. While racing reassures (or crushes) that confidence in a matter of minutes. Given the different ways practice and racing test you, you need both. At least, if you care to progress toward becoming your best. Practice to nudge you along day by day, one step at a time. Racing to make you brutally aware of how your day-by-day is going and to let you know if you are still heading in the right direction.

Two weeks to the day after we left Japan, I was back in New Jersey with my teammates, Tom, and Laurel. Considering that we had spent the last year training more than I previously thought was even humanly possible and had raced harder than ever but still came up short at Worlds, I had no idea what to expect on our first day back at practice together. I did, however, assume that we would not be starting year two of training by cleaning the boathouse and rowing only 4K as we had on day one of year one.

Forty-eight weeks. That is how much time we had to amend our shortcomings before the next World Championships. We had forty-eight weeks to gain experience, knowledge, and confidence.

Forty-eight weeks to gain speed one day, one training session, one stroke at a time. Forty-eight weeks to somehow do more than what we had done the year before, something dramatically different in order to achieve a different result than the one we earned in Japan.

Much to my surprise though, things were not dramatically different when I got back to New Jersey. At least not at first.

During our first meeting, we learned that we would (again) ease into things with team training in the mornings, followed by our own personal schedules in the afternoons. I learned that I would be able to go about my day job between practices. The job I was fortunate enough to still have despite my one-month hiatus for Worlds. That meant my days would still consist of morning practice number one. Followed by a one-hour break, sometimes a shower, then morning practice number two. After that, another shower at the boathouse, then a quick change into my office clothes so I could rush to work with wet hair and wrinkled pants.

Once there, I would work as many hours as possible before zipping back to the boathouse for afternoon practice. Practice number three for the day with typically another hour or two of training before showering (again) and making my way home to finish the day with dinner. Usually while watching some movie on DVD, scouring the mail for grocery sales, laughing at one of Susan's crude but irresistibly funny jokes, then bed. All to wake up early the next day to repeat the cycle.

That was how year two started. It was not until we were two months into our year two routine that things began to change.

Following practice one late afternoon in mid-November, Tom pulled our little group together for a meeting. He told us that we would be taking another trip out to California to train at ARCO again, but instead of ten days, it would be for two months this time. He told us which boats would be prioritized for the upcoming 2006 World Championships: the pair again and the double (two people, two oars each). Because we were still a relatively small group at the time, and it was early in the training year, just November, nearly everyone at that meeting was in consideration for one or both of the priority boats.

Explicit as always, Tom also told us we needed to "continue getting fit." Which meant we would finally be ramping up the amount of time we spent on actual training to an even greater extent than the year before. After our meeting, we all headed home to recover and rest in preparation for the next day's three training sessions.

With such a routine as ours, the days can start to run together—only discernible by our fitness and technical improvements. We still rowed small boats, though more pairs than singles, and our training distances gradually expanded. We carried on with our twice weekly race pieces, and our times were still posted every week without fail, so we all knew exactly where we stood, like always. However, because we had one year more experience, we began to track our progress from one day to the next *differently*.

Rather than only comparing ourselves to one another within our training group, we instead compared ourselves to and held ourselves accountable to some very specific speeds. Speeds Tom calculated and deemed necessary to perform relative to the world. Speeds based on world-record times. Translation: we trained based on paces that no one on the planet had ever before produced.

Tom made training toward world-record speeds seem totally normal. So we embraced our new challenge because it allowed us to compete against the world even though we never left our new home lake—Lake Carnegie. The lake that was just at the foot of the hill from where Susan and I lived. One mile at most rather than the seven-mile drive to Lake Mercer.

When Tom spoke, there was logic. So pretty much anything he said made sense in some way or another, which built trust. I believed him when he told me not to worry if my heart rate was higher than everyone else's when we ran. That it would come down eventually. Which it did. I believed him when he told me that not pulling with my arms would make my single go faster. Which it did. And I believed him when he told me that relaxing almost to the point of falling asleep would improve my steady state. Which it did. As far as I knew, he was either right or darn lucky. No matter which, my trust grew, so I paid close attention as he continued methodically building our team's plan. Because it was making us all faster.

As we continued to train, patiently, our speeds in every boat, on the rowing machines, and on our runs around the lake became faster. The time it took to complete assigned exercises in the gym went faster. When we raced two 8,000-meter pieces on the water in small boats, those went faster. And when we ran five miles of hills just one hour after those 8K pieces, those went faster too. Even with the cold New Jersey rain pouring down on us, slipping on the metal grates in the sidewalks, we were faster. Even more so because we were doing it together as a team.

The more fit we became, the more competitive we became, which naturally increased how much we respected one another. For our mutual respect, we stayed on rate when we rowed or erged even when no one was watching.[7] When we ran hills, passing was not allowed on the way down because it disrespected the work it took to get to the top. When it came to weight circuits, we raced them, smiling as our paces increased, me glaring up through my eyebrows as we all pushed through the fatigue that attempted to distract us from the task at hand.

We helped each other up when we fell in the woods and waited for everyone to be ready before we started training sessions. We invented erg-dancing to maintain a regular amount of lightheart-

---

7   To stay "on rate" is to maintain (and not exceed) an assigned stroke rate. Rowing at a higher stroke rate can provide a speed advantage, so staying accountable by being on rate minimizes variables when the aim is to compare efficiency between boats or between rowers.

edness, and we could not help but laugh whenever we got lost on adventure runs.

We even played practical jokes on the regular. Which is why, when Susan told me the US Anti-Doping Agency had showed up on our doorstep for me one Halloween night while I was upstairs putting on my costume, I did not believe her at first.[8] I laughed, thinking it was instead a genius costume. Only, once I saw two real doping control agents standing on our front porch did I realize she was serious. They were simply doing their routine checks that night, which, of course, we passed with flying colors.

Our training was hard enough, so we learned to revel in its more ridiculous elements. They raised our morale by injecting positive energy into something that could have easily been mistaken for emotionless and mind-numbing. Which made everything we did together all the more effective. It was through our combined effort and mutual respect that Tom's training plan became more than just a plan. More than just ideas on a piece of paper. Through everything we embraced together, we were making it real. And growing even closer as a team in the process.

Someone asked Tom in an interview once how he selects the team. As usual, his answer was simple and completely serious. "I don't," he told the interviewer. "They do. If someone enters this training center and finds it isn't for them, they leave. This team self-selects."

I cannot help but wonder if Tom broke his deadpan retort with some sarcasm about natural selection too. Selection at the hands of our own clumsiness. He sometimes joked that it made his job easier. Though I daresay "easy" is not a word anyone would use to describe any of the decisions he has to make.

When the amount of training you do every day expands the

---

8   An antidoping agency conducts periodic, random drug tests on athletes. Doping control agents collect the actual samples that are then tested in a lab for performance-enhancing strategies or substances. The aim is to maintain fairness within sport.

way ours did, from one to three hours of physical training to five or six hours (not including travel to and from, setup, breakdown, physical therapy, meal prep, sleep, and whatever else we each did when we were apart), you become increasingly tired. But since you have bills to pay, you still manage to work whenever you can because that is your only option.

Imagine coming home after your third training session of the day, one or two trips to the office peppered throughout, then mustering what is left of your energy to make dinner. Immediately after that, you crash into bed to get as much rest as possible because you know you are going to need it to tackle whatever the next day brings. Probably something even more tiring than what you just did.

Every now and again, even on days like these, friends do knock on your door to convince you to go down the street to karaoke night. Sometimes after you have turned off the lights and are in bed for the evening. And even though you know you should stay in bed, you go once in a while, because periodic distractions can be good. But then you go home early because you know you have the rest of your life to sing karaoke and only a small window to become gradually great at this one thing on your way to becoming your absolute best.

Following another holiday break filled with erging in my parents' kitchen, then another cold January of erging in New Jersey, we were delighted (and relieved) to be back out at ARCO by February first. Rather than for ten days like the two trips we took the year before though, this ARCO trip would last two months. Two whole months of nothing but rowing, running, lifting, resting, and repeating…

The week after we arrived at ARCO, our coaches called a team meeting. This time with video. And though this meeting was separate from practice, we still planned to meet down at the boathouse.

When we arrived at the boathouse, Tom and Laurel were already in the back of the erg bay with the TV set up. Once everyone was accounted for and had a place to sit, Tom explained that we were there to watch. Just watch and not comment. Only think. He then explained what we were there to watch. Two races. That was it. The women's eight and pair races from the 2004 Olympic Games. Both races won by Romania.

That is what Romania did. Not only was it their habit to go to the Olympics, it was their habit to *win* them. That had been their pattern for several Games in a row, and when it came to 2004, they won the pair by a large margin, then turned around and won the eight too. It was a historic and as yet unmatched feat in women's rowing to have won as they did.

After showing us the races, Tom continued by telling us that if we wanted to win gold at the Olympics, we had to believe we could. Not just think about it nor think we might want it, but to "see it clearly in our own minds." The medal around our necks. The small details of how that would feel. Because, as Tom said, once we saw it clearly, we would be even more willing (and eventually more able) to face the challenges such a pursuit would require.

"Preparation is confidence," he said. "You must learn to control what you can control and ignore what you can't control...Because when it comes to the Olympics, you have to be fast enough to win to even medal."

After what had happened in Japan the year before, Tom knew that we needed to continue building our confidence in our ability to succeed. He knew that the more we prepared, the more confident we would become. But in order to maximize either, he knew we first had to believe. As it was, once we started believing in what was possible for us, our ability to prepare would grow, and with it the kind of confidence we would need to win.

As I listened, I trusted Tom's explanation and believed that we really did need to keep preparing one step at a time. If we did that, we could move one step closer to becoming what we aspired to be—World or even Olympic Champions.

February 8, 2006,

Man am I excited. I can't wait. I am a bit scared though. I just need to focus on getting better! I can only control myself and my progress, while encouraging that of others. The point is to make the US Team as fast as possible. Oh man. Tired. Bed for now since I could think about that forever.

The Olympics...I think about it every day.

When I left our meeting, I could not have been more energized to keep taking steps toward what my teammates and I aspired to become. Through Tom's words of both wisdom and confidence, I had discovered a new level of focus. But rather than pressing forward as I endeavored to do, I had a small hiccup.

Four days after our inspirational meeting with Tom and Laurel, I was rowing circles in a pair with Anna M. (one of the 2004 Olympic silver medal veterans) when I felt something move oddly in my left shoulder. At the time, I did not think much of it, stopped only for a moment, shook it out, then carried on rowing circles while listening to Tom's coaching advice. Anna and I finished our row as usual after that.

Later that afternoon when I set off for a row in the single, whatever had moved oddly in my shoulder changed.

I had just launched in my single for a short afternoon row out on Otay Lake. The warm Southern California sun shone down on the nearly flat, calm water. Near perfect conditions. However, rather than enjoying a calm, technical row that afternoon, I only made it through the first fifteen minutes of practice before I knew something had gone irreparably wrong when my shoulder moved oddly earlier in the day. As my discomfort grew, I made the decision despite my reservations of disappointing Tom, Laurel, and my teammates, to turn and chicken-wing my single back to the dock.

As I approached the dock, I reached out a hand to stop myself as my boat glided in for a landing. But when I reached out, I could not put pressure on my dockside arm. As a result, my boat bumped the dock as it glided a little farther than it would have otherwise. Once my boat finally came to a stop, rather than planting a hand to help myself up and out of my tiny, unstable single, I instead rolled onto my belly as carefully as I could. It was all uncertainty and questions from there.

Did I break something or is it just a strain? Will it go away on its own? Why did this happen and why now? When can I row again? Not one of which could I know the answer to as I lie facedown on the dock awaiting assistance from Tom or Laurel.

When I awoke the next day with my arm still not right, Tom told me to cross-train for three days. After that, we would reassess. I had never cross-trained for an injury issue before. It was a foreign concept, so I had nothing to go on but Tom's advice. Which I trusted, so I cross-trained. For the next three days, I biked on my own and ran alone, but because my shoulder only limited my rowing, I was able to lift weights with my teammates.

Three days later, I reassessed by going for a short row with Anna G., who had been training full time ever since our return from Japan. Because she and I had gone fast during final pair selection the previous summer, we had rowed together quite often ever since. So "reassessing" with her made sense.

Miraculously, my shoulder, though not perfect, was getting better, and in just three days. To play it safe, rather than rowing with Anna a second time later that afternoon and risking a setback, Tom instead rambled off instructions for a run he said I could do while the rest of the team rowed. He did not tell me the run distance nor how long it should take. He simply told me to head up the road, then onto a trail, then down a hill. Then take a path at a fork. Then another path at another fork. Then another one. And another one...

"Oh, and Shoop, when you get to the bottom, be sure to grab a rock. If you encounter a mountain lion, make yourself as tall as possible. Throw the rock if you need to." Other than that, he told me not to worry because no one had seen mountain lions for years.

When I got to the bottom of the first hill, I grabbed two rocks—big ones—just in case, then ran along with a heightened awareness of every tiny noise. Although the rocks were heavy, I felt more comfortable with them, so I kept them with me for the entire run.

After forty-five minutes of continuous running through the Southern California hills (alone), I headed for high ground to get a look at how much of my run remained. When I reached the next peak, I realized I must have made a wrong turn. I was significantly farther from the boathouse than I expected. It was getting dark, so I picked up my pace.

When I finally made it back, Tom asked me where the heck I had been. As I told him turn-by-turn, fork-by-fork, I knew by the look on his face that I had gotten lost. I left my giant rocks in the locker room for the remainder of the training camp for good measure. My teammates laughed and were shocked at the same time. Because we all knew it was funny but also a little dangerous.

Two days after my rock run, my shoulder was feeling better, and I was back on the erg. Within two weeks, I set PRs on two out of three erg tests we took over four days' time. The fact that I could not only erg but also PR on back-to-back full-pressure erg tests reassured me that my shoulder was back in action.

When it comes to injury, the issue is not so much the injury itself, but more the uncertainty that it brings. *How long will this last?* The longer it lasts, the more severe your thoughts grow: *Will this last forever?* I was lucky. My injury hiccup lasted all of six days. Six days that I managed by taking Tom's (yet again) simple advice and focusing on what I could do one day, one step at a time rather than fixating on the uncertainty of it all. Controlling what I could control kept me from wasting energy on worrying about future what-ifs. Though easier said than done, it truly is a productive way to progress in the face of uncertainty. Particularly, as summer racing drew near again.

March 3, 2006,

It's a matter of strokes and guts. Believe it and want it. Know it. See it. Feel it. Keep working and improving. It is there!

As summer approached, and our fitness, technique, and times improved, all signs pointed toward the fact that we were getting faster. But since we rarely got to test our speed apart from practice, there was no way for us to know for sure without a race.

So, at the end of May, Tom gathered six of us (me, plus five of my teammates) and told us that we would be heading to Germany to race a World Cup. It would be our first speed gauge since Japan. A checkpoint to be sure we were making progress in the right direction.

As far as international races are concerned, the Olympics is at the top, followed by the World Championships, then come what are called World Cups. Because three Rowing World Cups occur every year, barring any unforeseen hitches, they serve as stepping-stones that ramp up toward that year's one World Championships (or Olympics if it is an Olympic year).

As far as the racing itself, World Cups run similarly to Worlds and the Olympics in that they apply the same heat, quarterfinal, rep, semifinal, and final race progression. However, World Cups are unique in that they allow a single country to have more than one entry in a specific event. So rather than just one pair or one double, like at Worlds or the Olympics, a country may enter multiple pairs or doubles (or any other boat for that matter) at a World Cup.

That is exactly what Tom planned for us. Rather than heading off to Germany that May to race an eight, we traveled overseas to test our speed in small boats—two pairs and one double from our training-center group.

When I awoke sitting vertically in my airplane seat at the end of our overnight flight to Munich, I could not wait for a shower and a clean bed. It was our first trip with such a small group, so I was excited by the prospect of a solid night's sleep to adjust to the six-hour time change as quickly as possible and to get out on the water. But when we landed, I learned my rest would have to wait. Rather than rest, we headed straight for the racecourse to find the equipment we had rented for racing, rig it, then go for a short row.

Two days and five short rows in the pair with Anna G. later, and racing started. Due to the number of entries in the pair, Anna and I knew we would have to race at least a heat, a quarterfinal, then a semifinal before finding out which final we would ultimately race. But because of our finishes in Japan, we knew not to get ahead of ourselves, so we took it one race at a time.

Although Anna and I had fared well together in the past, having made it to final pair selection the summer before, we had improved in fits and starts ever since. On some days, we would go from learning to feeling like we were terrible. On other days, we would go from improving to losing by ten to fifteen seconds during 2K race pieces. On all days, we compromised some, matched some, argued some, spent some time going fast, and also spent time going…not so fast. But as luck had it, in the days leading up to racing there in Munich, Anna and I had figured something out and so were showing signs of steady improvement.

Through our first day of racing, our improvement continued. By placing second in our heat, then third in our quarterfinal, we officially moved two more steps along the path toward possibly making the A-Final. Given how "under control" our effort had been through our first two races, our second- and third-place finishes reassured us that we were making progress in the right direction.

Immediately following our quarterfinal race that afternoon, I proudly changed out of my USA uniform and into my sweatpants and sweatshirt. Because we had to wait for the rest of our team-mates to finish their races, I figured I should get comfortable and off my feet to start my recovery since we would have to race again the very next morning. Once I changed, I gathered my things, then found a decent spot to rest by one of the boathouses. With a wall to lean against, I could easily watch racing while staying off my feet.

While I waited and watched, and the afternoon wore on, the wind gradually picked up, and a thick layer of clouds rolled in. Clear signs that the weather was taking a turn for the worse. With the longer I sat and watched—both racing and the clouds—my whole body began to ache. My face grew warmer, and although I was wrapped in my sweatshirt and pants, I wished I had more layers. Without any, I buried myself under my and my teammates' backpacks, hoping to block the wind. Still, I felt chilly, so I sank a little lower into my spot against the wall.

I began to wonder if I had pushed myself harder during our races than I realized. That our races were not as "under control" as Anna and I thought. Still, I sat, waited, and watched.

After we made it back to our hotel, I showered, then headed down the street with my teammates to dinner. By then, I knew something was wrong. As we moseyed down the street to a local restaurant, I fell behind my teammates' pace. Even at a walk, I needed to stop and rest. That was when I told everyone else to go on without me. I would meet them there. As my pace slackened, my face felt warmer while my body felt colder. Something. Was definitely. Wrong.

By the time I made it to the restaurant, my teammates were gathered at a long table in a giant back room the owners had set aside just for us. The room itself was large. The table was large. Our group, not so large. The menu, not so diverse. Mostly salty German food, none of which sounded appealing, considering how I felt. I simply sat there staring at the menu, feeling progressively worse.

Finally, because I knew some food was better than none, I opted for the simplest meal and the closest thing to a ginger ale that I saw: spinach pasta, no sauce, and a sparkling lemonade. When my drink arrived ahead of my meal, I took one sip of it. That was all it took. As soon as the glass bottle touched my lips, my stomach turned, chills ran up the back of my neck, and my mouth watered. I thought I was going to be sick, so I immediately put down the bottle, then spent the rest of that night's team dinner focused on holding myself together. I did not want to alarm anyone.

After my meal arrived, I did not touch it. I instead sat quietly and patiently awaited the end of what felt like the longest postrace meal of my life. When the time came for us to head back to our hotel, I took my sparkling lemonade with me but left the pasta.

As soon as I made it back to the room Anna and I shared, I was freezing, so I cranked up the heat as high as it would go, then turned the shower to its hottest setting. My plan? Stand in the shower to break my chill, then dive into bed and bury myself under my blankets.

Before I dragged myself into the shower, I unscrewed the cap to my soda, then chugged it as fast as I could. Within moments, I was on the bathroom floor sicker than I had ever been in my entire life. Chills. Fever. Body aches. You name it. Apparently, something I ate earlier that day was not right, and it chose to let me know it by wreaking havoc on my entire system. Of course something like that had to happen right as Anna and I were finally making steady progress together in the pair.

I cannot tell you how long I was on the bathroom floor before Anna found me. When she did, she convinced me to crawl to bed. Our next race was less than twenty-four hours away. I had to rest.

Anna only endured our sauna of a room that night by opening the window next to her bed, while I lie shivering, bundled like a burrito under extra blankets just a few feet away from her. The next morning, my fever broke, so we raced.

Within the first twenty-five strokes of our third race of that Munich World Cup, though we were matching well and moving well, I simply ran out of energy. I had eaten *nothing* in a day. And because I could not even drink water without being sick, my body gave out. As you might imagine, unlike the previous day, our result was not exactly a confidence boost.

Yet another day later, though I had held down nothing in nearly three days, Anna and I raced a fourth and final time in the B-Final— the final that would decide places seven through twelve. Despite what must have been some sort of food poisoning that prevented me from eating and drinking for three straight days, Anna and I managed to place eleventh out of twenty-five boats. To this day, I wonder how things would have gone had I not been sick as a dog. Our teammates in the other USA pair took fifth, while our double took eighth.

Though not one of our boats earned the results we had hoped for based on the improvements we had been making, it was where we stood at the time. Like the previous year's Worlds, it was a learning experience. One that taught me to be even more careful about what I ate when we traveled. One that taught me that no matter how prepared you think you are, surprises still arise. And one that helped us gauge our progress outside of New Jersey. It was just a World Cup and not Worlds.

The 2006 World Championships was still two and half months away. Which meant we still had two and a half months to prepare. To control what we could while ignoring the rest. As long as we kept learning and taking steps forward together despite whatever surprises or challenges arose, two and a half months would be plenty of time to earn more speed.

TWENTY-FOUR

WE NEEDED A TEST.

WE SPENT THE ENTIRE MONTH OF JUNE WORKING TO improve upon our World Cup results. If anything, our stumbles back in Munich drove us all the more. I reassessed my standards for how far I could push myself. I reassessed and found an even greater desire to become better. And given my unexpected bout with food poisoning, I even reassessed my eating habits and recovery methods. All of which pushed forward my ability to perform—when we rowed small boats, when we did race pieces at least twice a week, and when we worked our way through seat racing and toward final selection for the 2006 Worlds team.

With every step we took to improve upon our World Cup performance, Tom began assembling an eight from the cream that rose through it. An eight that included our three small boats from Munich, plus Caryn (a 2004 Olympic silver medal veteran), Caroline (my 2005 pair partner), and Mary (our veteran coxswain).

From the very first time we rowed together, the nine of us felt something special. Something that seemed better than the year before. Something focused, locked, and powerful, almost shark-like every time we left the dock. It was an eight I felt incredibly fortunate to be part of.

We had just one problem though. Because we rarely rowed the eight in practice and had never raced it with this new lineup, we had yet to truly test our speed in it. We may have felt like we were improving, but for those of us who had raced small boats in Munich, we knew that feeling faster and being faster were two very different situations. No matter how different we may have felt, that was all it could be. *A feeling.* We needed a test.

Our first test came in the form of a midsummer trip to the Henley Royal Regatta in England. The Henley Royal is undoubtedly among the most renowned regattas of all time. Nearly two hundred years old and one of the most anticipated events of the summer over in England, the Henley Royal is the rowing equivalent of Wimbledon.

Because the event is open to more than just national teams, we knew before we headed overseas that we might race teams who were likely slower than us. However, we also knew that we would, at the very least, race two national teams who had entered the event too: the British and the Dutch.

On July second, when we finished our experience at the Henley Royal Regatta by setting every course record there on the River Thames, beating both the British and Dutch national teams by large margins along the way, we began to consider that our new lineup's speed was more than just a feeling. It was a promising performance, considering that less than two months remained before Worlds.

Straight from the Henley, we traveled to Lucerne, Switzerland, to race another World Cup. This time though, we raced in a slightly different lineup in the eight than the one we had raced at the Henley. Even with the change, we took second in the eight in Lucerne. Taking second was again a promising performance.

Because of our results overseas and the fact that it was nearly mid-July when we returned home, Tom made his decision about who would get to race in the eight at Worlds—our lineup from the Henley Royal. From that day forward, the nine of us had exactly one month more of training to find more speed before we headed back to England for the 2006 World Championships (my second ever).

On August eleventh, following our one month more of rowing small boats and occasionally the eight, we flew to London for the main event of the year—the World Championships. When we landed there at Heathrow Airport, then made our way by bus to Eton, England, our confidence was as high as I had ever felt it. All on account of everything we had done just to get there. Our practices. Our extra races raced. The steps we had taken because we kept learning, took nothing for granted, and controlled the controllables to the best of our ability. Because of every small detail that drove us toward becoming our best, we were undoubtedly more prepared, which had helped us become undoubtedly more confident. So when I say that our 2006 eight felt like a shark every time we left the dock, I mean a literal shark. Complete with *Jaws* theme. That is how laser-focused and unified we were.

Sharklike focus during a practice row in the eight. (Image courtesy of Row2K, Row2K.com)

Ten days after our arrival in Eton, racing started.

When the nine of us met with Tom by our eight in advance of warming up for our heat, we could tell that the race was going to be an even greater challenge. A challenge already because we were a new and young lineup that had only ever raced together once before. An even greater challenge given the turbulent conditions on the racecourse that day. It was no typhoon, but the racecourse was awash with wind and waves.

Since we could not do anything about the conditions, we embraced the heightened challenge and returned our focus to what the nine of us could do—aim to find a hair more speed during our forty-five-minute warm up. Which we did.

A little under an hour after we launched for our heat, we crossed the finish line in just over six minutes. A time that turned out to be the fastest of all the women's eights that raced through the heats—all twelve of them. Still, we took nothing for granted because our margin of victory was only a narrow two-tenths of a second, a matter of feet, faster than the time posted by Australia—the team that had won the eight in Japan the year before.

Winning our heat to advance directly to the A-Final was new for six out of the nine of us in our boat. It was a big deal. Definitely a step forward from where we had been the year before. It meant that instead of having to race through a rep (as we had in Japan), we would have six days to rest, recover, practice, and find a little more speed before racing the final.

Racing to test our gradually growing confidence. (Image courtesy of Row2K, Row2K.com)

When I had sat at the start in Japan, I had only raced internationally one time. But by this 2006 Worlds, I had raced on the world's stage five times. So, as I collected myself at the start line of *this* A-Final, I more confidently focused on nothing but the veteran Anna M.'s back and our coxswain Mary's words…I was more ready than ever to give everything I had to help my team take another step forward.

Almost as immediately as I heard the announcer's start command, we were nearly five hundred meters into the race. The wind was howling. Waves were crashing. Splashing was inevitable. But to our advantage, it was a wind that pushed us along rather than slowed us. As long as we stayed technically composed through those most horrendous of conditions, it was all but certain that this A-Final would be the fastest I had ever raced.

The first five hundred meters were gone in just 1:25.59. A blistering pace that, if we maintained it, would have us across the finish line in a speed far faster than any women had ever gone. We all knew better than to take such a lead for granted though, so we kept pushing as if our lives depended on it.

In another five hundred meters, when we crossed over the midpoint of the race, I could feel my top lip beginning to stick to my front teeth. I grimaced with every stroke we took and push I gave...Our effort was working. We were still ahead. Now by nearly sixty feet. Almost the entire length of our boat.

Through the third quarter, the third five hundred (meters) of the race, notoriously the toughest portion, Germany began to push into our lead one stroke at a time, one inch at a time. When Mary saw them, she urged us for more. Which we gave.

As we closed in on the final 250 meters of the race, despite Germany's push, we were still in the lead. We had been there before. Just one year earlier, we led the pack with 250 meters (less than sixty seconds) to go, when not one, not two, but three boats passed us. So with 250 meters to go, when Mary urged us for more, we found more to give and dug in to what we had earned through every step of our preparation together.

As the waves crashed and the wind blew all the fiercer, we surged all the faster toward the finish line. One. One. One. One stroke at a time. Until there were no strokes left to take.

In our final few strokes, Mary called for *more* yet again. My vision hazed over. My lips peeled back from my gums. My ears pulled rearward as my head dipped in the boat. I had nothing left. This time, not on account of food poisoning but because of the effort I poured out onto the racecourse in search of the best we could possibly be.

Because of the speed that Mary, Caryn, Caroline, Susan, Anna M., Anna G., Brett, Megan, and I created together that day, we not only crossed the line before every other boat, but we covered those two thousand meters faster than any other women in history had ever rowed them—5:55.5.

On that late August, bluish-grey, and incredibly windy day in Eton, England, the nine of us became World Champions together, in world-record time, through some of the worst racing conditions I had seen or would ever see. Challenge accepted. Challenge achieved. Another step taken.

Celebrating together on the medals dock. (Image courtesy of Row2K, Row2K.com)

By winning and being surprised for the better on my second trip to Worlds, we moved, in theory, one step closer to the Olympics. Worlds was only a stepping-stone. A gauge to see how we were progressing toward the big show. Our glance toward the peak that was the Olympics. Although we were well ahead of the pack when we crossed that 2006 finish line, we had to keep learning. Because, in rowing, you can never be far enough ahead.

So back to New Jersey was the plan. Back to our routine. Back to our unified pursuit. The one we were gradually stepping toward by setting new standards, then exceeding them. Repeatedly. Back to believing in what we could become together and back to taking not a single one of our steps toward that for granted. For as long as we prepared and kept learning, the uncertainty we could all but count on might surprise us for the better. Again.

Before we would take yet another step by meeting back in New Jersey to resume our preparation, Tom sent us home for a month. It was the longest break of our two years of training together up until then. Tom knew things would ramp up again, so he gave us some much-needed physical (and mental) freedom. We had to recover if we wanted to keep stepping toward even greater challenges.

During the month I spent at home after the whirlwind that winning our first World Championships and breaking a world record was, I ran a four-mile road race. The run is an annual event held in my hometown. One still held to this day. Had you told me back when I was a freshman in college, back when I was slower at running than an elderly man walking, that I would one day voluntarily run a four-mile race, I would have cringed.

But I had taken many steps since then. So I chose to run the race because it would motivate me to stay on some sort of training pattern while I was away from New Jersey and my team. Plus, because I had run the race twice with my Virginia teammates back when I was in college, I was curious to see just how much more fit I had become since then.

On the morning of September 3, 2006, I stood amid a massive crowd of more than 1,500 women and eagerly anticipated the start of the Charlottesville Women's Four Miler. It was early but already hot. Tiny bugs were already sticking to my skin under the moist air that condensed on me in the form of sweat. I did not mind. It was the most prepared I had ever felt at the start of a running race.

Through my first two years of training in New Jersey with Tom, Laurel, and my teammates, I had vastly improved my ability to plan and set paces. So, when the pack took off, I gradually built my pace, patiently let dozens of other runners pass ahead of me and stuck to my plan. Despite being passed, I grew increasingly confident in my fitness. Then, when I began to overtake many of the early leaders before we reached even the first mile, my confidence grew a little more.

My gradual preparation over my first two years of full-time training (through both good and bad days) had built my fitness and my confidence, and it showed. By the time I crossed the finish line, I had covered that four-mile course in a speed more than two minutes faster than I had run it in college. I had my answer. I was not just more fit. I was far more fit. My run time was yet another piece of evidence that all of our preparation was paying off.

I had come a long way in just two short years. It was now the fall of 2006, and I had made two national teams. I had raced two World Championships and three World Cups and had already set a world record. Now, with two years of full-time training behind me, year three of preparation approached, and with it, our last World Championships before it would finally be the Olympic year.

When the end of my month away neared and I prepared to return to New Jersey, I anticipated a training routine complete with small boats and the occasional eight row. Plus running, weights, and erging. Perhaps the sporadic ride on the stationary bike and a training trip to ARCO. Jokes among friends and adventure runs, and likely even less time with our families. Not all that different from the past as far as training went, except for one thing—we had set a world record. Which meant we would be raising our standards yet again. Because like I said, you can never be far enough ahead.

TWENTY-FIVE

LEARN AND MOVE FORWARD.

AN ICE-SKATING RINK. THAT IS WHAT ANNA M. CALLED THE space in the boat just below where I was sitting. As she chuckled about it, I sat there shivering with my shoulders hunched to my ears concealing my neck. My clothes soaked through by our tumultuous row. My confidence frozen with every correction Tom threw my way. Everything hardened to ice by the time we returned to the dock.

Just one boat went out on the water that day. It was too windy and far too cold for small boats, so an eight was it. When we found out that just eight rowers and one coxswain were to go on the water, I imagine we all had the same thought.

It was a Saturday, which meant we knew we would be doing hard work. If you were in the eight that day, you would do race pieces on the water. If you were not, you would do pieces on the erg. Both situations were equally dreadful. But for as much as we all hated to be *that* cold, the eight was where we twenty or so athletes training with Tom knew we needed to be. It signified the upper portion of the team hierarchy, a chance to show your worth toward making the 2007 World Championships team. A particularly important team to make given that it was the last one before the 2008 Olympic year was finally at hand.

It might have seemed like a small thing—one row in the eight—but it was definitely not something to take for granted since every year, no matter how many times you may have been in any boat in the past, you have to remake the team. Every… single…year. For as much as I dreaded rowing through such bone-chilling conditions, it was exactly where I wanted to be because it was where I knew I needed to be.

On days like that Saturday, when you cannot fathom a more awful accumulation of conditions, when no amount of clothing is impermeable to the cold, no amount of confidence imperme-able to the corrections your coach makes, you discover just how dedicated you are to your pursuit. That is how training goes. Lots of soul-searching, freezing days. Plenty of ups and downs to keep you accountable and on your toes. As if Mother Nature herself again begs the question: "Are you certain this is what you want?" No matter how bone-chillingly cold it is, your answer is the same every time: *Yes.*

By March of 2007, following six more months of training and step-taking no matter the challenge, I managed to set two more personal records on erg tests. I was one of the few who did too. Apparently, it was a particularly tough segment of training that left everyone tired. Even so, I squeaked out some of the fastest speeds I had ever produced on the rowing machine.

But I had to keep taking steps. So shortly thereafter, I met with Tom to find out what I needed to do to put myself where I wanted to be—helping my teammates defend our World Championship title—and he told me a few simple things.

The first of which was, "Keep getting fit." I had just gone my fastest ever just four days prior to our meeting, and "fit" was his advice.

"You've stayed relatively injury free for almost three years now." Tom continued as he elaborated on his advice. "That's pretty good. That will help. Do that and keep figuring things out technically."

Even when you have been part of a World Champion, world-record-setting team, you still need to work to improve your technique. Because when you keep raising the bar, when your goal is to become the best you can possibly be, you must keep taking steps. Because you can never be far enough ahead.

Rather than walking away wilted from my meeting with Tom, I took his advice to heart. I kept chipping away at my fitness and technical improvements and sought more ways to take care of myself to remain injury-free. All of which would help me take more steps…

By May, when Anna G. and I were invited to race a pair in Austria along with two other pairs from our team, it seemed my patient persistence was paying off yet again. Considering that it takes four pairs of rowers to row an eight, my being among the three pairs chosen to represent our team, to check the progress we were making as a group, was a good sign that I was still headed in the right direction. It was also an important responsibility.

A few days before our small group left for Linz, Austria, to race our first World Cup of the 2007 summer season, Tom called a teamwide meeting. All twenty or so of us sat upstairs at the boathouse on the squeaky green pleather couches and listened as Tom laid out the summer's plan—everything that would happen from June fifth until early September (when Worlds would end). Once he had delivered us the basic plan, he emphasized that if we wanted to make the 2007 Worlds team, the month of June would be a critical time to perform. We would likely begin final selection then, and that is always a critical time.

Since the six of us going overseas would only return home from Austria on June fourth, though Tom did not specify it in our meeting that day, I figured our performance at the World Cup would also be critical.

Similar to the year before when we traveled to that food-poisoning-doomed World Cup in Germany, we landed in Austria following a night of vertical sleep in an airplane seat. From the airport, we headed straight for the racecourse to find the equipment we had rented, rig it, then row. Six practices and three days later, racing started.

With twenty-eight entries in the pair event, day one of racing began with six heats that were then pared down to four quarterfinals—three of which our three USA pairs won. In doing so, the six of us in our three pairs proved we had gained speed and improved upon the previous year. We knew better than to take our progress for granted though, so we headed to our hotel to rest, recover, and prepare for our next day of racing.

June 1, 2007,

Breathe. Visualize. Run. Stretch. Breathe. Stay Calm. Focus. Decide. Breathe.

By 10:30 the next morning, Anna G. and I were on a shuttle bus on our way to the racecourse. To further my race-day focus, I popped in my headphones and stared out the window while the bus meandered its way through the little town in the direction of the course. Though our 2,000-meter semifinal race was not until later that afternoon, Anna and I decided to leave early given the bus ride and how long we needed to warm up. Because we had been steadily improving in the pair again, we left nothing to chance, and so made our schedule and our plan down to the minute.

When we arrived at the racecourse, I found a spot inside the makeshift boathouse and made myself as comfortable as possible while I awaited our race. We were focused, and things seemed to finally be going our way. All that was left was to wait patiently, meet with Tom, grab our boat and oars, then shove from the dock to warm up for our semifinal. But when is the last time things went according to plan?

While Anna and I awaited our 3:15 p.m. race—me leaning back on my black mat inside the boathouse, headphones in, nothing but my race-day thoughts and songs running through my mind, Anna doing the same next to me—I thought I heard the faintest of rumblings in the distance. To better hear what was going on outside, I tugged my left earphone from my ear and let it rest on the side of my head.

"Was that…thunder?" As I looked at Anna, I heard it again. When I heard it for the second time, I was sure. *Thunder*.

Within a matter of minutes, Tom appeared in the doorway and made his way toward us. Tom, and the skies that grew blacker by the minute, confirmed it.

"Racing is temporarily delayed," he said, almost jokingly. Apparently, he too had come to find the humor in just how infrequently things seemed to go as planned for us. "Wait here, but be ready to move quickly should it come to that."

When the unexpected happens, as it usually does, my first thought goes to my hydration and food. *Should I eat something? Will it be hours or minutes? When?* Now with my nearly three years' experience at the national team level, I knew that all I could do was patiently manage the things within my control. We could not control the weather. We could not control the race officials' decisions. All we could do was wait and be ready.

As the minutes ticked by and the start time for our race neared, the race officials had technically not yet changed the race schedule. In fact, rather than pausing the entire race program, they opted to skip races instead. While we awaited updates, the time we had set to meet with Tom for our prerace meeting passed. Then, as the minutes continued to tick by, I began to wonder if our race might be skipped too. Fifteen minutes later, the time Anna and I had set to shove from the dock passed.

Then, when less than thirty minutes remained before our race start time, despite the faint rumblings of thunder that remained, and the dark clouds that hovered, racing resumed! When it did, the race organizers did not shift the schedule. They instead resumed on the original race schedule with plans to run the skipped races later in the day.

Because of this decision, rather than shoving at our customary fifty-five minutes before our race to methodically run through our to-the-minute planned forty-five-minute warm-up, Anna and I were left with just twenty-five minutes. Twenty-five minutes to gather our equipment, shove, warm up, and make it to the start line before our semifinal took off without us.

Tom was not joking when he told us to "be ready for anything." Anna and I knew better than to take him lightly, so we hustled.

On our way to the start, we streamlined everything by cutting straight to only the most imperative of warm-up elements. Because we did, we made it. Barely.

As we sat at the start line awaiting the announcer's start call, the sky loomed dark overhead. Thunder still rumbled faintly. The water…Dead. Flat. Calm. The green leaves of the trees that surrounded the racecourse reflected darkly upon the surface of the lake. Not a sound other than the low grumble of the storm and our breathing. My hands trembled. My mind was a tornado of adrenaline.

I opened my eyes wide, took a breath, stared at Anna's back, and attempted to relax my face. Then, when the start command buzzed from the loudspeakers and over the racecourse, we took off…a bit more jittery than normal because of our rushed warm-up. Top three was our aim. If we placed among the top three in our semifinal, we would make the A-Final and prove we had gained even more speed.

Anna and I focused one stroke at a time and pushed with all our might, while simultaneously seeking some semblance of calm, rhythm, and flow—a little more challenging than usual given our rush to the start line that day.

By the time we crossed into the final five hundred meters, the last quarter of the race, we were in a solid third-place position. Nearly a full boat length, almost thirty feet ahead of the Australian pair behind us. It was a decent place to be with less than two minutes to go…

With the finish line fast approaching, the Australian pair that trailed us began reeling us in, inching closer, one stroke at a time. With every inch they pushed, what rhythm Anna and I once had unraveled, which caused our boat to bobble from side to side then swerve within our lane. No longer flowing perfectly straight, we lost ground, basically handing the Australians an extra inch for every inch that they took on their own. As they continued to gain on us, we poured more effort in one last attempt to hold them off. Without matching each other perfectly though, our effort was less effective than it would have otherwise been. It came down to the final ten strokes.

After being solidly among the top three, poised for the A-Final for more than two hundred strokes, the Australian pair overtook us just before the line. Two whole tenths of a second was their margin. All of two-tenths of a second separated us from racing in the A-Final with our other two team USA pairs. Devastated does not begin to describe the way I felt as we crossed the finish line.

As our boat drifted past the finish, my mouth watered. It tasted of tarnished silver and warm drool. I was on the verge of throwing up. My teeth throbbed with every beat of my maximal heart rate. My feet felt as if they might explode from within my shoes. I could not sit still on my seat for the ache in my legs. My throat and chest burned as my lungs attempted to recover something that even remotely resembled normal breathing. My eyes, a little blurry.

For as excruciating as my self-inflicted anguish was, it paled in comparison to how severely I felt I had failed Anna. I was fairly certain both she and Tom would be angry.

It was a nightmare. When that Australian pair applied the pressure and began to cut into the lead we had on them, Anna and I questioned ourselves. Right when we needed to focus most, we fell apart.

That night, as I digested what happened in our semifinal race, I thought for sure that my hope to make the 2007 Worlds team was dashed. Passed in the closing strokes of any race, crumbling under pressure is the last thing you want on your conscience or your record. Which meant that Anna and I had one option: learn and move forward.

June 2, 2007,

Worst chip for the summer. Nightmare. Breathe it off. We didn't approach it well enough. Never think you are far enough ahead. You must go while you can. We technically fell apart when we needed to focus and lock and push. If I were stronger maybe it would have been fine…Learn and move on. But never forget.

By the time we closed out that Austria World Cup, our other two USA pairs came away with silver and bronze medals. As for Anna G. and me, because we adjusted our race plan to directly address our biggest areas of weakness, we were able to win our B-Final on flat, calm, glassy water in a most convincing way.

When Anna and I met with Tom after our B-Final race, he told us that "we annihilated the competition at a thirty." He almost laughed as he said it. We had won the B-Final by open water to take seventh place out of twenty-eight pairs, but we had done it at a rate of just thirty strokes per minute—a low rate for racing and a significant turnaround from our previous race. Based on Tom's comment, it seemed as though Anna and I had redeemed ourselves, which rekindled my hope for making the 2007 World Championships team.

Later that afternoon, I met with Tom in the lobby of our hotel to discuss what I needed to focus on as we moved into final selection for the 2007 team. As we sat across from one another at the small, square table, I realized it was the first time in my now nearly three years of training with him that the two of us actually sat for a one-on-one meeting. As usual though, I had no idea what he might say.

"Shoop," he began. "You seem like a disciplined athlete…" He went on to explain how I did everything he asked of me and how I embraced even the smallest details if I thought they could help me improve in some way. He then reminded me that the rest of June would be critical for selection, and he gave me a few small pieces of advice to help me through it.

He told me to keep gaining fitness, to keep working on my technique, and to do everything within my control to continue taking care of myself. But for all the advice Tom gave me that day, his tone sounded different, which gave me a strange sense. He had been my coach for going on three years, so I thought we had come to know one another. But in that moment as we sat across from one another at a small table in a hotel lobby in Austria, his comments felt like those of a stranger. All I could figure as we headed home for final selection was that I actually was on thin ice. I had to find more if I wanted to make the team again.

The morning after we returned from Austria, I woke up, took my resting heart rate, and went for a jog with Mary, who now lived with Susan and me in our little white duplex. Later that afternoon, following a postjog nap, the whole team met for practice and got right back to rowing. With final selection for the 2007 team upon us, those of us who had just flown home from Austria did not take a rest day.

Through what remained of June, I focused on what Tom had

told me. *Get fit. Figure things out technically. Be diligent and disciplined.* When I was assigned to row nearly every type of boat imaginable, including the single, pair, four, and eight during that time, I did so with the simple focus of taking the best strokes I possibly could. On every stroke, I aimed to make each one a little better than the previous.

In July, it was hot. The kind of hot that turned Lake Carnegie into a veritable cesspool of mosquitoes and stagnant, scummy water. The kind of hot that makes you feel sick to the point of nausea. Even so, we rowed, and I had no choice but to keep taking things one stroke at a time. Until seat racing for final selection arrived, which I also took one stroke at a time.

July 3, 2007,

Open your eyes and breathe. Right mind. More. One. Yes. Keep a positive mind and confidence.

It was August by the time Tom told us who made the 2007 team. When he did, I learned that my improvements since Austria were enough to earn me a seat in the eight again. Along with nearly every one of my teammates who had been in the boat the year before when we set the world record. With just one exception, one small addition to the team: Sam. Sam was by no means new. She was the same Sam who had won Olympic silver in 2004. The same Sam from our 2005 eight. After taking some time off following the 2005 Worlds, she finally returned to full-time training and made the eight again in 2007. With her experience back in the boat, we stood to make more progress as Worlds approached.

At 1:30 p.m. on the afternoon of August seventeenth, all of two weeks after we learned we made the eight, Mary, Caryn, Caroline, Susan, Anna M., Anna G., Brett, Sam, and I boarded a bus to head to the airport. But rather than bound for Worlds in Munich, Germany, along with the entire US team, the nine of us (plus Tom) flew as a small group instead. Traveling as a small group like we did would give us an extra day on the Munich racecourse—to focus and prepare to defend our world championship title at the 2007 World Championships. The main event of the year. The last World Championships before the Olympic year was finally at hand.

TWENTY-SIX

NEVER FAR ENOUGH AHEAD.

WHEN YOU CHALLENGE YOURSELF DAY IN AND DAY OUT TO ceaselessly find a little more than what you had the day before (or even the stroke before), you must keep things simple. If you do not, you allow that tiny person in your head who constantly attempts to plant doubt get the best of you. Which is exactly what happened as my third World Championships approached, and things did not feel quite right.

In the final weeks leading up to our departure, our rhythm felt forced. When we rowed the eight, rather than laser sharp and focused, we fixated on imperfection. For whatever reason, whether it was our relative inexperience, individual pride, or insecurities, we lost sight of the many strokes that were going right for us. Instead, we allowed the strokes that did not go right to dictate how we felt about ourselves as a team, and that planted tiny seeds of doubt. Seeds that made us question whether our win and our world record the year before were less about skill and more about luck.

Couple our two unpredictably inconsistent weeks of practice rows with the fact that our actual flight to Munich for Worlds was met with anything but predictability, it seemed as if the odds were stacking against us as we prepared to defend our world title.

When our eight plus Tom departed New Jersey for Munich, we looked forward to the additional focus of traveling as a small group. Especially, given our struggles over our previous two weeks of practice. However, when a flight delay out of Newark led to two subsequent missed flights in London, and being stranded for twelve-hours in the Heathrow Airport, only to finally arrive at our Munich hotel nearly a day later than expected, it felt as if fate did not want us to succeed in defending our world record and title.

Two years of training had turned us into World Champions and world record holders in the women's eight. But considering that many of our competitors had boats filled with veteran athletes who had spent years (sometimes decades) winning, we had not won all that much in the grand scheme of things. So when we finally hit the water for our first row on the racecourse at the World Championships in Munich that year, rather than feeling like a shark and full of confidence when we left the dock as we had the year before, we instead felt awkward, heavy, short, and unbalanced. With race day nearly upon us, our youthful insecurities led to anger, frustration, and doubt. Which further exposed our immaturity.

When we rowed, we questioned every bobble. We fixated on what was different than the year before when we had felt so confident. We searched for some specific reason to explain what was happening to us when, in fact, we should have focused on what we could do about it. At the time, what we really needed was a kick in the butt. Something to force us to stand up to the heightened challenge. Though we had shown speed once, our immaturity demanded more evidence.

Throughout nine more days of unstable and confusing practice rows there on the Munich racecourse, we tried everything. We tinkered with our technique, our lineup, our specific focus. Until the night before our heat arrived and no time to tinker remained. The nine of us gathered with Tom and Laurel in the small common area midway down the hall of our hotel floor. We sat quietly as Tom prepared to review the plan for our heat. For lack of a better phrase, you could cut our nervous tension with a knife. And our coaches knew it.

Before he spoke, Tom deliberately rounded our circle of nine with his eyes. He knew we were overthinking everything, so in order to quiet our doubts, he leveraged our respect for him to convince us otherwise.

"Keep it simple," he said. "Go out there and row well. Row better than you have so far. You are more than capable."

August 27, 2007,

One stroke at a time! One. Breathe. More.

The next day, rather than things working out as we would have hoped, we lost our heat. After all, there is a big difference between being told you are capable of something and believing you are capable of something. Immediately following our heat, we gathered in a dejected circle around Tom. He again read our thoughts by the looks on our faces. Some angry. Some sad. All frustrated and confused. So again he rounded our group of nine with his eyes.

"Look." He said in a stern tone. "Trust makes the boat go. It is something you earn. You are not given it." He paused, perhaps in reflection of the previous night's meeting. "And you cannot fake it."

We all stood silently, some faces still mad, some still sad, others now flat. Whichever we were, we all absorbed his words. I cannot be certain of what my teammates reflected upon in that moment, but I am certain of what I did. Because Anna G. and I had proven back in Austria that we were capable of improvement (and redemption) in a very short time, I believed that we as an eight could do so too.

Thoughts of everything we went through to get that far whizzed through my mind. The snow, the cold and cracked hands, the heat, the delirium, the blisters, the meters, the timed runs, the doubts, and subsequent recoveries. Our daily preparation and our will to do more. Our transformation from one devastating 2005 Worlds to become the fastest in the world. And we had only continued stepping forward since then. Yet there we were, letting one race, a matter of minutes, dictate our confidence.

The next time we rowed, our only option was to find more. Because I trusted that we had trained for more and I knew how fast my teammates were, I knew we had more.

August 29, 2007,

Breathe, sleep, and get through it.

A day and a half were all we had before our next race. But within its three practice rows, it proved enough. We took another step forward and won our rep to advance to the A-Final for our third World Championships in a row. Luckily, we had four more days before we would race again. Four days to practice. Four days to gain speed. Four days to diminish the doubts, anger, and confusion that still loomed.

On the day of the A-Final, Tom's words were intentionally stern during our prerace meeting. Just moments before we hoisted our eight to our shoulders to walk toward the dock to shove for the A-Final, Tom did not metaphorically hold our hands. Instead, he challenged us once more.

"Eight of you are the same. Screw rowing well. Go assert your will."

Tom's words could not have been better timed. They were the swift kick in the butt that we needed. They abruptly struck a chord and ignited something in us *as a team*. Instantly, all nine of our faces changed as if we found an entirely new level of confidence and will right then and there. A level that revealed an as yet undiscovered strength and speed in us as an eight.

In the days surrounding racing, we were each individually concerned with adjustments and focus. Our minds simultaneously attentive, while also unintentionally scattered. But when Tom told us to assert our will that day, he convinced us of something he had only suggested in the past. That when we truly believed in our capabilities and clearly saw what we wanted, we could make it real. To assert our will meant taking possibility and making it happen. Together.

When the bow of our eight crossed the finish line of the A-Final, spit flew from my mouth, my heart pounded in my chest, and I did not know what happened. It was not like the year before when we had won by a large margin of nearly sixty feet. Instead, the margin was close. Too close. Only once I saw Caroline's dad on shore yelling and waving his incredibly long arms did I know. An instant after I saw him wave, our verified race time popped up on the giant neon screen behind him.

United States of America, 6:17.20. Romania, 6:18.33. Great Britain, 6:19.66. Then Australia, Germany, Canada. The top five all within 2.7 seconds of one another. Like I said. *Too close.*

We asserted our will and learned something. But given how our race unfolded, I knew that even with how far we had come, there was still so much I could not yet know. So much we still needed to gain before the Games. The year before, we had beaten the Romanian eight by nearly thirteen seconds. But on September 2, 2007, they closed their margin to just 1.13 seconds. A disconcerting gap with less than one year until the Olympics.

What we knew was that Romania was a team that went to the Olympic Games and won. They had been winning longer than I even knew rowing was a sport. They were one of those teams whose boats were filled with veterans who had been winning for decades. And with a trajectory like the one they had just shown, everything we knew about them was holding completely true.

With the Olympics drawing nearer, it was likely that more Romanian veterans would return from retirement. Which meant they would likely pick up even more speed by the time the 2008 Beijing Olympics arrived. So even though my boatmates and I were now two-time defending World Champions and world-record holders, we needed to keep finding more. More speed. More confidence. More will. We had to keep pushing forward because—with less than one year left before the peak, the big show, the Olympics—we knew we could never be far enough ahead.

Another thing I knew? Without a doubt, by the end of our second consecutive win at Worlds, I wanted to be in the women's eight and win *the* gold medal at the 2008 Olympics. On the very night of our second World Championship win, I wrote a letter to Tom telling him just that. Maybe one day, I will give it to him. *Maybe.*

September 2, 2007,

Keep my "what it's all worth" perspective to guide my choices each day. I shall do a little each day to be better...Stay focused. Don't forget the drive and preparation. Hydrate, sleep, fuel well, get organized, rest, stretch, physical therapy, core. Breathe in the sunrises and sunsets. Exhale the weight of my mind. One day at a time.

Bearing down on the finish line at the World Championships. (Image courtesy of Row2K, Row2K.com)

World Champions once more. (Image courtesy of Row2K, Row2K.com)

TWENTY-SEVEN

THE BEAUTY OF THE TEAM.

ON SEPTEMBER 25, 2007, JUST OVER THREE WEEKS AFTER winning back-to-back World Championships, my teammates and I raced a three-mile run test, then met with Tom to discuss our travel and training plan for the year. Nothing like a run test and a meeting for your twenty-sixth birthday.

In our meeting, we found out that we were to row in Oklahoma for a week, have a week of on-your-own training for Thanksgiving, two weeks for Christmas, then spend the rest of December and well into March out in California at ARCO—a much longer training trip than in years past. This meant I would be at ARCO for early December. With my parents again in Virginia for Christmas. Then two weeks later, I would be back at ARCO just after the New Year.

Two weeks sounded like a lot of on-your-own training time for our last holiday break before the 2008 Olympic year. But for each of the previous three years I had spent training with Tom, he always had a plan. A plan that worked. So I trusted him.

Being that it was my third straight year to visit them in December, my parents were used to me training in their kitchen. They were used to watching holiday movies with the volume up extra high to drown out my noisy erg. But because our training had expanded each year, I made a tad more noise around the house than they were used to this time. Three days into my visit, my parents kindly requested I find somewhere else to erg.

From then on, rather than training in the kitchen within sight of the television to watch a movie with my mom while I erged, I spent the first five to seven hours of my day alone at the University of Virginia boathouse.

Each day, just after the sun broke into silhouette over the tree-tops that surrounded my parents' farm, then shone in through my old bedroom window, I would change into my erging clothes, pull on my sweats over top, brush my teeth, then head downstairs and peek out the kitchen window to see how much frost might have accumulated on my car's windshield overnight. When the frost was thickest, my dad would start my car and crank its heat before I even made it downstairs. A small but much-appreciated gesture.

Those few minutes awaiting that thaw gave my dad and me time to linger and chat a few extra minutes in the kitchen. With my mom still in bed, those cold winter mornings in the kitchen were one of the rare occasions we spent time together as the two of us. Not just over that two-week holiday, but since my move to New Jersey altogether. Once my windshield cleared, I would hug my dad, tell him I missed him, then head on my way.

The boathouse was a thirty-minute drive each way. Rarely was another car in the lot when I arrived on those mornings. To keep my day moving, I would head straight upstairs and set up an erg in the middle of the room, plop my bag next to it, set up my water bottles and iPod, then set up my erg's tiny monitor for whatever workout Tom assigned on our printed training calendars. I would then sit, take a deep breath, relax, and get to work.

Sometimes the morning's first eighty-minute session passed quickly. As quickly as one stroke at a time for nearly a half-marathon's distance can. Other times, it seemed to drag on as I wondered what my parents or brother or cousins or grandmother or friends were doing without me while I trained for hours on end. Alone in the cold boathouse. At whatever pace the meters ticked, I ended every one of my morning erg sessions with a sense of accomplishment because I had a purpose.

Following my first eighty minutes, rather than changing and heading home to resume my conversation with my dad, I typically took a forty-five-minute break to change into a dry set of erging clothes, then pulled my sweats on over top again, hood up this time to protect my sopping wet (from sweat) hair from the morning chill.

On the occasions when I deemed it warm enough, I would grab my snack and water, then take a solitary stroll around the boathouse property's perimeter. I would then explore the boat bays to see what might have changed in the three and half years since I had been a college rower there at Virginia. To further pass the time when I was supposed to rest between training sessions, I lingered on the seemingly insignificant details of the boathouse space. A space I had all to myself on those mornings.

Not a soul in sight. Silent. Just the delicate scraping of leaves—the ones that caught the draft that crept in through the tiny crack below the garage door—across the polished cement floor of the boathouse. The very same polished floor where I sat those years earlier when Kevin's goals sheet encouraged me to dream of going to the Olympics.

On one particular December morning, as I lingered in the very boathouse where I learned to row, I smiled to myself, thinking of all I had gained through rowing. And when I saw the *We're Gonna Do This* sign that Kevin made during my senior spring (the year we lost every race, then came back to place fifth in the nation), I grinned about who I was then and appreciated the path the Virginia team had put me on. Apparently, a path toward voluntarily and happily spending my Christmas holiday alone in that very boathouse as part of my pursuit to become the best I could possibly be.

Following my snack and stroll down memory lane, with my hair still sweat-soaked from training session one, I resumed my place on the erg for another eighty minutes.

The sign as it hangs today.

On most days, I could erg an entire marathon before lunch. I never skipped anything Tom told us because I knew I had to keep taking steps. And as always, with my directive over break being to "get fit," I had to do everything, plus more.

Sweat-soaked and with a sense of accomplishment for a second time, I changed clothes…a second time, ate another snack, then drove the thirty minutes back to my parents' house. After that, a shower, a real meal, then my ritual nap next to my mom on the couch. One that usually lasted two hours. Sometimes four.

Imagine. On New Years' Eve, your "easy" day, you have the option between one hundred minutes of cross-training or eighteen kilometers on the erg, nearly a half marathon. Then, following whichever you choose, you lift weights for ninety minutes. Then, because you have spent three years focused on one thing, wholeheartedly dedicated to one thing, chipping away at becoming your best at one thing, rather than having some social plan to ring in the New Year, you celebrate it by sitting on the erg at your parents' house for another 10K later that afternoon. After that, you spend whatever is left of your day resting, hydrating, and stretching, then crawl into bed long before midnight. All because, despite everything you have done so far, you know that your greatest challenges have yet to come and that you can never be far enough ahead.

As that two-week holiday break neared its end, I knew that final Olympic team selection was just five months away. So that was my New Year's Eve. When I awoke the next morning, it was officially 2008. The Olympic year.

By January 3, 2008, we were back at ARCO and back in pairs. Rather than the two-week or two-month trips of years past, this time, our trip would be nearly three months. Three and a half months if you included those two weeks back in December.

Because of the trip's extra length, we were assigned new roommates every two weeks. Our coaches made a habit of rotating us like that to keep everyone on the safe side of stir-crazy. You never know what tiny squabbles can happen when people share tiny boats and tiny rooms for months on end. Compound that with a high-pressure situation like Olympic selection, and it feels like the most intense game of musical chairs that you will ever play. Particularly, since there are fewer chairs but more (and better) people every year.

Our roommate-switching pattern did not bother me much while we were there at ARCO. In fact, I did not realize our coaches had any sort of underlying reason for making us move like that until several room switches in. I tended to get along with most anyone, and the switches allowed me to get to know my teammates better. Our pair-partner-switching pattern, on the other hand, warranted far more of my attention.

Because of the way selection still worked, we continued to rotate pair partners. Sometimes every few months. Usually every few weeks. Every now and again, every few days. No matter when we switched pair partners though, it was typically not someone arbitrary, as was the case with our roommates.

As for my pair partners specifically, with every switch we made, it began to seem as though they were among the youngest of the group. Or someone who had recently joined us. Or someone who had been injured or training with the scullers instead of with us sweepers. In many cases, she had yet to be part of the eight. She had yet to race an Olympic class event of any kind. But most importantly, she had yet to climb into the top end of the team on any of the race pieces we still did every week, twice a week. So when that very thing happened with just five months left before final Olympic team selection, I felt like I was starting over, right when I thought I was making progress.

It had been more than three years, and with just five months to go until final selection, I had to figure things out yet again with someone new.

Erin and I stared at each other from opposite ends of our boat and said very little. We each then grabbed our respective end, then rolled the boat over so we could adjust our shoes. We had been training together for a couple of years, and we were great friends. Yet somehow, Erin and I had not spent much time together in a pair. She had raced in the four in the past at Worlds but had yet to make the eight and was injured more often than she would have liked.

It was our first day back on the water out at ARCO at the dawn of the Olympic year and following our two-week holiday break. An incredibly exciting time. Yet all I thought as I stared at Erin was, *All this time and this could be it.* I had managed to take steps for three and half years. But that was the past. I still had to find more. I had to find a way to keep taking steps no matter how far I may have come…I had not made the Olympic team yet.

Erin and I carried our pair down to the water in silence. As we did, I stared at her braided, dirty-blonde ponytail and thought of how well we had gotten along, how good of friends we had been for the two years we had known each other. Most of all, I hoped we would continue to be friends through rowing together. Because when you are stuck in a space as small as a pair, whenever things go well in the boat, things tend to go well out of the boat. Whereas, if things go…not so well, you may as well forget whatever friendship you had. At least for as long as you are paired together.

When we shoved from the dock, our plan was simple. *Breathe. One stroke at a time.* Then, on each consecutive stroke, see if we can do it a little better. Blades in together. Lock on together. Push hard without hesitation. Together. I did not want to lose one of my best friends. I did not want to lose period. It was the Olympic year.

From our first stroke off the dock, we clicked. Somehow. We clicked. Erin was a few inches shorter than me. She had not made an Olympic class event yet. But she was incredibly determined to also find her best. So, from the time we took our first stroke, barely a row passed that I did not gain confidence in the speed we were creating together.

Follow, I thought. *Follow and push more. Keep it simple.* Erin had discovered something, and when we came together, the boat went fast. From there forward, much like the first time I rowed with Molly (who had retired two years earlier) all those years before, I knew to do whatever it was that Erin did. And so, it was with every push that my trust in Erin grew.

Following one of our first sets of race pieces together, Tom did not post our results right away. So rather than waiting around the musty ARCO boat bay for him to post them, a group of us headed to the dining hall to grab breakfast instead. Shortly after Erin and I found seats with our teammates at the end of one of the long folding tables in the dining hall, sandwiched between the cafeteria line and the drink machines, Tom and Laurel walked our way.

They did not speak at first but just hovered there holding their trays, staring as if they might say something, then reconsidered. Then their heads cocked slightly to the side. By their looks, I wondered if we had done something wrong.

"Good job today?" Tom simultaneously stated and questioned as he looked at Erin and me.

After that, he and Laurel walked away in silence. Erin and I looked at one other through semirestrained grins. His comment said enough.

When we saw the results later than morning, we discovered that we had won nearly every race piece by open-water margins. It was the first time in a while I had won that many race pieces in a row. It was the first time Erin had won many at all.

A few days later, Tom stopped me after our midmorning weightlifting session. I was alone when he did because weights tended to take me longer than the rest of my teammates. Yet another of his ongoing directives for me: get stronger.

Being among the last inside the giant white temporary tent of a weight room, Tom approached me as I was changing out of my borrowed lifting shoes and back into my tennis shoes. My shirt drenched in sweat, my hands still trembling from the heft of that morning's weights session.

"Shoop," he said as he leaned on the weight machine next to him. "It seems like you've learned something, and I think you can help your teammate Elle."

I did feel I was learning by rowing with Erin. More than ever. So, without hesitation, I agreed, "I do think Erin and I have discovered something, so if you think I can help Elle, I'm up for it."

Elle was all of twenty years old and had taken the year off from her college team to train with us. She had been a spare, our fill-in, during the 2007 World Championships but had not officially been in a senior team boat yet. As such, she had never raced internationally at the highest level. She was incredibly strong on the erg, but she was new and so had a lot to learn about technique.

For the majority of the next two months following Tom's request of me, Elle and I rowed a pair together. She was so young, so strong, so full of potential. And though she had not had the best of luck during her first four months of training with us— having been at the bottom whenever we did race pieces—Tom saw something in her, and he thought I could help her gain speed like Erin and I had.

On our first day in the pair together, Elle and I did not expect everything at once. But we did expect some sort of improvement. For that to happen, frustration was not an option. We had to focus on what was right in front of us. One stroke at a time. If we let frustration win, we knew we never would. So, drill after drill, Elle and I made small adjustments to our technique and tried everything Tom and Laurel suggested. Sometimes it worked.

Sometimes it did not. In both cases, we kept adjusting in search of our best. Our more.

January 8, 2008,

Things to remember: Control what you can. Ignore what you can't. Positive, patient self-talk. Convince your body of what your mind can see. See the goal. Put myself there. See it. Visualize it.

In the pair, you are never farther than a few feet from your partner. Sometimes for one hundred or more minutes on end. So much volume that the only way to make it through an entire row without running out of energy is to have a snack during one of your short two-minute breaks that you get to take only every twenty-five minutes. When you go for that long in that small of a space, frustration can easily arise, and the snack helps. Not just with the energy for the rowing itself but with the negative thoughts that might pop in when improvements are not coming easily.

Elle always reminded me to bring my snack. Because she cared like that. She also knew it was one small thing that could help us get along, trust each other, and find more speed.

January 31, 2008,

Fight for it. Keep my head up and stay positive. Tomorrow is a new day. Deal with the good and bad.

By this point, as January neared its end, I was used to being among the top three if not winning. Erin and I had consistently been at the top just before Elle and I were paired together. Meanwhile, prior to our time rowing together, Elle would finish last. Sometimes by as much thirty seconds. So, for as much as I would like to say that Elle and I eventually won, we never did. We did, however, significantly improve our speed. Through our persistence, Elle went from being behind to occasionally the top three while rowing with me. After which, she, the youngest among us, reshaped my perspective. Again.

"Shoopie!" Elle blurted as we tapped the boat along rowing a top-quarter drill.

The water was dead flat. The blue sky above and greenish-brown mountains that surround Otay Lake reflected on its mirrorlike surface. Our pair was perfectly set. Our blades were locked on in unison. Though rowing with Elle was more challenging than rowing with Erin, we were locked onto the water, matching each other's every move. Because we were the only ones down at the far end of the lake, it was nearly silent except the sounds the blades of our oars made as they dropped into the pristine water. Five top-quarter strokes later, Elle and I paused to let the boat slow down.

We stopped for a moment, then Elle turned her head toward me to finish her exclamation in a direct and serious tone. "Shoopie, you taught me to row."

Through the calm, focused, silence we had all to ourselves at the end of the lake that day, her words cut straight to my heart. In that moment, it felt as if we were the only two people in all of Southern California, if not the world.

When we stopped after the next twenty-five-minute segment of our row that day, I smiled, sipped my water, and took a bite of my snack while a teardrop welled in the corner of my right eye. Elle's words made me realize that all the adjusting, the intuiting, the teamwork, the ups and downs over each of my years were no longer teaching just me. It was all helping her too. To Elle, I was doing for her what Dirks had done for me those years before.

Dirks had chosen to retire following the 2007 World Championships. It was her decision, and one she did not make lightly. In a big way, what I was able to do for Elle, Dirks had made possible. Although she was no longer training with us, I carried with me everything I had learned while rowing with her, which enabled me to share her knowledge with others. And though I still felt new, I guess that meant I was becoming a veteran.

Elle and I sat there at the end of the lake an extra minute and talked about how much we loved rowing. I told her that I wanted to row for as long as possible because it built me up every day. I told her that I could not imagine my life without it. It was showing me that I could become the best version of me a little more each day. Which made it nothing short of the opportunity of a lifetime.

"I want to do this for as long as possible too, Shoopie. And I hope we get to do it together for a really long time."

Her words made me want to cry. She had no idea just how much she was teaching me. Elle was twenty. I was twenty-six. I wanted nothing more than for what she said that day and what we both wanted to come true. As I thought about what our future could bring, I sat ready, then we started our last twenty-five-minute segment of practice. Together. Smiling. The warm Southern California sun beaming down on Otay Lake as if Mother Nature too was smiling.

By the end of those nearly three months out at ARCO, I was faster. From Erin, I had learned quickness and agility. From Elle, true strength and raw power. From both of them, true joy in working to become our best.

March 16, 2008,

No matter how hard or quick you feel you are pushing, you can always push more. The Olympics will be harder than that. Be smart. These are obstacles and tests...one day at a time. Confidence.

A women's pair training on Otay Lake. (Image courtesy of Anna Mickelson Cummins)

When we returned to New Jersey at the end of March, Erin was the first person I got to row with. And though we had not rowed together in over two months, we did some more winning. After Erin, I spent a little more time with Elle. After that, as had become my pattern, came another new partner by mid-April. This time, she was someone who had been injured, who had been training with the sculling group, who was young, and who had taken a year off from her college team to train with us. She was also another partner who had yet to make the eight. Again, the only option: find a way.

The first day Esther and I rowed together in our pair, in truth, was terrible. Hardly anything went right. For a stroke or two here and there, we would match perfectly, then out of nowhere, the boat would go crazy. Tipping left to right. Crashing to one side for a few strokes, then balanced for a moment, then crashing to the other side. For every minute of our first hour-long row together, I simply could not make enough adjustments to figure anything out. Which made me excruciatingly aware of each minute of that row and of every word Tom spoke. Every suggestion he made.

By the end of our first sixty minutes in the pair together, I felt like a complete failure. Like I let Esther down. Like I had forgotten how to row altogether and was back to square one. A complete novice. And for the first time in years, I felt tears of sadness welling up before we made it back to the dock. But being several years into training, I was a little more mature, and so I did not rush to Susan's car sobbing. I spoke with Tom instead.

His words calmed me. He reminded me that we had more strokes to take before we raced that year's NSR2 together. The USRowing selection event that could potentially identify the first two spots on the Olympic team. The event I first raced with Dirks back in 2005 and had raced every year since. The event made immensely more important because it was the Olympic year, and just two months remained before final Olympic team selection.

Before I spiraled further into thoughts of how Esther and I could possibly successfully race the NSR2 based on our first row, Tom reminded me that it was practice. That we would go home and come back the next day. But with the NSR2 in just nine days, and since it was one of the most important races of the entire Olympic cycle, it was hard not to worry. At least a little. The fact was, Esther and I had all of nine days to figure it out.

The second day Esther and I spent in the pair, Tom followed us. He coached us until I felt as though everything I had spent the previous three years learning was completely different. Until it felt better again. By the end of our second sixty-minute row together, Esther and I docked, debriefed, then left.

A week and a half of practice, adjusting, and staying positive later, and Esther and I were as ready as we could be to race the NSR2.

April 21, 2008,

Stay strong, positive, and confident. Remember: you have done this a lot.

The first day of racing was conducted time trial style, each boat racing in single file rather than side by side with other boats. Against the clock, so to speak. For that reason, there would be a delay in our knowing how we performed. Only once we hit the dock would we know how we compared to the other boats. That benefitted Esther and me because it provided us time to think about what went well and what we could improve before our next race. A technical reflection made more valid without the bias of our result to impact how we felt about our performance.

For our first time down the 2K racecourse together, we were pretty pleased. So we cooled down and used that time to keep practicing. After that, we made our way to the dock, then figured we would check the results after we washed and put away our equipment.

When we approached the dock, I turned my attention to landing and reached out my arm to stop us. As I did, I was confused to hear someone congratulate us. By the time I looked up to see who it was, he was gone. At first, I thought maybe he felt bad for us or thought I was someone else, so I did not think much of it as I unstrapped my feet from within my shoes and prepared to get up and out of our pair. Then, as Esther and I carried our boat toward the boathouse, we were congratulated a second time. Then again a few steps later.

With three consecutive "Nice jobs," I could not help but wonder, *They couldn't all be confused. Could they?* In disbelief, Esther and I washed our boat and tried not to get our hopes up. *This has to be a mistake*, I thought as I walked over to the board where the results were posted.

I could not believe what I saw. Second. In just nine days of unrelenting positive focus, Esther and I had put ourselves in the hunt. A stark improvement from nine days earlier, when I felt I had failed her…

When we raced the final, Esther's youthful exuberance stoked a flame of aggression, possibility, and strength that had us surge toward the finish line a matter of feet and a close third behind Susan and Anna G. Though it would have been nice to place higher, I was far from disappointed. It was the most incredibly powerful closing 250 meters I had ever raced in a pair.

I could not believe how much we had learned and accomplished in such a short time. And even though Esther and I could have earned the privilege of racing a World Cup in Munich had we gone just two seconds faster, it was not what was best for us. Practice was what we needed more. I was excited to keep learning with someone as strong and willing as her. If nine days could take us that far, I could only imagine what we could do with a month. I knew we had more speed in us.

Therein lies the beauty of the team. Every partner sharing with and teaching me along the way. From some, physical. Others, technical. And still others, emotional. Separately, we were each the best at our thing, a specialist in our own rights. But together, our collective commitment and talents enabled us to far exceed what we could have ever been alone.

The next day, Monday, it poured down rain. The perfect day to take completely off following the NSR2. By Tuesday afternoon, we were back in the eight where I, for the first time in as far as I could remember, sat in five-seat. A seat typically reserved for one of the most powerful rowers in the boat.

TWENTY-EIGHT

DON'T TELL ME.

IF YOU COULD KNOW ONE THING ABOUT YOUR FUTURE, would you want to know it? If so, what would it be? One of my Virginia Rowing teammates asked me that back when I was in college. Initially, it sounds like a great idea. *Wouldn't it be amazing to see into my own future?* But then, if you think about it, if you knew so much as one thing, you would inadvertently behave in a way that would end up preventing it from happening at all. Even if that one thing you could see in your future was great. I know. Because me not knowing my future, is what made it happen.

Six weeks remained. Six weeks were all we had left before the final decision. Three and half years with barely a day off. Tired for three and half years. Living on a shoestring for three and half years. "No, I won't be able to make it home for your birthday." "No, I won't be able to be in your wedding." "No, I won't make it for your son's baptism." And "No, I just can't come home early for Christmas this year." Three and a half years focused on one thing, and now, a month and half would determine whether or not what we had done was enough.

In the last six weeks before the official naming date, where we would know if we had made the Olympic team or not, a small group left for a training camp in Breisach, Germany. Because of its remote location and foreign language barrier, the trip would provide an additional layer of isolation, which would only encourage even more focus. And focus was critical as the Olympics neared and tensions rose. Tensions surrounding who would make the team and also the pressure to perform at the highest level yet.

When I was asked to be part of the Breisach group, it meant I had a chance at making the team.

For the duration of the two-week trip, we were set to live in a hotel and train on a portion of the Rhine River. From Germany, we were to head directly to Lucerne, Switzerland, to race another World Cup. My sixth at that point, its timing would be our most accurate speed gauge yet, given that it would be just two months before the actual Olympic Games began.

During my time in rowing, I had become good at making myself at home in foreign places. I learned through experience that rooms can be closet-sized, beds can be hard, and pillows like cereal boxes. Air-conditioning was a luxury, and smokeless buildings were not the standard worldwide. So even if our accommodations ended up being comfortable, I arrived prepared for anything and willing to adapt.

I discovered I could hand-wash laundry and hang it to dry in the windowsill and was thankful Caroline introduced me to the wonder of earplugs early on in our training together. She slept best with the white noise of a fan and put herself to bed with earplugs and an eye mask even if it was dead silent and pitch black in the middle of nowhere in Germany. The earplugs were a kind gesture so I too could sleep through her fan.

To this day, I am thankful she shared those earplugs with me. As it turned out, a lot of our teammates talked in their sleep. How do I know? When you train with the US National Rowing Team, there are no sponsorships, no commercials, no big corporations to pay for your training, so everything is penny-pinched to the max. You have at least one to three roommates every time you travel for racing or training. So when the teammate in the next bed over shoots bolt upright in the middle of the night and asks you a grammatically correct, well-thought-out question in a full sentence (in her sleep), you realize that earplugs are well worth the investment.

Sleep was critical. I could sleep all night, sometimes eleven hours, and still take naps. Upward of two to three hours at a time. Though they were the kind of naps that made my room-mates think something was wrong with me, I now realize that my ability to sleep like that was a gift. Another thing that kept me healthy.

Two weeks of nothing but training in focused isolation in Breisach later, we left for the World Cup in Lucerne where a hostel became home.

Four weeks until final selection...

Seeing as how that trip to Lucerne was my sixth World Cup, you might think I had some idea of how things might go on this sixth time around. But if anything had held true by that, my fourth summer of rowing with Tom and Laurel as my coaches, it is that expecting the unexpected is an understatement. The number of times someone got hurt or sick or requested a personal day that set into motion a ripple effect of unforeseen lineup changes proved that. Oddly enough, it also usually created an opportunity to find more speed.

"Shoop, I need to talk to you." Tom pulled me aside when we arrived in Switzerland.

Hm, I thought, then I gradually spiraled out wondering what our impromptu meeting could mean. Esther and I had placed third at the NSR2 just two weeks before our Breisach trip. Was it possible that I had rowed so poorly during our two weeks there that I had forgotten all of the progress she and I made? Whatever his reason, being pulled aside and isolated from the team four weeks before the official Olympic team naming date was disconcerting, to say the least.

When you are being considered for a team boat like an eight, one that involves the team, being separated from the team is not where you want to find yourself four weeks before selection.

"You are not going to be part of selection here," Tom stated plainly as he and I stood by the edge of the Lucerne racecourse and a good distance away from the rest of the team. "There are some things I need to sort out first that you are just not part of."

Although I sensed trust in his voice, because my mind lingered on the "not going to be part of selection" portion of his statement, I did not process everything he said, so I did not fully understand what he meant.

Instead of doing race pieces in fours with the majority of my teammates, Tom told me I was to row a double with my 2007 boatmate and fellow starboard, Sam. His plan meant that she and I were to spend our first three practices in Lucerne sculling rather than sweeping with everyone else. Sam had an Olympic silver medal, was more than ten seconds (a significant amount) faster than me on the erg, and we rowed the same side of the boat. So it was not inconceivable that Tom was comparing us somehow.

A fleeting thought flashed through my mind: *Is he priming her to row in the eight instead of me from here forward?*

Imagine being partnered with someone you are in direct competition with. Someone who potentially stands between you and what you want most. But in order to get to where you want to be, you must not compete against one another. You must compete *with* one another. You must help each other go as fast as possible. That was our double for our first three rows in Lucerne.

Before my thoughts of what Tom had said to me spiraled further, I took a step back, breathed, and calmed myself. *Control what I can. Ignore what I can't.* This was not about Sam. This was not about me. This was about making the US team as fast as possible.

From the very first stroke Sam and I took together, I focused on making each one the best I had ever taken in my entire life. The most perfectly matched to Sam as possible. My fate in that double may have been uncertain, but that also made it an opportunity.

May 25, 2008,

Focus on what I can do every day. Make every stroke count. Every opportunity. Stay patient. Work together. Lots of speed to be had.

Sam and I landed back at the dock in our double long after the rest of the team was done racing in fours. Because we were the last of our US boats on the water, we quickly put our equipment away, then Sam and I went our separate ways. As I walked alone in the direction of the boathouse, Susan approached me with a wide grin on her face.

"Dude, Shoop. When you and Sam rowed by while the rest of us were meeting with Tom after our row, he told us to stop what we were doing and watch. He used you as an example and told us to do what you were doing. He pointed and said, 'Watch Shoop. Do that.'"

Apart from being my teammate, Susan was my roommate and friend, so I trusted her. I grinned internally as I took in what she shared with me—that Tom had suggested to everyone that I was doing something right when it came to rowing the boat. And not just right. So right that he used me as an example for everyone else to mimic.

Susan's words reassured me. Rather than being given the heave-ho, maybe something was going right for me at the best possible time.

With every stroke of the thirty-two kilometers that Sam and I rowed over the course of our three practices in the double together, I thought of nothing but taking it one stroke at a time and paying attention to Sam. I followed her every move and poured every ounce of my being into every small detail over every single stroke. It may have been disconcerting because it meant I was separated from the larger team, but being in that double was exactly what I needed there in Lucerne.

We had rowed an eight or fours during our two weeks in Germany. So the opportunity to be back in a small boat, though sculling, allowed me to slow everything down so I could fully focus on my own technique. Which made the impact of every technical or effort-related adjustment clearer—the distinction between good and bad strokes obvious. Out in our double, it was just Sam and me. The two of us, quietly rowing, and nothing more. And apparently, Tom noticed the steps I was taking in the right direction.

After three practices in the double with Sam, I was back in the eight and preparing to race the World Cup. This time in two-seat. A seat typically reserved for the smaller, more technically minded athletes. After all, by the time we prepared to race there in Lucerne, I was one of the smaller starboards among us. So it made sense that I sat two-seat, part of the bow pair.

Sitting ready at the start line for what could have been (for all I knew then) the last time I would get to wear my USA uniform, I stared at Erin's back, glared up through my eyebrows, breathed, relaxed my hands, and cleared my mind to nothing but two words: *Yes, more.*

Yes, more, was all I thought from our very first stroke together that day. I was testing my simplest, most powerful thoughts yet to see if something so simple as *yes* could be my key to unleashing more effort and more drive from within than I had ever found before.

For the first forty-five seconds of the race, my thoughts were powerful, my effort almost easy as I glared through my eyebrows, breathed, and pushed harder with every stroke I took. After those first forty-five seconds, my mind went nearly blank, and my body took over.

As we approached the first 500-meter mark, the first quarter of the race, we were a blur of six boats from six different countries, all nearly neck and neck. No one rolling over. No one giving up an inch. It seemed as though no one would break. But my job was not to worry about what was happening in the lanes next to us. My job was, *Yes, more.* To relax while also pushing harder than I ever had in my entire life. My entire purpose boiled down to just two words: *Yes. More.*

I raced the entire 2K, taking it one stroke at a time and thinking just two words: *Yes.* One stroke. *More.* One stroke. My mind blank otherwise. My ears ringing. Spit flying from my mouth as my cheeks relaxed at every exhale. My shoulders and arms as relaxed as possible so my legs could stay in charge. All the while, watching Erin's back. Which, with every stroke, every ounce of effort, became fuzzy as my vision further blurred and my ears rang on.

When you race side by side (six boats across the racecourse, each in its own lane as if it is a giant swimming pool) and not one of your opponents dies off nor cracks under the pressure of such a close race, there comes a moment in every stroke when doubt could creep in to make you question whether you—as you endure the excruciating torment of your sustained effort—will make it to the other end intact. On that day though, from where I sat behind Erin—the pair partner with whom I had found a new level of speed just months before—my confidence in our ability grew with every push she and I made together. So not one iota of doubt crept in.

I had Erin's back. She had mine. Along with our seven other teammates there in that eight, we all had each other's backs, and we were not about to let any one of the other five teams in the race make us question who we were. We did not need to be two hundred strokes tougher than our opponents that day, only one stroke tougher.

In the closing five hundred meters of the race, Canada and Australia pushed into our lead. But once we as an eight sensed the finish line, it was all but over. Our coxswain, Mary, urged us for more. Which, for all our preparation, we had. More spit flew. My heart pounded as if it wanted to leap from my throat. I pushed my legs with all that remained. Then, in a matter of strokes, amid a fury of six coxswains urging all six crews for more, all forty-eight pairs of legs and forty-eight oars among the six eights bearing down on that finish line, the bow of our eight surged across first. Not more than six feet ahead of Australia, who took second.

Yes, more, proved to be another step for me. Those two simple words left no room for doubt. Instead, they helped me control what I could so I could ignore the rest, which ensured that I let nothing anyone else did get to me.

June 1, 2008,

Commit to the plan. Say yes. In my head. Every stroke. "Yes. More." Stay positive. Believe the whole way. No matter what.

Winning that World Cup, maintaining control as the world applied pressure, was a healthy confidence boost. But of course, a World Cup was just an audition. Final selection was still ahead.

Two days later, I was back on the erg in New Jersey. The day after that, back in the pair with Esther.

Twenty-two days until final selection…

With the Olympic team yet to be named, we all prepared as if we were already competing in the Olympic Games in China. Beijing was supposed to be hot and humid with the thickest air imaginable. So, when a three-day heat wave hit New Jersey, we intentionally rowed during the hottest parts of the day to gain experience in conditions as similar as possible to those predicted for Beijing.

The first day we practiced in that heat, for forty-five minutes, I could not close my mouth. I could not even pant. As my tongue tucked against my bottom lip, my mouth hung open, dryly gasping for whatever oxygen it could find. My eyelids periodically squinted to squeeze out the pearls of sweat that diabolically snuck in at their corners and stung my eyes on every third stroke I took. Meanwhile, my brain begged for water. Twice, I made a futile wish for a third arm so I could row, drink water, and wipe the salty burn from my eyes. With only two arms, my only option was to row.

By the time we docked, my face had all but melted, as if I had overstayed my time in an excessively arid sauna. I was sick to my stomach for the third day in a row. When I stood, one foot on the dock, one still in the boat, my head spun a little. I momentarily closed my eyes, while I attempted to convince my mouth to accept the last swig of hot water from my bottle. As it dribbled down the back of my throat, it tasted as if I was drinking the overheated lake water itself. It was better than nothing.

Seven days until final selection...

One decisive week of race pieces for final selection would be our last opportunities to make the Olympic team. After that, our coaches would have everything they needed to finalize their decisions. Decisions they had been weighing over the past few years would come down to a few final days.

Of the thirty or so athletes who had rotated through the training center over my now almost four years there, we were down to the remaining twelve. Twelve highly competitive, highly trained, highly focused women vying for just eight spots. Eight spots that would be sorted out over the final seven days of Olympic selection.

During those days, we raced every other day, then finished with two race days in a row.

Day one dawned with intense winds blowing in all directions as if Mother Nature herself sensed our nervous energy. A tension finally released on day one through multiple 1,000-meter pieces in fours with various lineup changes. Changes that yielded a heightened nervous uncertainty for the simple fact that time to improve, and also to prove ourselves, was running out.

When it comes to final selection, no matter how far you have come, no matter how long you have been in any position on the team, you cannot take a single stroke for granted. You must breathe and continue taking steps to become better every chance you get. Even if just a hair better, because every moment is pure uncertainty. Every stroke an opportunity for anyone in any boat to have an aha moment and suddenly get faster. To find a new level of speed. To prove her worth just in time for the culmination—the peak you have patiently, gradually taken steps toward with only periodic course-correcting glances to the top.

On days two and three, the final twelve of us were split among an eight and a four to race three 1,500-meter pieces. Races just shy of the full Olympic race distance for the sake of our physical ability to manage that many all-out race pieces in such a short time.

On day four, when I found myself on the erg for two of the pieces while nearly everyone else was on the water, what else could I do but keep pushing forward. I could not do anything about what was happening out on the water and in the boat without me. Only what was right in front of me. My only thoughts, *Confident. Tough.*

Day five: 1,250-meter pieces. Three of them.

Day six: 1,250s again. Two of them.

Over the course of those final days, every time we finished a piece, we had no indication of what might be next. *Would racing continue, or is this the last piece? If not the last, what race distance is next? Is it my turn yet? When will I be switched? I know my turn is coming. It has to be. If not me, whose turn is it, and who will she switch with?*

When your turn to switch finally comes, as your nerves surge, you step up and out of one boat and into the next to swap places with one of your closest friends and teammates. Someone you race both with and against every single day. You then shakily get situated in your new seat and close the Velcro of your shoes a few extra times for good measure, then check your oar a few extra times for good measure too. Right when you feel you cannot possibly be any more nervous, you take a deep breath, then let it flow outward from every last one of your pores to calm your nerves so you can focus on what is most important. From there forward, you simply convince yourself that you have more to give on every single stroke. Because if you do not, someone else will.

When your piece is over, you wonder if you made this boat better while also wondering how things went over in the other boat without you. *Was it even better for them? Was it worse? Was it faster? Slower? Will I ever get to sit in that boat again? Did I just win or lose my last shot at the Olympics?* While part of you attempts to understand some overarching pattern, the rest of you manages everything you actually have control over: *Do I have enough water? Do I have enough food? Yes. More. Every stroke. Breathe. What else is there?* After all, you are allowed to have uncertain thoughts. The key is to breathe and manage them.

Until finally, you hear the words. "That's it. We're done. Take it to the dock." Tom's words came one day earlier than expected. "Take a break, go for a forty-minute jog, then wait upstairs in the boathouse. I will meet with you each individually."

By day six, having raced fourteen pieces in just six days, each result delivered at the end of each day, Tom and Laurel were satisfied with what information they had. Either that, or time simply ran out.

Once Tom spoke his final words, all of two hours remained until we each had our answer...

By midmorning on June twenty-fourth, following a forty-minute jog, we gathered upstairs in the boathouse but sat more quietly than normal, given the gravity of what was about to happen. Then, just as he told us he would, Tom called each of us one by one, down the hall, and out of earshot of the group for our individual meetings.

As I sat and listened and waited patiently, nervously, hopefully, it soon became apparent that people were being called not at random but in a very specific order.

Tom began with Mary. The veteran cox with an Olympic silver medal to her name. Her experience limitless. Having already coxed the eight for six years, it would now be a seventh straight for her.

Next, Tom called Caryn. Stroke seat. Also a silver medal veteran, no one better equipped to sit up front, facing Mary, and to set the rhythm. At nearly six foot four, her natural length, plus her rhythm that she had honed over her more than a decade of rowing by then made her the best for that seat. Calm, elegant, driven to perform.

After Caryn came Caroline, my 2005 Worlds pair partner. Now, the Olympic eight's seven-seat. Her technical dexterity, raw force, and sheer will to succeed made her the natural mirror for Caryn's rhythm.

Behind Caroline, came Susan for six-seat. My friend and roommate of nearly four years. Genetically gifted in every way. Her height. Her physical strength. Both attributes perfect to pass back and add power to the rhythm set by Caryn and Caroline. Plus, with her naturally comedic demeanor, she had a way of relieving our tension.

After Susan's came Anna M.'s turn. Five-seat. The third and final veteran among us, her strength and experience to back up

Susan's. But with an unwavering faith, calm, and an innocence rather than crude humor about her, she bridged the gap between the experience of the stern and the youth of the bow.

That began with Elle. Twenty-year-old Elle. The teammate and friend who taught me to push myself harder than I ever had in my entire life, who also switched from port to starboard shortly after we rowed together. Her natural and naive strength perfectly formed for four-seat. Strong yet still so much to learn. With guidance from those in front of her, she could focus on following and pushing with all her might. Which would let her pure joy for the sport shine.

Tom had called six names by the time he called Anna G. for three-seat. The port with whom I had rowed the most during my years of full-time training. We had been through an immense amount together, for better and worse. And through it all, I had come to trust that, like Caroline, Anna G. is someone you want in your boat and not lined up against you.

My tailbones pressed into the wooden bench as I sat upstairs at the boathouse awaiting the name that might follow Anna's. Tom had called three starboards by then, so only one spot for someone like me remained. While I waited, my stomach turned as I stared down the long corridor that led to where Tom was and hoped more than anything that he would call me next.

All this time, I thought. *This is it.*

As the sun shone in diagonally through the windows that overlooked the lake, my cheeks tingled in anticipation. Until I finally saw Anna G. walking my way, her shadow flickering each time she passed through the sunbeams that doused the long corridor with light. With each step she took, she walked taller and struggled to conceal her smile. Meanwhile, I counted down the remaining ten seconds before she told us whose turn was next.

I could tell by Anna's look that something great had just happened to her. So far, it was a great day for her and those whose names had also already been called. It would not be a great day for everyone though. Inevitably, at least four people would not hear Tom utter the words they so desperately hoped for.

When Anna nodded, I knew that zero seconds remained for me...

That nod confirmed it. Tom had requested me next.

As I walked toward the single most important meeting of my life, my ears pulled rearward, and a chill ran down my neck. A chill that continued along my spine between my shoulder blades and down my back. My heart pounded harder with every step I took, which caused my throat to pulse just below my jawline. A warm drool accumulated at the edges of my tongue as my nerves welled toward nausea.

At last, I sat awkwardly on the edge of a sticky green pleather couch opposite Tom.

"Well, you know why you're here, don't you?" Assessing the look on my face, he paused. "Wait...don't tell me your teammates didn't tell you?" He paused again, then chuckled. "Oh...come on."

For every year I had been a rower, Molly's comment had held true. No matter how much I thought I knew or how many times I had confronted something, I knew nothing was guaranteed. Because taking nothing for granted had gotten me that far, I did not get my hopes up. Not yet at least.

"Well, you made the boat." Tom said in the most nonchalant way possible. "I had no doubt. You've been consistent. You have a good sense of team. You're a disciplined athlete, and you have done everything I've asked without question..."

As Tom recounted some of his reasons for selecting me, he helped me see that I had more good performances than bad. Whereas I had fixated on my weaknesses and the times I stumbled, Tom had noted the innumerable more times when I demonstrated the opposite.

Like rising to the top of the pair matrix back in 2005. Or

pulling off eleventh at that Munich World Cup despite food poisoning. Or how Anna G. and I rebounded to annihilate our competition after being nipped in the pair back in Austria. Or even how now, in that very Olympic year, when paired with Erin, Esther, or Elle, we worked our way into the top three pairs on the team. But above all, because I trusted my teammates, our coaches, and our process, Tom thought I was consistent.

Because it could sometimes seem like I needed ten great days to make up for even one bad one, I lost count of my ratio of good to bad. So I feverishly focused on what I could do better. Though stressful, working one step at a time like that kept me from getting ahead of myself, which helped me improve.

The exact way everything progressed over the years—every up and down included—shaped me until I made the Olympic eight. And even though it may have saved a little stomachache along the way, *no*, I would not have wanted to know my future. Had even one small thing been different, everything might be different. Including the conversation Tom and I had that day.

As Tom rounded out his list of reasons for why he selected me, I realized that although it had been hard for me to see, when I stepped back and saw it as Tom did, I finally grasped how far I had come.

Once Tom confirmed my selection to the 2008 Olympic eight, I was excited to keep stepping forward to find even more. Lost in the moment of that very thought, I stood up halfway and shook Tom's hand, then realized he might not have said everything he needed, so I paused.

"Oh, sorry, you weren't finished…"

"Nope. You're good." He chuckled through his trademark side smirk.

No longer able to restrain my elation, I forgot to let go of his hand, so I nearly dragged him with me as I ran down the hall to tell Erin that it was her turn to meet with Tom. She would round out as my pair partner in the bow of our 2008 Olympic eight. After I told Erin it was her turn, I found my phone, then called my parents, whom I had not seen in six months, since Christmas.

The very next day, June 25, 2008, those of us selected for the women's eight—Erin, me, Anna G., Elle, Anna M., Susan, Caroline, Caryn, and Mary—were officially named to the 2008 US Olympic Rowing Team. We even signed contracts attesting to the historical significance of what we were about to experience together.

From that official naming day forward, the clock reset. Four weeks until we departed for the 2008 Olympic Games in Beijing…

Practicing on Lake Carnegie during the hottest parts of the day. (Image courtesy of Row2K, Row2K.com)

TWENTY-NINE

ONE FOCUS.

I DO NOT CONSIDER MYSELF SUPERSTITIOUS. I DO, HOWEVER, have certain things I do every day to help me perform my best. I do not always have to understand why they work. Nor does there necessarily need to be scientific proof that they should work. All that matters is that they do. I mean, I would not want to jinx anything. Especially not with one month to go before leaving for Beijing.

Our coaches were the same. They had seen distractions impede progress in the past, so they did everything within their control to ensure we stayed focused. The easy part was over. Our true test, the Olympics, was still ahead.

In the days following our official selection to the team, media from each of our hometowns, as well as from across New Jersey, was given a five-day window of access to our team for interviews, videos, and photos. After that, we were on complete lockdown. So when a magazine wanted to do an exclusive photoshoot with us outside of that five-day window, it did not happen. The request came after the five days allowed by Tom and Laurel had passed.

I could not help but be a little disappointed. It was the first time anyone took notice of us. We had trained for all that time, and no one knew except us. Our coaches were right though. We had won nothing yet. We still had work to do. We could not take anything for granted. No distractions, one focus, one unified goal.

Counting down the days before our departure, rather than rowing only the eight in our race lineup as you might think, we instead erged, ran, rowed pairs, and lifted weights. All things we had grown accustomed to doing over the years. All things that kept us accountable, aware, pushing for more, and gaining speed. Which made those times when the nine of us did get to row the eight all the more meaningful, all the more enjoyable. And faster than any of us had ever gone in our entire lives.

When the time arrived for us to leave New Jersey and head overseas, we first had a one-night stopover in San Jose, California, to go through Olympic processing and to collect our Olympic team gear. Uniforms, paperwork, all sorts of Team USA athletes from just about every sport. Plus, one night's sleep in a dorm. After our one night in San Jose and a twelve-hour flight, we would be in Beijing.

When we hit the ground in California, it was nonstop. First, a bus ride to San Jose. Then long lines, each of us awaiting our turn to sign up for, collect, and repack our newly allotted Team USA gear. With just three veteran rowers in our eight, few of us had experienced anything like Olympic processing before.

While I was standing outside the gym in San Jose—lined up single file with my teammates like a bunch of third graders preparing to walk into the school cafeteria—awaiting my turn to enter the gym to collect my share of team gear, I glanced over because I saw a man whom we all recognized working his way around the room full of American Olympians. I kept half an eye on him as he happily greeted and shook each athlete's hand, migrating ever the closer to my teammates and me. As the governor of California at the time, he was there to wish us well.

"Oh, you are healthy girls," Arnold Schwarzenegger said as he looked up at me and my teammates, lingering on his handshake with Anna G.

Not "tall." Not "athletic." Not "big." To him, we were "healthy." I took his words as the perfect compliment, an incredibly empowering suggestion coming from someone as strong as him.

We all laughed. I smiled at Arnold. Then, because it was my turn, I headed into the gym to gather my gear. Thirty minutes of clothing sizing and gear selection later, I checked out, only to be told I should head to another room for ring sizing.

Ring sizing? Athletic gear, a sweatshirt, a hat, maybe a pair of tennis shoes. Even sunglasses and sunscreen perhaps. *But a ring?* That I was not expecting.

The woman at the long narrow display table handed me a carbon-copy form covered top to bottom in fine print. Every word aimed at designing for and delivering to me the perfect team ring. After she handed me the form, she explained the ring display. I could tell by her tone that she was genuinely excited for me.

She explained that the basic ring would read *Olympic Team* at the top and bottom with the Olympic Rings sandwiched between those two words. She said I could choose from gold alloy, white gold, fourteen- or twenty-four-karat yellow gold. I could add other accoutrements if I wanted to make it fancier. And of course, I could pick whether I wanted it to include *USA*, my last name, *Rowing, Beijing 2008*, or even a little pictogram of two people rowing. Those were the easy decisions.

The tough one, the one decision that caused me pause, was just one tiny box. One little empty square midway down the carbon-copy, landscape orientation order form. The question it asked? *In the event that my teammates and I won, would I prefer my ring to read "Gold Medalist" instead of "Olympic Team"?*

I hesitated, then shot the saleswoman a concerned glance. Although I did not consider myself superstitious, it seemed like a loaded question. With my hand paused midair and my pen hovering over the order form's tiny checkbox, I glanced around for any one of my teammates. A quick consult was in order.

Apparently, we all had the same thought. Not one of us felt particularly comfortable with even the slightest assumption that we would win. My stomach turned as I eventually checked the little box indicating that I would want the words changed to "Gold Medalist." Like I said, I do not consider myself superstitious, but I knew better than to take anything for granted.

During the twelve-hour flight ahead of the biggest event of my life, I did everything I had learned over the years to prepare. Sleep mask. Ear plugs. Neck pillow. Extra ear plugs. Compression tights. Snacks. Book. Music. Movies. Friends to talk to. But even if I slept eight hours, I still had at least two movies' worth of time to be bored while seat-belted to the confines of my airplane seat. When we finally arrived in Beijing, I was more than ready to shower, sleep in a real bed, and then get back on the water.

"I don't know." That is what I tell people when they ask me what it was like to be in the Olympic Village before we raced. Instead of the Village, we made our home (yet again) in a hotel a short bus ride from the Shunyi race venue. For our first few weeks in China, it would be just us, the Italians, and the Canadians. The only three teams at our hotel. No one other than athletes, coaches, and support staff allowed inside. Metal detectors, security guards, and dogs were at every entrance. They even checked the underside of our shuttle buses with mirrors. I can only imagine what they were looking for. I chose not to ask.

As for our families, we would see them just once (briefly) before racing. No distractions. Remember?

Back and forth. Hotel. Sleep. Eat. Practice. Hotel. Nap. Eat. Practice. Hotel. Sleep...Two weeks of nothing but the racecourse and the inside of our hotel. Nothing but practice, preparation, and focus, our entire Olympic experience apart from our hotel and our race venue exactly the same as the one the entire Chinese population was watching on their national television station.

"I don't know," is also what I tell people when they suggest that the Opening Ceremony must have been amazing. That particular ceremony is considered among the grandest of all Olympic ceremonies, so it is a question I get asked a lot.

At 8 p.m. sharp on the evening of August 8, 2008 (a date intentionally reiterative as "eight, eight, oh eight"), a date and time symbolic of luck to the highest degree in Chinese culture, the Opening Ceremony for the Beijing Olympics began. But instead of walking into the Bird Nest (the main arena of the Beijing Games) that night with the throngs of spectators and other athletes from across the globe, my teammates and I stayed back at our hotel to watch the affair via projection screen while eating dinner.

We may not have experienced the same marvel as being *in* the stadium that night, but the maroon faux-velveteen curtains of our dining room with carpet to match were all the spectacle we needed. After our meal and well before the ceremony finished, we were in bed sound asleep. The biggest race of our lives was less than forty-eight hours away.

On the morning of our heat, I woke up feeling rested for the first time in four years. Our race was scheduled for late in the day, so I had plenty of time to prepare. I brushed my teeth, showered, stretched. I breathed deeply to expand my lungs fully like I had been for the previous few days. I was going to need every last bit of them for this.

I ate breakfast, then napped. I ate again four hours before racing to give myself time to digest. Even eating the blandest of foods and well in advance, I still had to take Pepto Bismol because of how hard I learned to push myself over the years—to the point of making myself ill. And another opportunity to find yet another level of performance was on deck that very afternoon.

I showered again, then stretched again, then purposefully put on my uniform in methodical anticipation of our upcoming opportunity to perform—our heat.

Finally, six years and seven months from the day I discovered rowing back in college, I launched with my teammates for the heat of the women's eight at the 2008 Beijing Olympic Games.

Warm-up time. The final forty-five minutes.

Sights set on the start line, the nine of us ran through our warm-up routine, according to Mary's calls. It was our final forty-five minutes of practice and preparation before our first true test together. Our final opportunity to find more speed, more ways to push ourselves, even if by the tiniest increments.

As we rowed toward the start, we were focused. I saw nothing but Anna G.'s back—one I had followed for millions of meters over the years. I heard nothing but our breathing, the boat, the water, and Mary's voice. I felt nothing but the strongest and most prepared I had ever been. So when Mary called for our first build of speed together during our warm-up, I made the conscious decision to find more. I was going to find a way to push harder than I ever had in my entire life. *Find more, Shoop*, I told myself. Which I did. Repeatedly. Throughout every single one of Mary's calls.

Forty-five minutes later, having found another ounce of speed together, it was time.

As we approached the start bridge, the very same energy that was driving me for more was also driving me toward nervous. So I breathed to align it, to unify its purpose rather than attempting to deny it. I needed it. It was there because I was about to do something I cared about intensely with a team I cared about intensely.

As I exhaled, my eyes softened. My face, feet, shoulders, and hands relaxed.

One last breath…

"United States. Take it to the dock." Those were the last words I expected to hear ring out over the loudspeakers at the start.

Wait? What? Why? What did we do wrong? Are we disqualified? We didn't do anything. I jammed every possible irrational thought into those three seconds.

We did nothing wrong. Simply, the thunder from the storm that had been brewing all day finally broke. With the storm finally upon us, the officials determined it was not safe to race. We would have to wait. For how long, that was left to question.

At first, we were told to pull to shore alongside the start area and hop into vans. Those vans would then cart us safely back to the boathouse. To us, that seemed like a waste of time. Considering where we sat, the fastest way home would have, in fact, been *to race.*

Rather than making our way toward shore and those vans, we opted to wait for the other three countries in our heat to take off. Then, on Mary's call, we too made our way down the course in our lane at a focused, calculated pace. It was the right decision on Mary's part to wait. Had we taken off four boats across, each country in its respective lane, we would have gotten caught up in the moment and raced anyway, which would have wasted our energy.

Buoy by buoy down the racecourse, the sky thundered, and so did we as we picked up speed with every stroke we took. I glared through my eyebrows toward Anna G.'s back and grinned as a chill ran through me. From the grandstands at the other end, our families sat and watched with no clue of what was happening. They knew nothing of the postponement due to the storm. All they knew was that it looked like we were losing by the largest margin they had ever seen. When in fact, the race had never started.

By the time we reached the finish line end of the racecourse, the confusion in the grandstands cleared, and the nine of us headed to the boathouse to await official word. With our boat away, we lingered in our team's one small waiting room on the second level of the boathouse. The room was small, a few bunk beds along its walls, buzzing white office lights above. Though an oddly sterile environment for a boathouse, it was the perfect reflection of how oddly confusing a situation we faced.

Are we going to race? Should I eat something else? How much time do we have? Can I go to the bathroom again? My mind filled with these small questions. As if you can predict the weather. All you can do is wait, hope for the best, and breathe. *Expect the unexpected. Control what you can. Ignore what you can't...*

It was late, and the storm was there to stay. Postponed. Come back tomorrow. All of that. Warmed up. Dying to race. And come back tomorrow was what we got. So we went home, ate dinner, and slept. When I awoke the next day, I repeated my entire race-day ritual.

One thing our race delay provided us was an extra day of practice to find a little more speed.

Just before three o'clock in the afternoon on the following day, which was August eleventh, we were back at the start line alongside Germany, Canada, and Great Britain. This time, though still overcast, there was no storm. The water was near flat. Only small puffs of wind delicately rippling the surface of the race-course. The start line was silent except for the final countdown from the race officials.

The male announcer's British accent chimed in as if to deliberately add tension to an already intense scenario. "Three minutes," was all he said.

Then exactly one minute later, "Two minutes...

"Raising start systems."

Just after the hydraulic start system emerged from the water with its metallic clanging sound reminiscent of a pop from a champagne bottle's cork, I turned and looked over my right shoulder to help Erin nudge the very tip of our bow, the tiny ball at the end of our sixty-foot-long eight, into the clear plastic cup of the start system. Designed to hold our boat still, it marked the exact line of the start. As Erin and I made our adjustments, the final sixty seconds before the start of the race ticked by.

Imagine turning your attention away from your team during your one final minute of focus before the start of the single most significant race of your life. How do you manage that kind of ticking pressure? You breathe and do your job methodically while distracting yourself from the fact that you better do it right (and quickly) so you can get back to your team and your one focus.

At last, the announcer began his final calls. "Germany...Canada...U-S-A...Great Britain...Attention—"

Brrrrrnnnnnt...Rather than "Go!" a horn blared, and a red stoplight at the front of our lane instantaneously switched to green. When it did, we pushed, propelling our boat forward, breaking the stark, simple, greyish-green silence of the start.

By five hundred meters in, we had nearly one entire boat's length of a lead on our competitors. By halfway, the bow of the next nearest country was only barely at Mary's back. We were nearly open water, more than sixty feet, ahead by then. Apart from *Yes*, my mind went blank long before the halfway mark of one thousand meters in.

We had not raced a full 2K on the water in the eight since that World Cup back in Switzerland more than two months prior. For as rested as I was finally feeling when we headed into our heat, that full 2K race hurt a whole heap more than my body remembered.

Yes. More. Blade in. Legs shoving as hard as possible. Spit flying from the corners of my mouth upon every exhale. My mind blank. My body mesmerized by my self-inflicted effort—a sensation that is both agonizing and addicting.

Yes. More.

In the closing 250 meters, the last forty-five seconds of the race, we still had nearly a whole boat length's lead. Nearly sixty feet ahead of Great Britain, Canada, and Germany. With only seven countries allowed to compete in the women's eight at the Olympics, only seven can ever hope to make it as far as we did. And among the ones we raced there in our heat, we were decidedly ahead. We asserted ourselves early, and no one but the British chose to chase us, to charge at us as the race thundered to its close under that overcast sky. Still, despite their efforts, we crossed the line to win by a considerable margin of just over two seconds. Job number one was done.

As soon as we took our final stroke across the finish line of that heat, having taken another step forward, we turned our focus to our next step: recovery. Almost immediately, we spun the boat to begin our recovery process in preparation for our next race. As we did, Erin reached forward from where she sat in bow seat to where I was directly in front of her in two-seat. She patted me on the back as I rolled the wheels of my seat back and forth to pump my now acidic-feeling blood through my legs. I knew she felt the pain too. But still, she mustered the energy for a small tap of appreciation. Challenge accepted. Job done. Step taken.

As the simultaneously cramped and throbbing feeling waned throughout our cooldown, we all smiled and savored the step we had just taken together. Having won our heat as we did, we knew we were heading straight to the A-Final. No need for a rep like the year before at Worlds. It was straight to the medal-deciding A-Final for us, which we knew would come six days later on Sunday, August seventeenth.

Just over ten minutes after our heat had ended, Romania— the team that had won the women's eight for each of the three previous Olympic Games (1996, 2000, and 2004), the team that had closed their margin on us by an inconceivable amount at the 2006 and 2007 World Championships, the team that could not be counted out in 2008 for their long history of winning in the sport of rowing—also won their heat. In a time nearly one second faster than ours.

Despite our world records and world championships, we were the underdogs when it came to the Olympics. By a long shot. No American women had ever won gold over the 2,000-meter race distance. Romania, on the other hand, had made it a habit.

From the day of our heat forward, we had six days to find more speed. Six days to wait. Six days to rest. Six days to practice and to test any newfound speed against a stopwatch. Given our aha moments in the past, those six days stood to be more than enough to make technical changes, if needed. Changes that could make us faster.

In six days, the actual biggest race of our lives would take place. We had won nothing yet.

THIRTY

THE HUNTER.

BEFORE WE LEFT FOR BEIJING, TOM GAVE MARY AN OLD RACE
video and requested that she get our boat together to watch it.
So she, Susan, and I invited everyone to our house to do exactly
as Tom asked.

On the afternoon we planned, our teammates gathered in our
living room and squished, one by one, onto our hand-me-down,
we-kept-it-because-it-was-free, cargo furniture. Once everyone
was situated, Mary told us what Tom had given her and what he
told her. That we were to watch the final of the women's eight race
from the 1984 Olympics. Though the quality of the race recording
was grainy, which made it tough to discern individuals, we knew
exactly where Team USA was.

As the event unfolded, we watched the US women race past
Romania and the Netherlands to bring home Olympic gold and
make history. This was precisely Tom's reason for having us watch
it together.

Up through 1984, women raced a 1,000-meter event (half the
distance that the men raced). After 1984 though, the distance
was made equal for both genders, a large step in women's rowing
worldwide. But in all the years following the change, not a single

American woman had won Olympic gold over the 2K race distance. This meant that we had the chance, there in Beijing, to become those first to do exactly that.

Prior to our heat, prior to even our first practice row on the Shunyi racecourse outside Beijing, we had gathered with Tom and Laurel at the far back of the boatyard. At first, I thought it was an odd place to meet given that it was a good distance from the water. But once I got there, I understood why our coaches had chosen it. They were introducing us to our boat, *The Hunter*. The boat we had borrowed for the occasion. The boat whose name serendipitously described what we had set out to do: to hunt the line. The boat we met for the first time at the way back of the boatyard on that first day before our first row in China.

When we met at the back of the boatyard, though not completely sure, we at least expected to learn our practice plan. Something that typically detailed distances, times, and drills. Which it did. But at some point midway, our conversation shifted away from that day's practice to Lake Casitas, the rowing venue for the 1984 Olympic race that we had watched together in our living room back in New Jersey.

We were reminded of how we had gotten to go row there a few years earlier. Of the old race tape and its history lesson. At which point, our attention turned to a partially filled, small plastic water bottle Tom had been holding while he spoke. As he unscrewed the cap, Tom explained a little more as he trickled the contents of the bottle over the bow of *The Hunter*. While he carefully poured, he told us it was a bit of water from Lake Casitas. From the very lake where the women of the 1984 Games won gold.

I do not know if Tom was being serious about the water he poured over the bow of *The Hunter* that day. But our belief that it came from Casitas was what mattered. Like I said, we were not superstitious, but a private boat christening could not hurt.

On the morning of our Olympic final, Sunday, August seventeenth, just six days of practice after our heat later, I woke up with a huge zit on my chin. Twenty-six years old, and there it was staring back at me, a zit. I could not help but laugh. It was one of those things over which I had no control. So I set about my race-day routine, which began with brushing my teeth and a little stretching in my morning hot shower.

After that, I ate breakfast, then stretched a little more. Followed by some long, slow, deep breathing to fully expand my lungs, my usual nap, then a carefully timed lunch. More downtime. Another shower. A little more stretching.

Just before it was time to leave for the racecourse, I dressed in my uniform and brushed my teeth again. I liked how the minty flavor opened my nostrils and refreshed my throat. It made the whole day feel new.

With my routine complete, I made one last bathroom stop, then headed downstairs to wait for the bus.

When our shuttle bus arrived, I showed my credentials, stepped aboard, and walked back a few rows to find a suitable seat. I settled in, put in my headphones, relaxed my face through a deep belly breath, and started my prerace playlist. A list of songs carefully selected over each of the years that combined to create that very moment. Because our race was one of the last events of the 2008 Olympic rowing program, the shuttle bus was mostly empty that afternoon, except for my teammates and me. Staying focused on the way to the racecourse came easier that way.

From the moment I stepped off the shuttle bus, I headed upstairs to that small, oddly sterile waiting room with the bunk-bed-lined walls and killed time until our scheduled prerace meeting with Tom.

A little over an hour to go before race time, Tom strolled into the small, white room where the nine of us were waiting. He stood quietly, holding us in silence slightly longer than usual. His behavior highlighted the gravity of that moment. Until he finally spoke.

"This is just another race," he said. "Do what you do best and go race."

The corner of my mouth turned up slightly as I listened intently. I glared upward through my eyebrows with a focused grin. My cheeks contracted and relaxed with each of my intentional breaths. I was ready.

One woman at a time, I rounded our huddle to take in each of my teammates' expressions. With every glance around our circle, my sense of preparation, my confidence in us as a team amplified. Our time had finally come. No more thinking. No more waiting. Time to *do*.

By the time we were done with our prerace meeting, though I do not remember much of what else Tom said, I felt as though I could do absolutely anything. When you leave a meeting like that, every single otherwise normal thing you do feels unexpectedly powerful. Everything from standing to breathing to walking to the look on your face to carrying your equipment.

With *The Hunter* resting upon our eight shoulders, we walked toward the launch dock. One focus. Nothing could break our concentration. Nothing mattered but the nine of us.

"Toes to the edge. Up and over heads. And down," came Mary's voice. Familiar yet uniquely meaningful.

We rolled the boat down and gently set it to rest on the water with a soft *shushing* splash.

Once all eight of our oars were in place, Mary's voice calmly arose again. "Down and in when ready."

Each at our own times, we adjusted our seats, stepped into the boat, then sat down. As I settled in, I readjusted my oarlock and checked the Velcro of my shoes. I reopened and reclosed it. Twice for good measure to get the *just right* amount of comfortable wiggle room for my feet. While I waited for my teammates to complete their adjustments, I recalled something Tom once told me: "Shoop, you take care of the middle. The others, they'll get you across the line."

I took another deep breath as I thought of Tom's words, then "Hands on. Shove in two…" came Mary's last call to push away from the dock. Our last launch.

When we heard her request for "Ready all eight…" We sat poised, blades buried in the water, ready to take our first stroke for our last warm-up together in that lineup.

We passed under the pedestrian bridge that led us into the warm-up area. Then, tracing the little mound of land that separated us from the racecourse, we headed in the direction of the start line. I was focused, attentive, relaxed. I felt stronger than ever.

We cruised purposefully along, our pressure increasing with each push. Mary's voice kept us aware of just how prepared we had become. When she called our speeds, my confidence grew… again. In response to her words, my legs tingled. Every hair on my arms stood on end.

As I listened, I heard Mary's voice, the sounds of our boat, the water, our movements, our breaths. The air boomed with the sounds of cheering. Sounds that emanated from the rows upon rows of spectators. Sounds from the masses seated in the grandstands that lined both sides of the closing 750 meters of the racecourse. It was more than I had ever heard before. We could not have been farther from the complete isolation of our little lake in New Jersey.

As Mary prepared us for another ten-stroke builder, ten strokes to warm ourselves up for race speed, I took a deep breath to help me sit as tall in my seat as I could. Not the way I would actually row, but taller in order to satisfy my curiosity. I *had* to see over the little mound of land that separated us in the warm-up area from the racecourse itself. It was at the peak of my next inhale that I caught one tiny glimpse of the crowd that awaited us, then returned to my race-day posture.

Everything tingled after that. Every hair, including the ones on the top of my head, stood up. The corner of my mouth turned up even more, then my cheeks relaxed again. My gaze went back through my eyebrows until all I saw was Anna G.'s back. All I heard was the nine of us.

Just as it had before our heat, our forty-five-minute warm-up made us faster. More confident. All the way to the start line of, in Tom's words, "just another race…"

"And sit easy all eight…Shoop, give me a little tap. Cafaro, a tap. Good, bow pair. Together. Good." Mary's instructions to align us in our lane offered a momentary reprieve.

"Two minutes…" the female announcer's voice flatly warned as the hydraulic start system emerged from the water.

Erin and I managed the system together. Aligning our bow ball into the tiny cup just as we had for our heat.

"One minute…"

"Squared and buried all eight…" came Mary's voice shortly thereafter.

When you choose to take on a challenge as large as the one we were about to face, you enter into it with respect by recognizing that *it will be hard*. Possibly the hardest thing that you will have ever put yourself through. That way, its demands are less likely to catch you off guard. If they still do, you find a way to be okay with it because you entered into it knowing that it would not be easy.

Sitting at the line with one minute to go before the start, my nerves momentarily resurged. One last distraction attempting to perforate my consciousness. One final effort to disrupt my focus. In that moment of ultimate challenge, worry tried to call my bluff one…last…time. Tried to question just how durable my desire to succeed had become.

In through my nose came a deep belly breath. My eyes gently blinking closed as my exhale passed my lips. Fingers loose. Face, feet, hands relaxed. My major muscles pulsating in attention, sitting ready for their call to action.

My thoughts, *You want this. We have come all this way. This is what it has all been for. We are in this together.*

The tears. Blisters. Sweat. Frozen, cracked, and bloodied hands. The frustration. The anxiety. The long days. The weddings and births missed. The rush to work between training sessions to be able to afford groceries. Convincing myself that the cheapest thing on the menu actually is what I want and ordering water by default because it is free.

The snowy Friday nights with one hundred minutes left to pedal on the stationary bike. Literally going nowhere but with nowhere else in the world I would rather be. Teammates by my side.

The sore…*everything*.

The breakthroughs. Those two words of encouragement when needed them most: "Good job."

The laughs. The smiles. The joys. Embracing being the goofy underdog because of the mismatched outfits I chose, either because I awoke in the dark, or it was all I had.

Everything it took just to have the chance to sit in that seat, let alone at that line. The realization that everything that knocked me to the bottom had made me all the stronger.

You already made your choice. Only one option remains: go harder than you ever have in your entire life…and hope that your teeth don't fall out.

Other than a light lapping along the hull of *The Hunter*, the water was nearly dead flat at the start. Just a greyish-green color that reflected the simultaneous stillness and tension of that moment.

I adjusted my butt on my seat, then took my last deep belly breath. Jaw loose. Neck and shoulders relaxed. Every ounce of my being focused. Every ounce of my being ready. Finally focused on only one thing: this moment.

Then through the silence came the female announcer's voice for the last time.

"Great Britain...Canada...United States of America... Romania...the Netherlands...Australia—

"Attention—"

In an instant, the horn blared, the red light beamed green, and all six boats took off. The nine of us in *The Hunter* in lane three. A lane reserved for only the fastest of teams, a pole position that indicated how much faith the world had in our capacity to win. Yet we nine took nothing for granted.

One minute. That is as far as I made it before everything fell silent except for the ringing in my ears. No memory. Nothingness except, *Yes. More.* Every single stroke down the course. Relax. Push. Float. Breathe. Repeat. I did not have to think about what to do. My body knew what to do. The rowing, the race plan, those were things I had done countless times before. Instinct.

By four hundred meters in, you are going to push for the lead. Why? Because we're American. It's what we do. Tom had told us that countless times before. Having subconsciously practiced those words time and again helped my body know exactly what to do when the time came for us to hit our stride, our lengthen, our sweet spot where we would nail our strongest, most efficient rhythm. *Ever.* Which is exactly what we did upon Mary's call.

When we lengthened to our race pace, it was obvious just how attuned to one another we had become. We worked as one. We were all that mattered. Our teamwork, our singularity of focus. Our care for one another both in and out of the boat took what we had visualized and turned it into reality. One...stroke...at a time.

In rowing, if you attempt to push before the whole crew is ready, your effort is lost within the weight of the boat and the other people in it. When you realize how much more effective working in perfect unison is, you are patient. You feel, you anticipate, and you give exactly what the boat needs, what the crew needs, what the team needs, when it needs it most.

Somewhere in the middle of the race, Mary's voice temporarily broke my void. "We are in the lead. This is all we need right now…"

I could not believe it. I simply could not believe we were ahead, so I did something completely uncharacteristic. Without turning my head, I cut my eyes to the right, then back to center. Mary was right. We were in the lead. At that moment, we were better than anyone else…in the world. Still, we took nothing for granted.

Mary continued. "No one is gaining on us…and they don't know that we have another gear."

Her words could not have been more perfectly timed. They convinced me that although I was already giving absolutely everything, I did have another gear. She reassured my confidence.

"Third five hundred…"

The ringing in my ears resumed. Back to nothingness except my subconscious: *Yes. More.*

We knew it would be impossible to hear Mary during the last forty-five seconds of the race. In fact, we planned for it. Once the time came to sprint, it was pure instinct.

"Last two-fifty!"

Mary banged the side of the boat with the palm of her hand to signify that fact, and the air boomed all the more. As the energy of *The Hunter* and the roar of the crowd merged, I knew we were finally hunting the line.

Yes, more, turned to *Gold*. My mind unexpectedly switched the words on its own to the only thing left. Over and over, the little person in my head repeated not, *Yes. More*, but *Gold!* One stroke, one word at a time. *Gold!*

"Trust…believe…believe…" Mary's raspy voice implored through the hollow *shushing* that enveloped my ears as the crowd roared.

I had breathed early and had taken care of the middle like Tom told me, which left me with nothing but rubber for legs as they flopped, hollow on the deck of the boat. My lips peeled back from my gums, exposing what little strength was left of my entire being. *Blade in. Gold. I will not let my teammates down. Gold. Gold. Gold…*were now my thoughts as we closed in on the final twenty strokes.

"Four strokes…" Mary's words lifted my confidence once more.

As my head dropped just before the point of passing out, I saw them. The bubbles. The finish line. The nine of us shoved one more as-hard-as-humanly-possible stroke to be absolutely sure we passed it. The instant Mary made the call, I flipped my head left, then right. So loosely that my braided ponytail hit me in the face as my mind attempted to gather the meaning of what I saw.

No one is behind us. The race is over. No one can pass us now. We must have won? We just won? The Olympics! I must find a way to cheer this time.

I mustered just enough of what remained, then yelled. The corners of my mouth sticky with spit. I reached forward, grabbed Anna G., then kissed her on the cheek. We had been through so much together. I turned around to Erin and grabbed her for an awkward hug. I then grimaced, pulled my feet from my shoes, and threw off my socks. I dropped my legs over the sides of the boat into the water to distract their throbbing. I pointed toward Susan and to Elle, to Anna M. I gazed up toward Mary, Caryn, and Caroline, wishing the nine of us could hug each other in that exact moment. Then I wondered about Tom, Laurel, and my family.

Miraculously, my teeth had not fallen out. Even if they had, I would not have cared.

The bubbles that mark the finish line. (Image courtesy of Row2K, Row2K.com)

Three weeks and two days after leaving our lake in New Jersey, three years after our 0.38 second demoralizing loss at my first World Championships, six years after I began the sport altogether, my teammates and I became Olympic champions at five in the evening on a Sunday on a lake just outside Beijing, China. The first American women to bring home Olympic gold over 2K.

The nine of us hugging for the first time after winning gold. (Image courtesy of Row2K, Row2K.com)

THIRTY-ONE

JUST ANOTHER RACE.

AFTER THE RACE OFFICIALS ENSURED THAT WE WERE OKAY, we rowed toward the media dock and got out for only a brief moment to answer a few questions from the press. Still panting. Still catching my breath. Socks wet. My heart still recovering. We then crawled back into *The Hunter* to row another ten strokes to the medals dock where the medals ceremony would take place.

Of the twenty-eight sports that were part of the Beijing Olympic Games, three had the medals ceremony gear requirement waived. With rowing being one of those three, we did not have a day to think about nor a night to sleep on what we accomplished. Instead, within minutes of finishing the biggest race of our lives, we stood side by side at the center of the awards dock still wearing our sweat-soaked uniforms. We were nothing but raw, unscripted emotion as we awaited our turn and the singing of our national anthem.

We had won World Championships. We had set records at just about every major race around the world. But these were the Olympic Games, existing in a category of their own. Which is something I could not comprehend until standing there on that dock in the presence of one of the pioneers of women's rowing.

The fact that Anita DeFrantz was one of the first women to medal in rowing for the United States when she and her boat-mates brought home bronze at the 1976 Montreal Olympics is just the tip of the iceberg. Over the course of her lifetime, she has amassed a résumé that sets her apart as a heroine both within and outside of rowing. Not the least of which is that she was the first woman to become vice president of the International Olympic Committee. To put it mildly, her ethereal presence is awe-inspiring.

That is the person who was to present us with our medals. The one who would officially welcome us to the club.

As our ceremony proceeded in boat order, I watched Anita present my teammates with their medals, then shake their hands. She whispered quietly to each of them, then moved, almost floating, from one woman to the next. I watched her smile. I watched my teammates smile back at her. I clapped for each one of them with sheer joy in my heart. Then, before I knew it, it was my turn.

As I had seen with my teammates, I expected a smile, my medal, a kind word, a handshake, then for Anita to move along to the last in our lineup. So I grinned, albeit shyly, then glanced up at her. All it took was that glance. I only caught her in the eyes for an instant. But an instant was enough to make my grin quiver. My eyes started to fill.

Fully aware of my welling tears, Anita placed the medal over my head, then shook my hand and told me simply as if it was fact, "Your life is forever changed."

My real-life fairy-tale moment broke the dam. I could no longer restrain them. My tears had to flow. Anita kept my right hand a little longer, which made my whole arm shake. My right leg then followed suit as my whole being caught on to the fact that something truly did change. With the weight of our accomplishment finally upon me, it swung down and hit me square in the chest in the form of an Olympic gold medal. No matter how clearly I had visualized it, there was no way for me to prepare for that much reality.

I attempted to collect myself to turn full attention to Erin, bow seat, the last to receive her medal. I put my right arm around her, my left around Anna. They put theirs around me. I cried even more. Apparently, years of tears had been reserving themselves for that one moment.

If you go back to the recording of us singing the national anthem, you will see the nine of us standing proudly. But while my teammates sing, you will see me sniffling, then catch my breath in time to finish the last few words of the anthem with them. According to the commentator's take on what he saw that day, we were "true Olympians." Those who toil in silence far from the spotlight. Because, as Laurel always said, "We do it for something more."

Attempting to collect myself while we sing the national anthem. (Image courtesy of Row2K, Row2K.com)

After we sang the national anthem, we posed for a few photos, then got back into *The Hunter* to row to the dock one last time as a crew. Where, having yet to share the moment with our coaches, we hoped they would meet us. We all knew we had one critical thing left to do together. As we rowed back to the dock, Mary knew what was coming. I am certain she did not mind.

Within two minutes of landing, not only did the nine of us have time to get out of *The Hunter* and hug each other but also to hoist Mary over our heads to give her the ritual heave ho into the water. After tossing Mary, we all jumped in, smiling, laughing. Most importantly, together.

When Tom finally arrived at the dock, he too knew what was coming. But before we were able to send him flying into the water, he gave us a group hug, then the shortest, most powerful, postrace talk in history.

"By the way…" starting and ending as if he knew what we were capable of all along, "that wasn't just another race. That was the *effing* Olympic final. You just won an Olympic gold medal."

He was right. We were not the hunted. We were the hunters who went after nothing but the line. Nothing mattered but our one focus and each other.

Later that night, my Olympic gold medal slept next to me on my pillow.

Tom's group hug. (Image courtesy of Maggie Hogan)

The Hunter.

THIRTY-TWO

SAVOR THIS MOMENT.

THE NEXT EIGHT DAYS WENT BY IN A BLINK. SURREAL DOES not begin to describe it. Even with time and perspective since, I have yet to wrap my head around what my teammates and I were able achieve. So imagine what it feels like when it is fresh. Body still sore from the challenge, then waking up in an actual *Dream World*. That was the theme of the Beijing Olympic Village. Backlit signs displaying those very words were on every wall, corner, and building facade. Everywhere.

Before we moved into Dream World, our entire Olympic experience had consisted of three things: our hotel, our race venue, and whatever events in which the Chinese team was performing well. Whatever they were winning got the most airtime on Chinese national television, which was all we had access to from the isolation of our hotel. For that, I had watched a lot of weightlifting, shooting, and volleyball during the first week of the Games.

After moving into the Olympic Village though, our choices expanded. Instead of just watching events on TV, we could get passes to attend pretty much any sport we wanted. And being athletes, we had access to special seating right up front. At first, I planned to forego being a spectator in favor of sightseeing.

But as one of my teammates put it, "Those things have been here for thousands of years. The Summer Olympics, just this once."

My teammate Jen was right, so I changed my mind. Instead of sightseeing, I checked for athlete passes every day, with volleyball being the first sport I knew I would go to if I could get tickets. It has been one of my favorite sports since high school, and while there in Beijing, I found out Mary also appreciated it. We both had followed the US women's indoor volleyball team during the first week of the Games and had talked about cheering those women on if given the chance, which came earlier than expected.

On one of our initial days in the Olympic Village, Mary and I headed to the dining hall with our gold medals hanging around our necks. But because we were shy about wearing them, we hid them beneath our USA T-shirts before we left our room. When we got to the dining hall, athletes from all over the world were everywhere. The massive room was full, so we grabbed food, then split up to find seats.

I found a spot first, so I waved Mary over. But when she headed my way, she had a strange look on her face.

"Hey, Shoop," she whispered. "The volleyball team is over there. What if we go sit with them?"

Shrugging my shoulders in a "why not?" sort of way, I agreed with her gumption. "I'll go if you do."

After we carefully approached the table where the volleyball team was sitting, Mary asked if we could join them.

"Of course," they said.

While most of them sat quietly, two engaged in conversation with us. We told them we had been watching them compete all week between our races and that they had been inspiring. As our conversation unfolded over lunch, we learned a few things from each of them. Including the fact that a few of them were on their third Games and planned to retire after Beijing. We also learned that they were down to their final matches and that if they won their next one, they would play the team that had beaten them out for a medal in the previous two or three Olympics in a row. This year though, as long as they won their next match, they would finally meet their nemesis in the gold medal round. A medal would be guaranteed regardless of their outcome.

After they shared this information with us, they realized that they had not yet asked about our event or how we had done. When we told them how our races went, they immediately asked about our medals. Instantly, Mary and I looked at each other and shyly grinned as if to dare one another, on the count of three, to show them.

When we pulled out our gold medals from under our T-shirts at the same time, their faces dropped. They then leaned in to reverently assess them from a short distance but did not dare touch them out of respect for the honor. Instead, their voices softened as they stood in awe of what we had done. It was the very thing a few of them had spent multiple Olympic cycles, more than a decade, pursuing.

"Let's go get ours," one of the veteran volleyball players said.

They thanked us for sitting with them. We thanked them too, then wished them luck.

A few days later, Mary and I gathered a group together to cheer on our fellow USA teammates as they took on their nemesis, Brazil.

From its very outset, the match was rowdy. It was the gold medal round, and Brazil is known for its passionate fan base. The seats in the 13,000-person stadium were packed. The air was thick with shouting, humidity, and though we were not the ones competing, our own sweat on account of the intense back-and-forth play. Brazil took the first set, then the US, then Brazil again. Until finally, Brazil took the fourth set by a narrow margin of four points to clench the match and also gold.

On my feet for nearly every point, my legs ached. From my

cheering, my throat was bare by the end of the match. On account of our small moment at the dining hall, I felt intrinsically connected to the women out on the court that day and was happy for them as they finally brought home a medal of their own. Silver.

I cannot recall when, but I bumped into part of the volleyball team after their final match. They thanked me again for showing them my medal and told me that Mary and I had inspired them. Apparently, before they took the court for the match that determined whether they would play for bronze or gold, they came together as a team. They spoke of their goals and what they wanted to achieve. And as part of that conversation, they brought up meeting Mary and me. They knew what we had done, and they wanted their chance at a medal too.

Before that chance encounter following the volleyball team's final match, never would I have thought those women would have looked to us in the way Mary and I looked to them. Let alone that they might discuss our lunch together to motivate them to play their way through the biggest match of their lives. But that is the Olympics. It is the absolute pinnacle of athletic achievement. An honor that garners the utmost respect and connects us all.

Though we did not attend the Opening Ceremony, we dressed and went to the Closing. By the end of the Games, rather than the regimented groups that mark the beginning, everyone walks in together. New friends. Old friends. Countries and sports mixed. The finest in the world, gathered in one place, dressed head to toe in the colors of each respective nation's flags. Proud to represent the world. And me, I walked among them somehow.

As I looked up at the Olympic flame from the base of the giant torch that hung high above the Bird Nest stadium that night with the throngs of athletes mingling around me, I thought about something Anna M. had said during one of our last rows together in our eight before we had raced the final. She had called our attention as we paused midpractice.

"Savor this moment," she said, "because you never know if you will get to be here again. In a boat like this ever again."

Anna M. spoke with a wisdom suited to someone in her second Games. She planned to retire after racing, so she felt something the rest of us could not. I could not understand her perspective at the time because I planned to return. Just as Elle and I had discussed back at ARCO in our pair, I planned to row for as long as I possibly could. How could I not? Rowing had changed my life. It was allowing me to discover the person I was proud to become every day, one day at a time, through the decisions I was making and the actions I was taking.

I loved it more than anything and had already told Tom, without hesitation, when he asked about my future plans that, "Without a doubt, I am absolutely coming back."

As I awaited the ritual extinguishing of the flame at the Closing Ceremony that night, I attempted to take it all in. More than seven billion people on the planet and only ten thousand earn the chance to compete at the pinnacle that is the Olympics. And of those people who make it that far, less than 3 percent *might* win.

As for my teammates and me, the nine of us, we raced our way to not only American history but to something that less than 0.000005 percent of the people on this planet might ever have the chance to become. Most importantly, we did it together.

THIRTY-THREE

BELIEVE.

AFTER I ARRIVED HOME FROM CHINA, AN ENTIRELY NEW kind of whirlwind began. Interviews with the local news in my hometown. Visits to the Pentagon, the White House, Bethesda Naval Hospital. An open-top bus tour through the streets of Chicago on our way to be guests on *Oprah*. New York City for events and fundraisers. Interviews on satellite radio, trips to schools and companies to share the story of how it all happened. To answer the question, "What was it like?" So many questions and comments, many of which were similar. Until the day I visited a family friend who has known me since I was a kid.

As I had grown accustomed, I took my medal with me when I went to visit her at her home. For the majority of the morning, we sat upstairs and caught up on several years' worth of experiences. She told me of her art and her new kiln. That she had started making pottery. She told me of many things and also asked me many things, but never once did she ask me about my medal.

Thinking maybe she had forgotten, I eventually pulled it from my bag and handed it to her. She held it in her hand at half an arm's length and stared diagonally downward at it. She quietly surveyed its gold and pure white jade shining brightly in the morning sun.

Then, after a long breath, as if stating a pure fact, she calmly said, "You know, Lindsay. This medal is a social validation of the person you have always been. You have been in there this whole time. You just needed the right outlet."

Olympic gold in my calloused hands.

Our conversation carried on from there like I had never handed her the medal at all. As though she never felt the physical weight of it in her hand. So I wrapped it and put it back in my bag, then we discussed my future plans. I told her about my travels, the media, the events, all the incredible, yet short-lived, things that happen right after you return from winning the Olympics. We laughed. We brainstormed for another hour or two. Then we hugged goodbye.

As I drove in the direction of my parents' house, I thought about what she said, and I began to realize that she had been right. That I was in there all along but could not see it myself. Now knowing what I know, I wholeheartedly believe that possibility lives within each of us. We simply need to find the right outlet—the one that enables us to rediscover what time can cause us to question—then use time itself to rebuild ourselves (and our confidence) gradually, one day at a time.

For me, rowing has become my chosen medium. One for which I am eternally grateful. So grateful that I send a thank-you card to my college coach, Kevin, every year on his birthday. I thank him for providing me with the opportunity to change the way I think, feel, and share. To be proud of the person I can become through what I do each day. To dream of possibility and to believe, even when the circumstances suggest otherwise.

In essence, I thank him for having given me the opportunity to join the Virginia Rowing Team, because it set me on a path toward becoming the best I can possibly be. A path forged by removing my self-imposed limits and taking it one step at a time.

When I think back to the night that my teammates and I swore we would get tattoos if we won the Olympics, I realize that even though we had made it that far, we had yet to fully embrace our possibility beyond what we had already done. Which might be why our first World Championships ended with that disappointing fourth place by a matter of feet after leading for the majority of the race.

It was only when our coaches explained that we had to clearly see what was possible for us, to see what we wanted, that we began to make real strides toward it. Our first step was to change our minds. To risk believing in where we wanted to go and then to embrace that challenge despite its uncertainty. It was then, with possibility in our hearts, that we became willing to train as if we could win despite not knowing if we ever would. This allowed us to grow daily, one step at a time, until we became far greater than we would have been otherwise.

Far greater than I might have thought when I nearly flipped my single at the Canadian Henley. Far greater than when I struggled to run up O-Hill behind my University of Virginia teammates. And certainly far greater than when I lie awake that night back in college disrupted by my thoughts of, *What I could have been had it not been too late for me...*

Funny enough, just about every time I speak with a new group of people about how I competed in the Olympics, someone inevitably asks if I have gotten the tattoo. If not the most, it is one of the most asked questions.

As I write this, the answer is "No, not yet." But when I do, it will not be the Olympic Rings. It will instead be one word, written in thin cursive, on my right wrist. A daily reminder of what is possible through changing the way we think through removing our self-imposed limitations, then taking action in the direction of our dreams. For it is never too late to discover the person you are proud to become every day. Or at least to start believing he or she is in there.

My one word? *Believe*...After all, to be better great than never is to believe in the possibility within, then to take it one step at a time from there.

September 8, 2008,

It's been a few weeks, but we are still riding high. It is tiring but worth it. I feel empowered, like all of my personality traits and emotions have intensified. I want to help people and be a part of everything. I want to inspire young minds. I understand the journey now. How much it is all worth.

Do not ever lose sight of what has to be done each day to get there. Enjoy the process. Every day. Simplify. Adjust. Ready for anything. Prepared for anything. Adaptable. Never forget the cold, long, hard days. The forty degrees and raining. The hypothermia. The tears, anxiety, and being down on myself. Deal with the good and the bad, and never forget what it has all been worth.

Always remember. Always share. Always see the positive. Always work hard. Always be a champion in every aspect of life. I hope this will never fade. My life is forever changed.

Our team ring. My daily reminder of possibility. (Image courtesy of Shivani Parmar, shivspix. com)

My college coach Kevin and me back when I was in college.

AFTERWORD

ONE MUGGY MAY DAY IN SOUTH CAROLINA, AS A SUMMERLIKE sun beamed down from above, I stood on the tiny yellowish-orange beach by Lake Hartwell. A team I was coaching at the time had just launched for a practice row in final preparation for the conference championship. As they rowed by, I looked on and thought to myself how infinitely proud I was of what they had achieved together in such a short time. It was while I stood lost in thought, absorbed in my internal gratitude for them, that I heard someone call my name, so I turned to investigate the source of the call.

When I turned, I saw my college coach's wife, Barb, striding steadily down the steep green hill toward the lake's shore where I stood. As Barb descended the slope toward me, I stepped forward and onto the grass to brush the yellowish-orange sand from the bottoms of my bare feet.

Once she knew she had my attention, she hollered. "Hey, Shoop! I have a question for ya…Are you going to NCAAs?"

Confused by her question, I thought for a moment. She knew that my going to NCAAs depended on how each of our respective teams performed in the coming days at the conference championship. The team I was there with had yet to win it, while the team she was there with had won it many times. So she had grown accustomed to traveling to NCAAs.

Barb continued, "If you're not, don't worry about it. It was just a thought."

In all the years I have known Barb, nearly eighteen, I cannot recall her ever asking me about NCAAs. Which made me curious that day, so I followed up. "I'm not sure. Why? What's up?"

"Well," she said. "There's someone I want you to meet. His name is Dan Shoop."

I perked up when she said his name. I had recognized it from many years before. I had seen it on one of my very first visits to the Virginia Rowing office when I first joined the rowing team back when I was in college—eighteen years prior to that very day.

A painting hangs in the University of Virginia Rowing office. It is a large picture of a Virginia women's eight from one of the first NCAA Rowing Championships ever held. The artist signed his name to the lower righthand corner of the painting. The artist's name? Dan Shoop.

For the eighteen years that had passed since I first saw that painting, I thought Dan Shoop was a stranger. Someone my college coach, Kevin, had commissioned for the painting. Turns out, as I learned from Barb that day by Lake Hartwell, Dan Shoop was not a stranger at all. He was, rather, Barb's track coach—one of her greatest mentors since she was just twelve years old.

The instant I realized how significant Dan Shoop was, I excitedly interjected that I would, without question, be going to NCAAs. "You mean *that* Dan Shoop? I'll be there, for sure."

Though Barb told me not to worry about making the trip all the way to Indiana for NCAAs if the only reason was to meet Dan, I knew without a doubt that I had to go. I was honored she had thought to ask, and Dan's and my shared namesake was eerily serendipitous.

My decision settled, Barb shared with me that she had told Dan all sorts of stories about "the other Shoop" (me) over the years. She told me he had done research about our shared namesake and that over the years, through his own digging, he was convinced that he and I were related. Truly, how could I not fly to Indiana to meet him? Two days later, I booked my flight and rental car.

Within two weeks of Barb's serendipitous invitation, I found myself driving northward out of Indianapolis on my way to Carmel, Indiana (Barb's tiny hometown), with Barb in the passenger seat navigating. As we drove, she pointed out where she grew up, her childhood home, her school. As she spoke, she told me all about Dan and how she had known him nearly fifty years. She told me of his health, their friendship, and that over the course of their years of knowing one another, never a month, if not a day, went by without them speaking or visiting.

One hour's meandering drive later, I was sitting in Dan Shoop's living room side by side with him in matching recliners, while Barb sat diagonally across the room from us on the couch. The three of us passed that day sharing stories and laughing. We toured Dan's home, one filled with paintings that he had created over the years. Dan recalled stories of Barb and a lifetime of other athletes he had coached. He spoke of each one with a fine detail that demonstrated his genuine care and his joy in coaching.

By the end of our time together, Dan asked if I would send him a picture so he could get to work on a painting of me. I grinned, flattered, then agreed to send him a picture as soon as I got home. I was honored to meet him, and so, as we hugged goodbye, I looked forward to visiting him again one day.

Following our afternoon of laughing and having learned of how Dan and Barb had stayed in such close contact over the years, I understood just how important to Barb he was. They came into and impacted one another's lives, not by grand gestures but by small ones. Small moments and small connections that, when accumulated over time, came to have the most meaning and most significance.

For Barb and Dan, their one initial interaction followed by innumerable successive small moments led to nearly fifty years of friendship and significance that I am sure will endure well beyond. Less than seven months after my and Barb's mini road trip to Carmel to share an afternoon with Dan Shoop, he passed away.

At his memorial, it was said that Dan lived "a life of significance." Not because of one grand gesture but because of his innumerable small moments, the countless ways he impacted the lives of others…

Likewise, something as significant as an Olympic gold medal does not happen because of some great power nor one grand act. Rather, it happens because of each step, moment, and connection shared along the way. Indeed, a life of significance is not made by one big moment, but through the accumulation of small ones. Those taken one step a time and that end up having far greater impact than any of us might ever imagine.

ACKNOWLEDGMENTS

TRULY, ANY SIGNIFICANCE IN MY OWN LIFE WOULD NOT HAVE happened had it not been for each person who has shared moments with me along the way.

First, this includes my family. My parents and my one-and-only big bro, we Shoops, the Utzes, Granny Betty, the Cutrights, the Milams, the Robertsons, "Pee-Dee" Perri, and "Cebollilla" Cynthia. My Beijing Soul Sisters—Mary, Caryn, Caroline, Susan, Anna M., Elle, Anna G., and Erin—and Molly, Julie, and Marge, for being naive optimists and true champions in every aspect of life with me to this day. To each of you for *every day*, for being part of and for putting up with my stories.

To Kevin, who reached out to me in one small moment that turned out to be life-changing, and for continuing to be one of the greatest mentors of all time. To Barb, who has continued to be a beacon for genuine joy in the small moments, and for sharing some of them with me.

To Heidi, who first revealed the meaning of patience, consistency, and the little things. To Tom and Laurel and their small words that guided me to discover things for myself. To Dirks, who taught me to row. To KJ, Wendy, Brett, Cooke, Portia, and

Sheryl for freely sharing lighthearted wisdom. And to the original seven, plus one—Cooke, Kaido, Sharon, Mols, Suz, Melissa, and Kara—for braving the Lake Mercer tsunamis with me.

To Becky and Victoria, for singing and dancing with reckless abandon. To Cynthia, Caryn, and Jen for the unwavering support that injected confidence through the final stages of this first story.

To Paul and Mickey for helping me sift through my (numerous) words. To MagV for the bolt-of-lightning creativity during titling time. And to the athletes and coaches I have been lucky enough to coach and to coach alongside. Thank you. Truly.

The first seven years I spent writing this story made me realize how many people have had an incredibly meaningful impact on my life. Most of whom probably have no idea just how much so. I am grateful for those who have challenged, supported, and questioned me, and have never once given up on me. All of whom have helped me discover the person I am and continue to become.

I could easily write multiple volumes about how each specific person has impacted me, but it would still not be enough. Instead, I simply say, thank you. You have positively influenced my life in far greater ways than I could ever truly thank you for. However, this does not mean I will stop searching for ways to do just that.

Oh, and Suz, for the record, I found more than five dollars. I found something priceless.

ABOUT THE AUTHOR

LINDSAY SHOOP is a coach, author, speaker, and lifelong athlete. She is an Olympic gold medalist, a three-time World Champion, and a National Rowing Hall of Fame inductee.

With a focus on performance optimization and longevity throughout sport and life, Lindsay hosts clinics for coaches, athletes, and teams of all ages and skill levels. She is a commentator for USRowing and a speaker for events at major universities and corporations.

Lindsay lives in Florida, where she daily seeks to mentor, inspire, and improve the lives of others by sharing her journey of self-discovery from ultimate defeat, to Olympic gold.

Made in the USA
Monee, IL
08 March 2021

61252661R10225